Psychosocial Aspects
of Depression

Psychosocial Aspects of Depression

No way out?

Lars Fredén

Department of Social Science
Linköping University, Sweden

1807 1982

175 YEARS OF PUBLISHING

JOHN WILEY & SONS

Chichester · New York · Brisbane · Toronto · Singapore

Library of Congress Cataloging in Publication Data:
Fredén, Lars, 1949–
  Psychosocial aspects of depression.
  Includes bibliographical references and index.
  1. Depression, Mental. I. Title. [DNLM:
1. Depression—Psychology. 2. Psychology, Social.
WM 171 F852p]
RC537.F685   616.85′27   81-16444

ISBN 0 471 10023 4   AACR2

British Library Cataloguing in Publication Data:
Fredén, Lars
  Psychosocial aspects of depression.
  1. Depression, Mental
  I. Title
  616.89′5   RC537

  ISBN 0 471 10023 4

Photosetting by Thomson Press (India) Ltd., New Delhi
and printed by Page Bros. (Norwich) Ltd.

Contents

Introduction

Why should anyone write a book on depression? There are probably as many reasons as there are books on the subject. In my own case the process that led to my undertaking such a task probably began around the middle of the 1960s, when reports of the crisis in the Third World roused the conscience of so many of the young, of whom I was one. I felt a generalized urge to improve the lot of those in need. Sociology proclaimed itself as a discipline with an international flavour and concerned at least in part with effecting change in society. And sure enough this very subject became the most popular at universities at the end of the 1960s. I was one of about a thousand students who were studying sociology at Uppsala University at that time.

Along with many others I discovered that helping people in the Third World was both a difficult and a problematic business; but the desire to be of use persisted. I worked during two summer vacations in a large mental hospital and found that a great many people were badly in need of help much nearer home, in the psychiatric hospitals of my own country. Many of them were committed patients. I witnessed their degradation and the often inadequate help they received, frequently consisting of heavy medication and little else. At the same time I began to study psychology, hoping not only to learn something about psychiatric disorders but also to learn something about myself. I found the psychological explanations (dominated by the behavioural approach) inadequate. I returned to sociology and wrote a dissertation on 'Social recruitment in a psychiatric hospital'. My interest in social psychiatry and mental disorders continued to grow; I felt that I was learning more about myself and the world around me, and I realized that this whole area was badly neglected by the behavioural scientists. As a research student in sociology I became interested in the psychiatric concept of illness and in the theories of schizophrenia propounded by Laing, Cooper, Esterson, and others. I was still somewhat ignorant of the medical aspects, and was permitted to attend the basic course in psychiatry for medical students. I found this fruitful and, because of its markedly somatic orientation, frightening.

When the time came to choose a subject for my doctoral dissertation I had no hesitation in turning to the field of social psychiatry. The specific choice of depression was determined in part by my failure at that time (1973) to discover any substantial sociological or interdisciplinary research in this particular field (apart from the more theoretical macro-studies of the type undertaken by Durkheim). On the other hand, a good deal of research which could be regarded as sociological was being devoted to schizophrenia, alcoholism, and other specific disorders.

I was anxious to study depression in *sociological* terms since it seemed to me to be a mental disorder determined primarily by conditions in the social environment; in other words, I assumed that certain social conditions can predispose people to depression. I had noted with considerable interest the dichotomy in traditional psychiatry, according to which one major type of depression, the 'endogenous' depressions, cannot be explained in terms of external circumstances, while a second major category, the 'exogenous' depressions, lends itself to explanation in terms of conditions extrinsic to the individual. Given my sociological focus, it was natural that my earliest studies of depression were concerned with this second type.

After surveying current psychiatric research and finding much cause for criticism (see p. 108), I decided to extend the scope of my project. My optimistic goal was to study all depressive states, their psychological and sociological background, and their present manifestations, and then to comprehend all these elements in a macro-sociological theory. In other words, I wanted to try to set reductionistic psychiatric research to rights and to provide as all-embracing a picture of depression as possible. But this period of hubris was relatively short, and I was brought gently down to earth as a result of frequent seminar discussions at the University of Uppsala. Gradually the social–psychological outline of my project emerged from these talks and from the study and analysis of Ernest Becker's theory of depression. In the present book I have nevertheless returned, albeit more humbly, to an attempt to bring a diversity of arguments together into a comprehensive whole.

No other theoretical approach seems to me to command the explanatory value of Becker's theory. I might have considered starting from Mead's symbolic interactionism, or from one or other of the labelling theorists, from behavioural theory, Beck's cognitive theory, one of the neo-Freudian theories, Merton's anomie theory, or from Marx's alienation theory. But in view of my chosen social–psychological focus, all these theories were either too general (sociological) or too limited (psychological), or the connection with depression was too slight (e.g. Mead).

If I were to single out my main reasons for settling on Ernest Becker's theory as my point of departure and my chief theoretical base, the four following points must be mentioned:

(1) The theory is multidimensional
(2) The theory corresponds to my own experience of depression (theoretical, empirical, and practical)
(3) The theory draws several theoretical orientations together into a whole
(4) I appreciated Becker's view of man as it emerges from his theory.

To start with the last of these points: Becker sees man mainly as a consciously acting being. Man creates and is created by his social circumstances in a historical perspective.

We can see that life as we know it, cultural life in a human world, does not act *on* the person: it acts *through* him. We live and we become (in part) the objects we help to create. Constituted of the fiction, we in turn constitute it. Our life-style and our world create each other. (1964, p. 160)

This situation embraces even the critical scientist. It is unavoidable in Becker's view that a personality theory should be at least partly determined by social and moral dimensions.

We know man needs action and objects, and as we shall see later, choices and conviction. But whatever we find out about human needs, the facts remains that the *kind of people we make depends on the kind of poeple we want*. The social and moral dimensions of personality theory are inescapable. (1964, p. 167)

Becker's knowledge of sociology and the behavioural sciences seems to have been both deep and wide. His theory represents a synthesis of many theoretical orientations: existentialism (e.g. Heidegger, Kierkegaard), neo-Freudian theory (e.g. Rank, Adler, Bibring, Fromm), game theory (Szasz), and symbolic interactionism (e.g. Mead, Goffman, Dewey, James), to mention but a few.

When attempts are made to combine ideas from such a wide variety of theoretical sources, the result may all too easily be a confusing tangle. Becker's great strength, and one that is extremely rare, is that he succeeds in synthesizing a multiplicity of ideas in such a way as to produce a picture of human behaviour that is both unusually clear and unusually profound. Becker refers to the great body of knowledge that is available today in anthropology, social anthropology, and psychiatry, and proclaims his not unambitious goal as being to provide 'an excellent general theory of human nature' based on the discoveries that have been and are being made in these fields (1971, p. vii).

I was working on my theory of depression, drawing on Becker's model, while I was also planning and carrying out a comprehensive interview study. Together with nine other interviewers I talked to a number of discharged patients (referred to henceforth as the patient group) and to a fairly large group of normal controls during the spring, summer, and autumn of 1975. The interviews were semi-structured: some questions were open-ended, some were structured, and most of them were provided with possible but quite specific formulations geared to the different dimensions that we wished to cover, mostly connected with social relationships and actions important to self-esteem.

The object of study in this investigation was the social situation prior to a depressive period. I was influenced to a great extent in this choice of focus by my theoretical point of departure, in particular by Becker's emphasis on the 'range of possible actions' and the emphasis of the behavioural psychologists on the 'repertoire of behaviour'. These two concepts are both pertinent to the way people cope with stressful life situations. Had our respondents been able to solve their depressions by recourse to alternative actions? Were they able to direct their lives towards alternative solutions? Were they able to look at their problems from some fresh and more constructive standpoint? Our questions concerned the kin and close non-kin companions of the respondents, the nature of their relationships with these people (dominance, demands, depth), and the activities in which they took part. Naturally questions were also asked about the depression itself and its apparent (or claimed) cause or causes. I then tried, with the help of statistical and theoretical analysis, to form a picture of the depressive process.

With a few exceptions the 273 interviews were held in the respondents' homes. Almost all those interviewed were extremely cooperative and appeared to be genuinely interested in the study. We did not intend to interview anyone who was still severely depressed; in fact we found that most of those who had previously been depressed had now acquired a certain perspective in relation to their earlier problems. There were some exceptions to this, and a few of the respondents were still depressed when the interviews were held. Many of the interviews turned into long talks about various experiences and events in the respondents' lives. Many of them seemed glad of the opportunity to talk to an outsider about their severe problems. Many of the interviews began to resemble individual psychotherapy, most of the interviewers being in fact student psychologists nearing the end of their training. Most of the interviews took about one and a half hours, and a few as much as three hours.

The present book has three more or less equally important constituent parts, two of which—my own earlier study and Ernest Becker's social–psychological theory of depression—have already been mentioned. The third component is drawn from various studies of depression which I have found to be relevant and interesting. It is here that I have deviated most from the Swedish edition (Fredén, 1978), of which the present book is a revised version. In this new English edition I have given far less space to my own empirical investigations, although I am keenly aware that the interviews held in connection with that study have greatly increased my understanding of the problems discussed in the following pages.

It has been my aim to reach a comprehensive but at the same time consistent explanation of depression by applying the broad theoretical frame of reference to the psychological and sociological material that my own and other people's research has made available. Many studies and books have penetrated more deeply into the nature of depression than I have done here. Most of these, however, have focused on either psychological or sociological empirical findings, or on psychological or sociological theories. What I have tried to do in the present book is to build a bridge that links all these four scientific orientations.

Acknowledgement

Quotations from (a) *The Revolution in Psychiatry*, (b) *The Birth and Death of Meaning*, and (c) *The Denial of Death* by Ernest Becker are reprinted with permission of Macmillan Publishing Co. Inc. Copyright (a) 1964, (b) 1962, 1971, and (c) 1973 by The Free Press, a Division of Macmillan Publishing Co. Inc.

CHAPTER 1

What is depression?

Any two people discussing depression are likely to find themselves at cross-purposes, simply because they are not talking about the same phenomenon. Also, in everyday speech we refer to depression in so many different ways: we say that we are feeling blue, or low, fed up, depressed, sad, or lethargic. Nor is the use of different terms the only problem: the same word can have different connotations. One person says he is 'depressed' for a few hours, because he has had a bad day at work; to others 'depression' refers exclusively to a serious disorder (a biochemical or hereditary defect) which has reduced the subject to a lasting state of passivity. These diverging definitions of depression are reflected in scientific circles where opinions, although not as far removed from one another as in the example quoted, nevertheless differ greatly when it comes to explaining the roots of depression. There is more agreement, however, about the way depression manifests itself, namely in a state of low spirits which lasts for several days at least and makes it difficult for the depressed person to carry on his normal everyday activities.

In my own investigations, to which I shall be referring frequently, I started from a definition of this kind. To be classified as a depressed person, the subject had to have 'been feeling really low, so much so that he found it difficult to cope with his everyday life', and this state should have lasted for at least fourteen days. The third criterion was that the subject should rank as 'depressed' on a chosen rating scale. For this purpose I used a scale that is fairly simple to apply, namely Zung's rating scale as designed for the World Health Organization, which I shall describe in discussing the medical approach. Subjects had to answer 20 questions, each with four alternative answers, reflecting the depressive syndrome as described by adherents of the medical approach. Since the various schools differ less when it comes to describing the *manifestations* of the depressive state, I shall concentrate in the following brief survey of the various approaches on the different propositions put forward regarding the *causes* of depression.

1.1 THE MEDICAL APPROACH

There are two pivotal questions in the traditional psychiatric view of depression. The first is whether the cause of the depression is to be sought in external or internal (biochemical) factors; the other is whether or not the patient reacts positively to antidepressive treatment (drugs or electroconvulsive therapy).

In traditional psychiatry there are two main schools, exemplified in England

1

by the Newcastle school which takes a dichotomous view of depression, and the London school which represents the continuum hypothesis. According to the dichotomous view, some depressions are endogenous, having internal (e.g. biochemical, genetic) origins, while others are exogenous, depending mainly on external circumstances. According to the advocates of the continuum hypothesis, on the other hand, it is impossible to draw any clear causal boundaries between different types of depression; there is rather a continuous scale of external and internal causes.

The adherents of the medical approach use many different concepts in referring to depression, and these can vary from one country to another. The concept of 'neurotic depression' (see p. 107), for example, has wider implications in the USA than in the Scandinavian countries. The picture is further complicated in that the concepts represent a motley blend of (a) etiology (causal relationships), (b) symptomatology, (c) prognosis, and (d) reaction to specific treatments. A comparison of endogenous and exogenous depression based on these categories could look like this:

Endogenous depression	*Exogenous depression*
(a) Biochemical causes (hormonal, genetic imbalance in certain neurotransmitter substances)	Psychiatric 'social' causes (a traumatic psychiatric event)
(b) Among the most prominent symptoms often mentioned are: motor inhibition, guilt feelings, paranoid delusions, waking early, deep depression, loss of weight, failure to react to changes in the environment, agitation, and attempted suicide	Among the most prominent symptoms often mentioned are: anxiety, self-pity (putting the blame on others), difficulty in sleeping, suicide risk, and, above all, fixation by the depressed person on a specific precipitating object.
(c) Bouts of depression recurring at regular intervals (on an average 2–3 attacks of 6–12 months' duration)	Recurrence rare (depression seldom lasts longer than 6 months)
(d) Reacts specifically to antidepressive agents (psychodrugs and ECT)	Reacts 'non-specifically' to certain drugs

Thus we can see that the psychiatric diagnosis of depression, and in particular the partial diagnosis, is based on a mixture (perhaps we should say a confusion) of cause, effect (symptom), and treatment. Naturally, in real life it would anyway be difficult to find a 'typical' case in which everything fitted from (a) to (d).

Adherents of a biochemical explanation generally refer to what is known as the catecholamine hypothesis. In the transfer of nerve impulses from one nerve cell to another, the neurotransmitter substances act as a necessary aid. Some of these transmitter substances—the catecholamines, i.e. dopamine, noradrenaline, adrenaline, and serotonin—are heavily concentrated in the brain stem, and it is now held with some certainty that they act as transmitter substances there. It has also been found that a low catecholamine count correlates with a depressive state. Moreover reserpine, which reduces the catecholamine level, causes depressive symptoms. Antidepressive agents intervene in this process and speed up the restoration of the amines to the nerve cells.

A great deal of research is at present being done into these questions, and some of the assumptions underlying the catecholamine hypothesis (assumptions which I have not mentioned here) have had to be revised. We should also remember that a lower level of amines in the brain cells tells us nothing about the causal links. The changes in the neurotransmitter substances may equally well be the result of a long period of stress or a profoundly traumatic event.

Thus it seems that the diagnosis of endogenous and exogenous depression is chiefly based on: (a) whether there is depression in the family, (b) the degree of depression (severe/mild), (c) motor reactions (inhibited/normal), (d) reaction to antidepressive agents, and (e) whether any triggering factors are present. It is mainly on a basis of these factors that conclusions are drawn about the causes of the depressive behaviour, i.e. whether the cause is an internal (biochemical) or an external (psychosocial) one. And among these factors the possible link between the depression and some specific object (precipitating factor) generally plays the most important part in determining the diagnosis.

Among the adherents of the medical view of depression a tendency to stress the treatment angle instead of concentrating on possible causes has recently become more marked. A distinction is made between primary depression, secondary depression, and 'normal' low spirits. People with primary depression generally react positively to antidepressive agents. Those who are suffering a secondary depression, which has often been preceded by a non-affective psychiatric illness such as schizophrenia, may actually find that their problems are aggravated by such psychopharmaceutical aids. In cases of 'normal' low spirits, antidepressive agents have no particular effect (Akiskal and McKinney, 1975).

Primary depression has certain conspicuous symptoms. Zung defines depression as:

(1) A mood disturbance which is characterized by pervasive feelings and complaints of being depressed, sad, down-hearted, and fearful.
(2) Physiological symptoms which include: diurnal variation, disturbances of sleep, decreased appetite, decreased weight, decreased libido, constipation, tachychardia and unexplainable fatigue.
(3) Psychomotor disturbances, which are either that of retardation or agitation.
(4) Psychological disturbances which include: confusion, emptiness, hopelessness, indecisiveness, irritability, dissatisfaction, personal devaluation and suicidal rumination. (1973, p. 332)

This definition of depression provides the basis for Zung's rating scale, which was the decisive criterion in my interview study for categorizing depressed subjects in the control group.

1.2 THE PSYCHODYNAMIC APPROACH

The psychodynamic view of depression stems from Freud's *Mourning and Melancholia* (1957). Freud regarded depression as a state in which the subject turns aggression inwards upon himself instead of upon the person who is really the object of his aggressive feelings. Any hate or disappointment previously attached to this person in his mind can no longer be expressed openly; these feelings have become forbidden. But since the aggression has to be released somehow, he turns it inwards on himself. This is most likely to happen to those who are very self-absorbed (narcissistic): 'How could anyone abandon *me*?'

Freud's seminal work deals mainly with the difference between grief (mourning) and depression (melancholia).

In grief there is an *actual* loss of an object, consequently a feeling of the world being 'poor and empty', but there is no fall in self-esteem, no self-accusation. In melancholic depression, there is usually an *emotional* loss of object due to disappointment or related factors. (Bibring, 1953, p. 13)

Jakobson, who has been working along the same lines as Freud, prefers to extend the concept of grief to include sadness. In grief or normal low spirits our thoughts turn back to earlier, positive experiences, and we have a keen desire to witness the return of the lost object. But this is not what happens in a 'real' depression. Sadness, in her view, is quite unconnected with any aggression either towards the external world or towards ourselves. This last is the distinguishing characteristic of depression: 'The mood disturbance arises from the discrepancy between the self representations and the ego ideal (supergo) or the wishful image of the self' (Jakobson, 1971, p. 89).

Thus the main source of the disorder is an interior one: an imbalance between aggressive drives and libidinal impulses (self-love and to some extent object-love). The solution lies in becoming aware of our own ego ideals, but unfortunately these are often unconscious. Jakobson also discusses the difference between the neurotically and the psychotically depressed. She concludes that psychotic depressions are based on physiological changes (endogenous) which affect the balance between the internal drives (aggression and libido).

Edward Bibring represents another branch of the psychodynamic school, regarding depression mainly as an ego phenomenon. The important factor here is the relation between the individual and his social environment rather than any conflict within the individual himself. Another important difference in Bibring's neo-Freudian view is that a single underlying mechanism is ascribed to 'normal' low spirits, to neurotic depression, and to psychotic depression: all types of depression have their roots in loss of self-esteem which can lead to the inward-turning of the aggressive impulses. Internalized aggression is thus a secondary phenomenon.

Depression is the ego's emotional expression of helplessness and powerlessness. It is the result of the gap between a great longing to be valued and loved, to be strong, assured, and good, and the realization—real or imagined—that these goals are unattainable. Depression occurs when we are incapable of living up to our own ego ideals. This is because we have set the goals too high and sometimes because the social situation has changed.

In *depression* the narcissistically important aims are perpetuated, but the narcissistic core of the ego, its self-esteem, is broken down, since the ego-functions—which usually serve the gratification of the particular narcissistic strivings—appear to be highly inadequate, partly due to reality factors, partly due to internal reasons. (Bibring, 1953, pp. 32f)

Thus in depression the core of the ego—i.e. self-esteem—is impaired. Bibring assumes that the factor which most disposes a person to depression is the experience of helplessness in early childhood due to failure in the satisfaction of vital needs. The adult who has been so deprived will need continual confirmation of being loved and liked. If these (narcissistic) needs are not satisfied, depression is very likely to ensue. Also temporary but strongly felt experiences of helplessness during the first years of life (the oral phase) can be sharply revived later, if something happens to remind the adult of the earlier traumatic event. A particularly critical event is physical loss of the mother or her emotional absence (inability to satisfy the child's primary needs). If a child experiences such a loss between the ages of 6 and 36 months, the adult will find it more difficult to support a subsequent loss. The loss in adult life which re-evokes the earlier loss may be 'real, fantasied or symbolic' (White, 1977).

How does the mourning reaction fit into this scheme? Bibring suggests that when a person loses someone he loves his ego faces the loss of an object that previously helped to satisfy his need to be loved, and it is a loss about which absolutely nothing can be done. There is thus a great gulf between what the deprived person wants to do and what he is able to do.

1.3 THE BEHAVIOURAL APPROACH

There are two main ways of viewing depression in terms of learning theory. According to one (represented by Lewinsohn and MacPhillamy 1974; Ferster, 1973; Akiskal and McKinney, 1975; Ullman and Krasner, 1969), depression is seen as the result of limited access to actions that provide positive reinforcement (reward), perhaps because the individual is unable to perform a reward-bringing action. The depression is then triggered off by the loss of positive reinforcement and/or by the experience of punishment (negative reinforcement). Social–psychological arguments are also suggested by some followers of this school. Ullman and Krasner point out that our society has few sanctioned roles to offer to those who find life lacking in meaning. And the same authors mention the risk of the depressive role becoming chronic in those who are unable to find alternative actions and objects when their earlier behaviour is no longer providing positive reinforcement. The conclusion to this argument appears to be that a person with a limited repertoire of behaviour to which he can turn in a variety of situations is more likely to become depressed if he can no longer gain positive reinforcement from a particular type of behaviour.

The chief proponent of the second and increasingly popular way of approaching depression in learning theory has been Martin Seligman (see Seligman, 1975). Depression is now seen as the result of a loss of *control* over the means of acquiring positive or negative reinforcement. Seligman calls this state *learned*

6

helplessness. However, he admits that learned helplessness corresponds only to what is known as reactive depression, and even then applies mainly to cases in which the subject lacks initiative, has a feeling of powerlessness and takes a gloomy view of the future. Despite this limitation the concept of learned helplessness fits a large proportion of the depressed. It means that people see success and failure as lying outside their own control and having no connection with their own actions. It is the expectation of uncontrollability which is crucial to the development of learned helplessness. Seligman argues that people who were denied the opportunity to control their own environment in their early years are more likely to react with learned helplessness in adult life.

Paul Blaney (1977), who is himself a follower of the behavioural school, has made a critical survey of these theories. He finds that neither of them commands adequate empirical support. Many of the experiments cited in support of the theories could serve equally well to support explanations in terms of loss of self-esteem (see psychodynamic theory and Becker). Furthermore, Blaney is doubtful whether we can distinguish between the rate or *amount of reinforcement* and *control over the reinforcement* as crucial factors: consider a man who receives very little pay for a job which he has had to accept in order to quality for some particular social benefit; if he becomes depressed, is it because of the meagre size of the reinforcement (his wages), his lack of control over the reinforcement (he is forced to take that particular job), or a bit of both? Moreover, as Blaney points out, if he cannot control the situation, the man will be losing an essential element in the reinforcement. What, then, is the key factor in this context: control or reinforcement? Why the behavioural psychologists find it difficult to answer this question will be discussed at the end of the chapter, where I shall compare the behavioural view with Ernest Becker's approach.

Akiskal and McKinney seek to combine the behavioural view with a biochemical model. They hypothesize that the helplessness, together with a reduction in certain neurotransmitter substances (cf. p. 2f), results in the impairment of the neurophysiological substrates of reinforcement. This impairment then becomes manifest as depression. One of the arguments on which this hypothesis is based is that the symptoms—e.g. psychomotor disturbances, helplessness, etc.—are very similar in all types of depression. Also, monkeys which had been given a preparation to reduce their neurotransmitter substances showed certain typical kinds of behaviour: they took less part in social interaction, initiated fewer responses, appeared to care less about their surroundings, and became less physically active.

Forrest and Hokanson (1975) argue that the depressed seek to 'control' aversiveness and threats from other people by their own self-punishing behaviour. They find it easier to turn their aggression inwards on themselves than to turn it outwards on other people.

Coyne (1976) has an even more elaborate hypothesis: when an individual is exposed to stress he needs a great deal of support and validation from other people, but his persistence may ultimately become aversive to the very people whose help he craves; becoming aware of their annoyance he intensifies his signals of distress, which in turn will increase the aversion of those around him. His mode of expression arouses guilt in other people, but inhibits them from expressing the anger they feel. The depressed subject often arouses aggression in others in this way, since he is incapable of benefiting from the support they give him. He cannot arouse sympathy without at the same time arousing aversion.

1.4 ERNEST BECKER'S APPROACH

In interpreting various studies in the following chapters—among them my own earlier empirical investigation—I shall make frequent reference to the theories of Ernest Becker. Chapter 10 contains a comprehensive analysis of Becker's theory and I will therefore limit myself here to a brief presentation of such definitions and concepts as are relevant to our present argument.

Becker argues that depression is a result of threats to *self-esteem*. Self-esteem is engendered by the feeling of control over our own actions; self-worth thus acquired is not easily toppled by temporary disturbances. But if an individual's self-esteem is radically reduced, he will find it difficult to act, he will become passive. A strong and stable awareness of self-worth is a powerful element in the defence against depression.

Another important element in the avoidance of depression consists of access to a broad range of possible actions with which to encounter difficult situations such as the loss of an object or an accustomed activity. One of the merits of Becker's theory is that he gives us comparable concepts on both the psychological and social levels. To be able to choose between alternative actions in social life presupposes genuine access to such alternatives and a preparedness for action (an awareness of possible kinds of action). I will use the term *range of possible actions* to signify action preparedness combined with the existence of a variety of key-actor-related actions over which the subject has control.

Also of central importance in Becker's theory is the concept of *rigid action patterns*. This means that the individual has too small or restricted a range of action (on the social level), that he focuses doggedly on certain fixed solutions to possible actions or set answers to possible questions (on the psychological level). One of Becker's major assumptions is that people strive to acquire self-esteem and to avoid anxiety. These two fundamental human motives are also to some extent contradictory: the person more likely to react to adversity with depression has generally been particularly concerned to avoid anxiety and this in turn will have reduced his self-esteem.

I shall use the term *depressive personality* to describe those who are more disposed than others to react to stress with depression. I realize that this envelope term might be misunderstood, arousing as it does associations of inherited weakness and of permanence. It is therefore important to emphasize that my intention is exactly the opposite: *depressive personality* is used here as a social–psychological concept and it designates people characterized by low self-esteem, a limited range of actions, and rigid action patterns. It does not refer to a state that is determined once and for all; the depressive personality can and does change continually in the course of interactions and social communication.

1.5 COMPARISON BETWEEN THE PSYCHODYNAMIC APPROACH, THE BEHAVIOURAL APPROACH, AND ERNEST BECKER'S APPROACH

I have now briefly summarized the various approaches but have hitherto neglected to compare them with one another. The reader will certainly have noticed several fundamental similarities, particularly between Becker and Bibring. However, Becker differs from Bibring in the impulses he has received from symbolical interactionism and existentialism. The influence of *symbolic interactionism* expresses itself in the importance Becker assigns to *action*. Identity is a result of the individual's contact (or interaction) with other people; it has no connection with any kind of instincts or drives. The influence of existentialism can be seen in the importance Becker assigns to our awareness, as humans, of our own death.

A feature of depression which Becker does not mention, but which Bibring and others have discussed, is the lack of realism in the ideals and aspirations of the depressed in relation to the actual opportunities available. But this characteristic is not altogether unconnected with Becker's concept of the rigid action patterns which I will examine further in Chapter 11. Another important element in psychodynamic theory which Becker touches on only briefly is the re-evocation of earlier traumatic events in adult life which can precipitate depression.

There are also great apparent similarities between Becker's approach and Seligman's theory of learned helplessness. Both emphasize the importance of experiences in which people perceive a link between action and consequence. However, a more careful analysis reveals significant differences between the two approaches.

According to Seligman, depression *manifests itself* in 'learned helplessness'; Becker argues, on the other hand, that people who have been exposed to what could be called 'learned helplessness' are *more predisposed* to depression. In describing the state of learned helplessness (= depression) Seligman ignores what to Becker is at the heart of the matter, namely the lack of self-esteem. Nor does Seligman try to establish the kind of cultural or social circumstances in which learned helplessness is likely to occur. Becker seeks to go beyond the individual (psychological) framework, discussing among other things the incidence of depression in different social groups. He goes a step further, too, in trying to identify the typically human element. Seligman is not concerned with anything that might constitute the given framework for all human action. Because of this lack of precision, learning psychologists have drawn conclusions about human behaviour from animal experiments. Becker claims that all human action can be understood in the light of our fear of death, and thus of life; this stems in turn from our ability, unique to us as human beings, to look into the future and to envisage our own deaths. Because we can do this, our ideas about the meaning of life assume enormous importance; a feeling that life lacks meaning lies at the root of most depression. Seligman never mentions this question. Nor does he discuss the primary human motives or needs. Becker assumes that the striving for self-esteem and the avoidance of anxiety are fundamental motives common to all human beings. Becker's concepts seem to me essential to any understanding of the *origins* of learned helplessness or the limited range of actions, or of the *connection* between rigid action patterns and a limited range of actions, or of the devastating *effects* of low self-esteem. Perhaps the most important—or, at least, the most obvious—difference between the two approaches is that there is no equivalent in learning theory to Becker's concept of the rigid action pattern. If we try to define this in learning terms, we can get the paradox that 'too little learned helplessness encourages a depressive development'.

The weaknesses in Seligman's theory depend in the first place on his failure to recognize that people base their choice on different motives, that their actions are determined by the social context, and that they have the unique ability to reflect upon the meaning of life. This is also one of the reasons why learning psychologists find it difficult to distinguish between control and reinforcement (see p. 6). Which goals seem most important to the individual? What external opportunities are available? What is crucial in the long run? And so on. If these questions were asked, it would certainly be easier to solve the theoretical problem, but it would no longer be a question of a purely behavioural approach.

By now it is probably apparent to the reader where I stand with respect to the different approaches. Of the medical model I am altogether critical. It has a pessimistic, defeatist view of mankind that denies us any responsibility for ourselves and defines the psychiatric problem as one of human biology; people are not treated in a social context. My negative view of the medical model has also been influenced by the real world as I have found it to be. Medical treatment provides, at best, temporary relief. It enables people, at any rate for a time, to cope with their disappointment or loss. But it often obscures what is really happening and leaves the patient in a state of lethargy. Nobody has tried to delve into his everyday life, to help to make his existence more meaningful; instead he is probably told that 'the whole thing will go over in time'.

The behavioural approach also deprives people of reponsibility and 'free will'. And yet it does not seem to me to be as 'dangerous' as the medical approach. It probably provides a partially correct explanation of depression, albeit in an extremely simplified form. Typical of learning theory as a whole is that it explains a very great deal in very general terms; its explanatory value in the case of specific psychological states is therefore extremely meagre.

When it comes to the psychodynamic approach I am somewhat ambivalent. Nor is there a single such approach. Bibring's theory is probably the most fruitful, perhaps providing a better *psychological* explanation of depression than Becker. The great advantage of Becker's theory lies in the social–psychological explanation, the probing into factors in everyday or social life that can generate depressive reactions. I shall discuss a criticism of Becker's theory in a special section (p. 153f). Briefly, however, it seems to me that Becker pays too little attention to the role of early *affective* experiences in the development of the personality, and to the reactivation in adult life of feelings connected with earlier adverse life events. I also suggest that the concept of inward-turned aggressions can help to explain depression, provided it is seen in a cultural context and not made to fit into a theory of instincts as in traditional psychodynamic theory. Finally, one criticism applies to all the approaches presented here, including Becker's. Very little attempt has been made to combine the psychological and social–psychological concepts in a broader social setting. Nobody has tried to identify the kind of power structure, the type of economy or culture, etc., that is most likely to promote unrealistic ideals, learned helplessness, and a limited range of actions.

CHAPTER 2

What characterizes those who become depressed?

In this chapter I shall briefly present some studies of depression which I have found particularly interesting and enlightening. Naturally, I can only touch on a few investigations and I make no claim to be providing a representative survey of all depression research. In particular, I shall focus on research that links up with my own social–psychological approach and will also include a summary of my own earlier study. The reader may be a little surprised to find a summary at the beginning of a book, but it seemed to me that some understanding of at least the main features of my basic propositions would provide a useful platform from which to tackle an analysis in depth concerned to a greater extent with specific conditions. And in any case, this is not a summary in the traditional sense. Some of the points discussed here (e.g. the role of education) are not in fact followed up in the present book, while others will be developed later (e.g. the theoretical model which partly builds on the discriminant analysis summarized on p. 17ff below).

There are two questions to which I will try to find an answer in this chapter: What type of person becomes depressed despite a favourable social background? What type of person does not become depressed despite many external factors that might suggest such a likelihood? But one question must precede both of these, namely: Who has an unfavourable social background?

2.1 CHILDHOOD BACKGROUND

In seeking explanations in people's backgrounds for their present psychological or social problems we are apt to think first of broken homes, poverty, and alcoholism. And certainly such background factors are common in cases of alcoholism, criminal behaviour, and the more serious personality disorders. However, there seem to be various less immediately obvious factors which may pave the way for depression in adult life.

Fromm-Reichmann worked for several years with the families of patients diagnosed as suffering from manic-depressive psychosis. She combined the therapy, which was based on a psychodynamic approach, with research, and in 1954 she, together with a group of colleagues, published a comparative study of schizophrenic patients and their families (Cohen *et al.*, 1954). If I had to choose one word to describe the early family life of the adult manic-depressive patient, that word would be *circumscribed*. Family members were expected to entertain high moral values and to behave in a correct manner according to fixed norms.

The children were also often socially restricted, since their families were in some way socially set apart. Heavy pressure was also brought to bear on the children to succeed, above all in their professional careers. Gibson (1958) continued the work of Cohen *et al.*, conducting a more controlled psychological investigation. His results agreed with Cohen's. The parents of the manic-depressive patients were extremely eager for social approval, and they used their children to acquire prestige for themselves. There was also intensive competition within the family. As I see it, this background provides a narrow range of possible actions, which in turn makes it more difficult for the future adult to find openings or solutions to the problems that confront him. These ideas will be developed further in Chapter 5.

An example of a very different type of research into the implications of childhood circumstances for future depressions is provided by the work of Munro (1966a, 1966b). Munro found no difference between depressed patients and the physically ill as regards size of sibling group, position in sibling group, age of parents at patient's birth, or death of a parent before the patient had reached the age of 16. Many clinical studies based on the medical model have been aimed at discovering the importance of early object loss, but no definite support has been found for the connection between separation from a parent and depression in adult life. Such research is hampered by its own method; it requires easily comprehensible and classifiable data that lend themselves to quantification. Furthermore, there is no theoretical base such as attaches to the psychodynamic model, where the concept of early object loss was developed, Nevertheless, when Munro briefly turns his attention to parent–child contacts, he finds that the most depressed subjects report a highly significant excess of disturbed relationships with both mother and father during childhood.

According to the psychodynamic theory the loss must have been early (between the age of 6 months and 3 years). Also, during that period the mother represents the child's main source of security and she is therefore the 'object'. Nor is it only a question of physical loss; the effect is the same if the mother is emotionally absent, failing to provide a secure base. According to White (1977), many researchers confirm that loss in adult life afflicts people much more severely in the form of depression if the subjects have suffered early childhood loss. A sociological study by Brown and Harris (1978), based on a quantitative analysis, also supports some of the psychodynamic hypotheses: in a group of women who had suffered 'a severe event or major difficulty' in adult life, 47 per cent of those who had lost their mothers before reaching the age of 11 developed depression, compared with 17 per cent of those whose mothers had been accessible to them at that age. The loss of the mother after the age of 11, or the loss of the father at any age, had no connection with the development of depression.

2.2 EDUCATION

Here, too, we can refer to Cohen *et al.* (1954), who found that the depressive adults in their study had been put under heavy pressure in childhood to succeed at school, to achieve a higher position in society than their parents (which meant their fathers) had enjoyed. And in fact the twelve patients in the study had generally done well at school and, later, at work. Following Cohen *et al.* (1954) and Gibson (1958), Burns and Offord (1972) tried to establish on empirical grounds whether the depressive patients really had done better than other children at school, and found no difference between the two categories as regards school grades, IQ during childhood, or the level achieved at school. Woodruff *et al.* (1971) compared educational and occupational achievement between pairs of brothers, one of whom had become depressed. The depressive and non-depressive brothers had achieved the same educational and occupational levels, except where a diagnosis of manic-depressive psychosis had been made; in those cases the depressed subjects had achieved a higher level of education than their brothers.

The two last studies both miss an important point that is brought out in the psychodynamic approach, namely that it is the pressure on the child to succeed at school rather than his actual performance that is important. It is the sense of failure to satisfy high expectations that has caused the depression.

A more general study conducted by Linsky (1969) provides indirect support for the psychodynamic hypothesis. Linsky's American study is also one of the few studies I have come across that is predominantly sociological in its approach. In 27 communities Linsky compared the average educational level with the opportunities available for qualified work (measured in number of higher-prestige occupational positions). A substantially higher number of depressive disorders was found in communities that included many highly educated people but offered few opportunities for professional careers. The result did not appear to be affected by geographic drift or the availability of psychiatric services. Linsky concludes that those with a depressive personality

are inflexibly aligned with dominant cultural goals of success and with beliefs concerning the moral rightness and efficacy of traditional means for achievement. Their alternative therefore when success is blocked by the social structure is rejection not of that social structure but of themselves. (Linsky, 1969, p. 130)

People who have had impressed upon them during childhood the importance of success, of aiming high in occupational terms (Cohen *et al.*, 1954), are more likely to become depressed in a social setting that provides inadequate means of fulfilling these aspirations (Linsky, 1969). The risk is all the greater since these cultural goals are inextricably linked with the idea of the individual's responsibility for his own failures ('You can't keep a good man down'), so that people blame themselves for their lack of achievement instead of trying to do something about the external circumstances.

2.3 SOCIAL CLASS

Christopher Bagley (1973) has made an extensive survey of studies concerned with the relation between social class and depression. Material from the first half of the twentieth century shows an over-representation of manic-depressive patients in the higher social strata. Bagley also refers to an earlier study of his own, which confirms this result. He compared different types of depression, from severe depressions with elements of the psychotic (e.g. agitation, hallucinations) to milder depressions with elements of anxiety, and noted whether or not manic episodes occurred. There was only one group in which he found any connection between depression and social class. An unexpectedly high proportion of patients diagnosed as psychotic and suffering from manic phases came from the upper social strata.

In some general studies of depression—Brown and Harris (1978) and Birtchnell (1971), for example—depressive subjects appeared to be over-represented in the lower social classes. Several other studies, e.g. Fredén (1978) and Schwab *et al.* (1967), suggest that no social class is more liable to depressions than any other.

The varying results obtained in these studies of the relation between social class and depression can be explained partly by differences in the methods of selection used and in the way depression was defined. Schwab *et al.* (1967) have shown that definitions based to a great extent on the patient's own statements, and giving more weight to psychosomatic factors, result in an over-representation of the depressed in the lower social classes, whereas definitions based on the psychiatrist's general clinical assessment will have the opposite effect. People with a depression of the manic-depressive type are probably more common in the higher social strata, and many studies have been based on just this group of patients. Moreover, more of those who seek psychiatric treatment for depression appear to belong to the upper social classes, while there is more depression among non-patients lower down the social scale.

As regards factors which can precipitate a depression (i.e. factors that threaten or impair self-esteem), the *significance* that the different social classes attach, or are compelled to attach, to different types of loss and different kinds of problem is what matters most. Self-esteem seems to be exposed to much the same risk in all social classes, but not necessarily from the same sources. Problems connected with general home conditions and health are more likely to lead to the development of depression in the members of the lower social classes (Brown and Harris, 1978). The problem itself may be the same, but difficult social conditions can give it greater significance further down the social scale. Marital problems, on the other hand, appear to generate depression more readily in the upper social strata, perhaps because the cultural love ideal has a stronger hold on the members of these classes.

I suggest that people belonging to the lower strata of society generally have access to fewer action alternatives than those belonging to the upper strata, whereas the latter tend to develop rigid action patterns. I will discuss this hypothesis further in Chapter 7, where I will suggest that the two negative assumptions cancel each other out, so that no social class has a disproportionate share of depressive disorders.

2.4 PERSONALITY

The typical picture of the childhood family situation of the manic-depressive patient which Cohen *et al.* (1954) and others have given us, naturally also has profound implications for the personality of the adult. What is emphasized by the psychodynamic school is that manic-depressive patients are extremely rigid in their attitudes and views. They possess a few very well-established dependent relationships, from which they need to derive a great deal of attention and love. They often come into conflict with themselves, since they want to satisfy other people's demands while also putting great pressure on themselves to succeed. In a psychological study J. Becker (1960) found confirmation of these personality traits of manic-depressive patients. At the time of the experiment the patients were not depressed and exhibited the following personality traits among others: attitudes of submission to authority, extreme emphasis on discipline and on rigidly defined roles and statuses for family members, and they place a strong, positive conscious valuation on achievement. Unfortunately the above-mentioned studies are concerned exclusively with manic-depressive patients. In my view the personality traits described predominate in this particular diagnostic group (see p. 118ff) but also often occur in others. Following an existentialist line of argument, Scher (1971) emphasizes that for the depressed personality the future generally seems to be 'frozen' and determined. Such a person has become an object among other objects, or 'a thing among things'. He has no will of his own nor any responsibility; in other words he can do nothing about his situation.

Beck has perhaps been quoted more than any other writer when it comes to describing the depressive personality (Beck, 1967). What he sees as the dominating characteristic of the depressive personality is his possession of 'a negative view of himself, a negative view of the world and a negative view of the future'. As a result of this 'negative cognitive set' external difficulties assume huge proportions and lead to depression. Beck also stresses that the depressed person generally has *one* predominant way of perceiving his environment, one 'cognitive scheme'. He selects such impressions as fit this scheme, instead of choosing one of several possible schemes which agree with the external impressions.

What Beck's theory lacks is any suggestion of what may have generated these typical personality traits; there is thus no link-up with specific social conditions. This is exactly what we do find in Ernest Becker's theory, which thus appears to me to be less static than Beck's. The depressive personality in Becker's sense is not fixed once and for all; rather, it is continuously changing, sometimes in a positive direction but perhaps more often in a negative one, depending, however, on external circumstances. Let us briefly summarize again what Becker sees as characteristic of the depressive personality: first, low self-esteem; secondly, a rigid action pattern; and thirdly, a limited range of possible actions. The concept of the 'rigid action pattern' embraces and explains the various features emphasized both by the psychodynamic theorists and by Beck. It means that people have certain set answers and solutions to the problems of life, and that their way of life is circumscribed and subject to strict routine. The rigid action pattern follows from the limited range of action; at the same time it is itself a factor that restricts the range of action alternatives. Another important element in Becker's theory is that the depressive subject is intensely eager to avoid anxiety even at the cost of acquiring self-esteem. Thus Becker's theory of personality is concerned with the interaction of human motives with different ways of experiencing the world and of tackling reality. And this in turn is determined by the prevailing conditions of social and existential reality.

2.5 SEX

A study of sex and depression provides us with an opportunity to apply Becker's theory of personality. It is very much more usual for women to develop depressions than it is for men to do so. Perhaps we could say that a tendency to become depressed is part of the female personality. This statement may be correct in itself, but it suggests something predetermined and beyond our power to influence. What we have to establish is how and why the female personality and the depressive personality so often coincide. And the conclusion I come to is that female depression is to a great extent a question of rigid action patterns. In the upbringing that parents and society impose upon her, the woman is assigned a *fixed* position geared towards *other people* (husband, children, and parents). She learns as a girl and as an adult to hold herself back and not to question things too aggressively. The position of the woman, mostly in the home, easily becomes set into a series of routines. Even if she has a job, the general attitude is the same, while in any case the jobs that women do usually require less of them in the way of independence than the typically male jobs. It seems to me that this sort of situation is likely to result in rigid action patterns, so that women generally find it more difficult to escape from difficult life situations and are therefore more inclined to turn the grief and the guilt or disappointment in upon themselves.

2.6 THE SOCIAL ANTECEDENTS OF DEPRESSION

How prepared are we and what weapons do we possess for coping with the more difficult personal crises in our lives? Naturally, the various factors affecting personality development which we have just been discussing are very important in this context. In my own investigation, however, I was particularly interested in the implications of the social relationships and the kind of work and leisure-time activities in which the subjects had been involved in the period preceding and during the appearance of the severe problem. What action alternatives were immediately available?

Before summarizing the results of the study which I, together with a group of colleagues, conducted in 1975, I will describe something of the methodological background of the investigation.

We interviewed one group of people who had sought psychiatric treatment for depression for the first time during the period 1971–1975, and matched them against a control group taken from the same catchment area. After the interviews, this second group was divided into 'depressed controls' and 'non-depressed'. To qualify as a depressed control, the subject must have been 'low' for at least two weeks *and* must have suffered from at least a mild depression according to Zung's rating scale (see p. 3) *and* must have regarded the feeling of depression as interfering with his or her daily life. Fifty-one members of the control group proved to have been depressed at some time during the last five years and 124 were deemed not to have been depressed. Sixty-seven treated patients underwent full interviews. The choice of participants in the control group was based on the composition of the patient group. Three people were selected at random from the census register, corresponding to each member of the patient group as regards age, sex, and place of residence.

The purpose of most of the questions was to discover the social relationships and action alternatives that were available when the depressive problems arose. But we then came up against a difficulty: how should we decide exactly *when* a depression had become an incontestable fact? One subject had perhaps felt continuously 'low' since childhood. Another had been feeling increasingly repressed by her husband for a long time but reached the decisive stage in the depressive process when her marriage ended in divorce. This may have been the first time she had used the word 'depressed' about herself but she had quite likely already been in low spirits for several months.

It is thus impossible to pinpoint any exact moment when the possibility of depression becomes a reality. I chose to solve this problem by relying to a great extent on the interview subjects' own assessments. They were asked to say when during the last five years they had experienced a depressive patch for the first time. If they were unable to answer, then we asked whether there has been a generally negative period, and if so when. The period concerned might have lasted for anything from one week to one year. Once we had identified a depressive or negative period, most of the subsequent questions concerned the social pattern prevailing in the period of six months that preceded it. The answers which the respondents had already given about the present situation provided them with a point of reference in trying to reconstruct the earlier period.

Although there were still some difficulties, most people seemed to have very little trouble in describing the social pattern of their lives in the period preceding the onset of depression. The evidence of close relatives or friends confirmed what they told us.

I shall discuss some of the most interesting points that arose regarding partner and parent relationships in later chapters. At this stage I will simply summarize some of the results of my earlier study, in which I employed the technique of discriminant analysis.

First, a few words on this method of analysis. Discriminant analysis makes it possible to find the particular *combination of variables* that best differentiates between certain given groups. I wanted to identify the social–psychological and the independent variables that most clearly differentiated between the depressed and the non-depressed. Of the original 42 variables, nine proved important in this

Table 1   The combination of variables that best differentiates between the depressed and the non-depressed

	F to remove
1 Depth in partner relationship	47,2
2 Occurrence of depression prior to the study period	37,4
3 Demands in partner relationship	17,8
4 Dominance in parent relationship	8,7
5 Initiates social activities	3,4
6 Previous stressful events	2,8
7 Partner lacking importance	2,7
8 Mother at home or working	1,6
9 Independent work	1,2

Depressed: $n = 107$;   non-depressed: $n = 118$.
Percentage of 'grouped' cases correctly classified: 82%.

context (see Table 1), although there are, of course, other variables which also clearly differentiate between the depressed and the non-depressed. However, the discriminatory ability of these other variables has been absorbed by the strength of one or other of the nine. For example, many respondents who mentioned the demanding nature of the partner relationship mentioned the *same* thing, although with slightly less force, in connection with the parent relationship. In such cases only the first variable was included in the analysis. Two factors which cannot be treated either statistically or theoretically on a par with the other variables have been excluded despite their recognized implications in a depressive context, namely sex and dominating problems or precipitating events.

The value indicated in the table is the variable's relative importance in distinguishing between the groups. A high F-rating thus means that that particular variable alone can go a long way towards 'explaining' why certain people become depressed and others do not. I have put 'explaining' in quotation marks, since the analysis does not give us grounds for claiming that a particular variable *causes* depression. It may well be important, but it is probably itself the result of other factors (personality factors perhaps, as discussed in the previous section).

Checking these nine variables against the cases in my study, I found that more than eight of every ten people would have been correctly classified, i.e. those who would have been predicted as likely to become depressed were depressed, and vice versa. In other words, it would be possible to predict with reasonable certainty which people would become depressed and which would not on a basis of information about the variables in Table 1.

The main point of interest to emerge from the discriminant analysis was the significant role of the partner relationship in connection with depression. The isolated ratings (not shown in the table) obtained by 'Demands in parent relationship' and 'Depth in parent relationship' show that contacts with parents are also very important.

As can be seen from the table, several other variables help to distinguish the depressed from the non-depressed. One of these is 'Occurrence of depression prior to the study period'. This variable can be regarded as both a dependent and an independent variable. In the latter case, it can be assumed that a period of depression is a step towards the development of a depressive personality and that it thus implies an increase in the risk of depressions occurring later. At the same time, the earlier depression may have depended in part on factors revealed by the other variables; the social situation may have been basically the same on the earlier occasion.

That the variable 'Initiates social activities' proves to have a discriminatory function is more difficult to explain, since the result is the opposite of what we might have expected. About 40 per cent of the depressed as against 28 per cent of the non-depressed said that they often initiated various social activities. It emerged from the analysis that this variable had little connection with the other discriminatory variables. There was also least agreement here between the statements of the respondents and those of their close relatives or friends, which seemed strange since one would have expected this to have been an area where friends would have the best chance of knowing the facts. In most cases it was a question of whether the respondent or his relative or friend had actually taken the initiative with regard to a particular leisure-time activity. The patient group accounted for the biggest difference: according to their relatives the patients did not take the initiative as often as they themselves claimed. In the control group (particularly the depressed among them), respondents laid claim to less initiative than their relatives or friends gave them credit for. One explanation of these results may be that the patients thought they had taken the initiative, but for some reason the message did not get through to their relatives. Another possibility (which need not contradict the previous explanation) is that the patient group did not take very much initiative but that they wanted to appear in their own and/or other people's eyes to have done so. This interpretation accords with the results of the comparison between respondents' and relatives' answers to questions with a negative content (demands, dominance). It is further supported by the fact that, in the patient group, women in particular claimed to have taken the initiative (45 per cent as against 26 per cent of the men). In the control group, on the other hand, it was somewhat more usual for the man to take the initiative, which is only to be expected in view of the sex roles prevailing in our society.

The last two variables in the discriminant analysis, 'Mother at home or working' and 'Independent work', do not make any significant difference to the discrimination already achieved. A few more of the depressed people appeared to have had in their childhood mothers who worked outside the home (38 per cent as against 28 per cent of the non-depressed, which is not a significant difference). This may suggest that more of the depressed were denied some of the security or stimulus they needed in childhood because both their parents were working outside the home, which was particularly common in working-class families. The studied population grew up during the 1930s, the 1940s and the 1950s, at a time when the old extended family had almost entirely disappeared as a form of community living, when normal working hours were eight to ten hours a day and there was very little organization for child care. It must have been even more onerous then than it is now to have to work both inside and outside the home.

Thus we found that variables connected with the partner relationship distinguished between the two groups most clearly. The depressed had less successful contact with their partners and they felt that their parents subjected them to heavy demands; some of them said that their partners were not particularly important. This result did not surprise me, partly because the questions referred to the period immediately preceding the onset of the depression. The great majority of the respondents were women, which probably meant that for most people in both groups the partner represented what we can call the 'most significant other'. If the character of the respondent's relationship with her partner is negative (e.g. noted for inadequate depth contact and heavy demands), it is hardly surprising that she will have less chance than other people of coping with a stressful situation. And it appeared to be particularly common that the negative partner contact was the very factor that had to a great extent contributed to the stressful situation, which in Becker's terms means a situation resulting in reduced self-esteem. Negative ratings as regards 'depth', 'demands', and 'importance' in the relationship all suggest in different ways limitations on the range of possible actions. That the apparently contradictory ideas of 'demands' and 'lack of importance' have the same effect is presumably because in the first case the subject is not allowed to perform certain actions and in the other is not encouraged to take action herself.

It is not surprising that for much the same sort of reasons parent contact also seems to have a considerable effect on the possible development of a depression. This relationship may not now, in adult life, be as important as the partner relationship, but it is likely in most cases to have been very important at an earlier stage when it may have set off the development of a depressive personality. Even in adult life our parents generally come next in importance after our own family.

With the help of the discriminant analysis we can also examine the variables that hang together or that appear to stem from some common underlying factor. The variable 'Depth in partner relationship' has most links with other variables, in the first place with 'Independent work' and 'Demands in partner relationship', and to a lesser extent with 'Demand in parent relationship' and 'Proportion of dominating leisure-time contacts'. Thus, depressed people who have little or no independence at work, whose partner and parents make heavy demands on them, and who have rather a lot of dominating friends, will generally enjoy poor contact with their partners. *But* the reverse is not equally likely. We cannot draw any conclusions about causality in this purely *statistical* connection, but a few interesting suppositions suggest themselves.

It seems reasonable to suppose that people with depressive personalities (low self-esteem, rigid action patterns, and a limited range of possible actions) will find it more difficult to establish depth contact and easier to perceive demands imposed by others; they are also less likely to take jobs requiring independence. That lack of depth in the partner relationship emerges as the most important factor may depend on the very great expectations which are linked with the idea of success in this particular area. It is also possible that the depressive personality has been partly moulded by the negative relationship (dominance, demands, lack of depth contact) with parents, although this relationship may often have 'improved', perhaps because the subject has decided to be more humble or because he has resigned himself to the state of affairs as it is. But in our culture we are not expected to show the same degree of respect or subservience towards a spouse as towards a parent, and hope for an improvement in an unsatisfactory relationship is more likely to persist. There may be a third reason for the importance of 'Depth in partner relationship' as a discriminatory variable, namely that the probability of being able to talk openly within the partner relationship is much greater for someone who has been able to acquire assurance and self-esteem in *one* of the two major spheres of action outside the immediate family, namely in the parent relationship or at work. It seems to me that these three possibilities together provide the best explanation of the results of the discriminant analysis.

Another variable that to a great extent embraces the discriminatory powers of the other variables is 'Occurrence of depression prior to the study period'. A very large proportion of the depressed who had experienced many previous stressful events also had inadequate depth contact with their parents, while many of those who described their relationship with their parents as demanding had also been depressed prior to the relevant period. The opposite relation was not equally strong. This suggests that a negative parent relationship and/or involvement in very stressful events played an important part in generating earlier depressions. We can then assume that in many cases the earlier depression, together with the negative relationship with parents and the stressful events, set off the development of a depressive personality.

2.7 WHAT SORT OF PEOPLE BECOME DEPRESSED DESPITE A FAVOURABLE SOCIAL BACKGROUND?

According to the discriminant analysis in my study, 28 of the 107 depressed patients and depressed controls should not have become depressed according to our prediction. These people became depressed although they had good relationships with partner and parents and although they had not suffered a previous depression. Perhaps they had in fact suffered an earlier depression *or* had an unsatisfactory relationship with their parents *or* a non-confiding partner bond, but the two satisfactory variables had cancelled out the single unsatisfactory factor, thus falsifying the prediction. I therefore examined separately all those who 'should not' have become depressed but who had done so. Two main groups emerged:

(1) Those whose personalities were not notably depressive but who had suffered some stressful event which had presumably had a powerful effect on their self-esteem

(2) Those who appeared to have very low self-esteem and who were therefore very sensitive to pressure.

One or two cases were difficult to assign to either of these categories (for example M, described on p. 119 below), but most of the 28 subjects appeared to belong to the first group. Among these people it turned out that difficulties at work or the serious illness or death of a close relative had been the direct cause of the depression. There were also one or two cases where an unexpected divorce, a difficult relationship with parents or children, or a troublesome pregnancy had been the triggering factor. The common experience was thus that some extremely severe life event was required to make these subjects depressed, and in fact most people would probably have reacted in the same way in similar situations. There was very little to suggest the development of a depressive personality; none of the people concerned appeared to have particularly low self-esteem and they had resources within themselves to help them to recover from their depression. This impression was supported by the fact that a higher proportion of the unpredictedly depressed, in comparison with the predictably depressed,

—were depressed for the first time
—took the initiative themselves in seeking help
—did not consider themselves to be particularly depressed.

They gave evidence of initiative and even insight into their own situation, differing in this respect from the typical depressive personality. The fact that they did not regard themselves as being particularly depressed, despite a diagnosis of serious depression according to the more 'objective' assessment of Zung's rating scale, may have suggested lack of insight, but I interpreted it rather as the expression of a strong determination to overcome the depression. Again, this is in marked contrast to those who more or less 'choose' depression as a way of obtaining support for their own self-pity. These last, paradoxical though it may seem, use their depression as a way of acquiring self-esteem. The depression gives them, so they feel, some value; at least they have become someone about whom other people are concerned. In all this it seems to me that most of the unpredictedly depressed in my study differed from the typical depressive personality. An example of strength and a determination to cope with a difficult situation was provided by one 40-year-old woman whom I shall call S. In the end she could not cope any more, but who would have been able to do so?

One summer a few years ago S finally acquired a much longed-for adopted child. She and her husband had hoped for a long time to have a child of their own. The years passed and the adopted daughter failed to develop at anything like the same rate as her contemporaries. She took up a great deal of S's time. In fact, S reorganized her whole life in order to help the child. She cut down her social activities drastically. She had always been fond of reading, going to the theatre, and being generally active in lots of ways. All this she gave up for the child's sake. A few years later brain damage was finally diagnosed. S was deeply disappointed in her child and yet loved her dearly. Her whole soul and all her strength had been devoted to the task of caring for her. But to what purpose? The greatest cause of sadness to her was her own feelings. She felt she had failed to cope with the expectations and conflicts in her feelings for her daughter. Nevertheless, S suffered only a mild depression, which she tried hard to combat on her own. When she did finally seek psychiatric help it was to get support in solving the family's problems rather than because of her own depression.

The second group which was 'wrongly' classified as non-depressed differs in many ways from the group just described. Nor was the second group as clear-cut; the one common feature, nevertheless, seemed to be low self-esteem. Three traits appeared to dominate among the members of this group: some were very sensitive to stress and criticism, some were isolated and tied to their homes, while some appeared to the interviewers to be prevaricating and playing down the problems in their relationships with other people. It can, I think, be assumed that they all suffered from low self-esteem, and that very mild threats to their self-esteem were enough to make them depressed. It also seems likely that if they had answered the questions more truthfully, some evidence of negative aspects in their relationship with parents or spouse or of an earlier depression would probably have come out. Their reason for wanting to give the interviewer a more positive picture of themselves was presumably their low self-esteem. Perhaps, too, they still had some hope that everything would turn out for the best and were afraid of jeopardizing this possibility in any way.

It is relatively easy to understand the low self-esteem of those who were isolated in their homes. According to Ernest Becker's theory, low self-esteem stems in the first place from the narrowing down of the range of possible actions. The home-bound who are cut off from the world outside naturally find it difficult to envisage alternative openings, and presumably have little access to value-enhancing reinforcement. They have no self-value (self-esteem); their value is embodied in relationships with others (husband and children). It does not, therefore, take much to make them feel utterly worthless.

It was more difficult to understand those who were oversensitive to stress and criticism. Why did these people (they were all women) apparently have so little self-esteem, although the outward facts of their lives (work, parent contact, partner contact) should have given them a satisfactory idea of their own value? I concluded that it probably depended on circumstances not covered by the questions in the investigation, mainly perhaps conditions during childhood such as exaggerated demands, lack of consideration and care during the first years of life, and traumatic events. And perhaps, too, these women may have cherished one particular aspect of the typical female sexual role, namely that of living only for other people.

In general, then, most of the people who became depressed, despite apparently positive circumstances, in a period preceding the onset of the depression had been exposed to considerable pressure. The threat to their self-esteem had become too great even for their non-depressive personalities. Many people in the second group, on the other hand, probably did have depressive personalities, but circumstances in the period preceding the onset of depression were not particularly difficult, or at least they had not wanted to admit to any problems. A very small straw was enough to break the camel's back.

2.8 WHAT SORT OF PEOPLE DO NOT BECOME DEPRESSED, DESPITE NEGATIVE RELATIONSHIPS?

In our material, of 118 interview subjects, 14 who 'should' have become depressed according to our discriminant analysis did not in fact do so. Most of them seemed to me to have non-depressive personalities, but in the period preceding the negative patch in their lives they had suffered *temporary* problems in their partner relationships. They formed a fairly homogeneous group. They were all women and because of conditions on the labour market had all with one exception had to be separated from their partners for a while. Once the social situation improved, their relationship problems also resolved themselves. The other woman's depression ceased when she left the boyfriend she had been living with for a couple of years. She declared that it was the quarrels and rows that had caused her depression. Since she took the initiative to move, her 'low' period did not need to develop into a full-blown depression. The very fact that the problems in the relationships were temporary, and that the subjects had the determination and the ability to find solutions to their problems, seems to me to prove that there was no question of depressive personalities.

Typical of these cases, too, was that none of the women described particularly serious problems. It is possible, even probable, that if they had been confronted with the same severe problems as those described at the beginning of the previous section (p. 22), they too would have reacted with depressive symptoms. Brown and Harris's results suggest very strongly that over and above any unfavourable background conditions, a 'provoking agent' is almost always required before a depression develops (Brown and Harris, 1978). They found that those who ran the greatest risk of depression had a non-confiding relationship with their partners, had suffered early loss of mother, and/or had more than three children under 14 living at home. *None* of the nine women in this highest risk group who had *not* been exposed to a 'severe event or major difficulty' developed a depressive disorder. The severe events or major difficulty are the equivalent of the threatened or impaired self-esteem in Becker's theory. Thus Brown and Harris as well as my own earlier investigation support Becker's assumption that depression is triggered off by the threat to or the loss of self-esteem. What this can mean in concrete terms will be studied in more detail in the next chapter.

CHAPTER 3

What stressful events tend to precipitate depression?

The interviews in my study were to a great extent unstructured. After asking the interview subjects to recall a depressive or a negative period, we also asked them to tell us something about the background to this low patch in their lives. We tried to discover whether the problem was in itself connected with the subject's relationships or with his work or leisure-time activities. Some of the responses to these questions were quite long and detailed. The interviews were then summarized and I divided the complex of problems into nine categories (in doubtful cases I talked it over with the relevant interviewer), based on the 'precipitating events' most often suggested in the psychiatric literature of depression.

Beck (1967) suggests that the precipitating events can be classified in three groups. The most common type of situation is the one that impairs a person's self-esteem (e.g. failing to pass a test, being left by a lover, losing a job). Other situations which can trigger off a depression are those which interfere with important plans, and lastly Beck mentions physical illness which can turn a man's mind to thoughts of physical deterioration or death. As I see it, and I base my view on Becker, common to all these precipitating events is the fact that they have a negative effect on self-esteem or self-respect. The sufferer is unable to realize his earlier intentions or to do what he thought he would be able to do.

Brown *et al.* (1973a) are very dubious about reliance on what patients or their relatives have to say about precipitating events. Such people, they claim, tend to exaggerate the depressive implications of the various events. The authors solved this problem in their own study by including only events which they had defined beforehand and which could be linked with a particular point in time. But in a later report (Brown *et al.*, 1973b) they discussed the problems connected with their approach, problems which they partly resolve in their later studies (Brown and Harris, 1978).

Nor is it reasonable to reach any sort of final conclusion about the proportion of patients involved in a total environmental effect without a complex analysis that takes account of a whole range of other possible social influences such as long-term social problems not the result of a life-event in the period studied, frequency and range of social contacts, quality of marriage, amount of social support, and so on. (Brown *et al.* 1973b, p. 171)

Another objection to these researchers' approach is that whether or not the stated cause appears trivial to an outside observer, it can still have very significant consequences for the person concerned. The implications and significance of anything that happens to him is determined by his own particular and very personal yardsticks. Thus it seems to me that we are more likely to get nearer the 'truth' by listening to someone relating a particular event to his own earlier experiences than by letting an 'objective' researcher try to pick out significant events beforehand. At the same time I have concluded from my own and other investigations that people with depressive personalities often find it very difficult to say why they are depressed. Becker's theoretical arguments point to the same thing: the depressed person generally singles out isolated events but finds it very difficult to perceive the really big problems and the complicated inter-relationships. We also have to remember that the different studies have had different purposes; Brown and Harris's chief aim was to see whether there was a causal link between life events and depression. In my study I was more interested in the *type* of problem that predominated in different groups, and how these tied up with the immediate social conditions.

The solution I chose in my own study consisted of elements drawn from various existing approaches. The patients' own accounts steered my subsequent classification to a great extent. In cases where several problem areas were mentioned, I tried to decide what appeared to have been most important in the depressive context. I did not try to isolate single triggering factors, but assumed that the respondent's problems could equally well have evolved as part of a composite process (limited, however, to a period of six months before the onset of depression). Nevertheless, problems classified as 'Other problems', 'Difficulties at work or study', and 'Family problems', in other words problems which often consist of such composite processes, proved difficult to assess. It was also this kind of problem that produced the most disagreement between the interview subjects and their relatives (see Table 2).

Twenty-seven respondents in the non-depressed group had to be left out of the

Table 2   Dominating problems

	Non-depressed (%)	Depressed controls (%)	Patients (%)
Loss of close relative	11	12	7
Loss of work	2	4	4
Problems at work	28	26	6
Somatic illness	17	10	9
Separation	2	18	21
Problems in the partner relationship	4	8	7
Family problems	13	16	12
Nothing special	3	2	12
Other problems	20	6	22
	100	102	100
	$n = 97$	$n = 51$	$n = 68$

calculations, since they could not claim to have experienced any negative periods during the last five years.

Separation proved to be one of the most common factors underlying depression. Only a very small proportion of those interviewed appeared to have coped with a separation without becoming depressed. Only two of eleven people in the control group *failed* to develop a depression, when the dominating problem was separation. But in answer to another question, when we had singled out some typical stressful events in advance (in the same way as Brown and Harris), we found that many of the non-depressed had been abandoned by their partners in adult life, without suffering depression. Among the patients the work situation did not very often appear to have been the direct cause of depression; in the control group, on the other hand, it had been. Two factors confirmed that problems at work seldom lead to serious depression, namely that the patients with this problem were not hospitalized, and that the state of the depressed for whom this had been the main problem was not particularly acute. The highest rating on Zung's scale of depressions attached to the problems 'Nothing special', 'Separation' and 'Difficulties in partner relationship' in that order. The 'Nothing special' category included all those who were unable to pinpoint an event or a problem which could be connected with their depression. From the answers to another question about dominating problems, it appeared that roughly three of four depressed people claimed some connection with problems in their personal relationships. I imagine that if we could go more closely into the cases of those who were unable to cite any reasons for their depression, we would very often find relationship problems there too (see also pp. 116–121). My general conclusion from these results is that the great majority of people who become depressed have *set their hopes on other people*. When the expectations are not or cannot be fulfilled, it is regarded as a personal failure. Another result which provided some support for this assumption emerged when we asked about earlier positive periods and their antecedents. Many members of the control group replied 'Had a child' and 'Work was going well'. In the patient group the main comments were 'Had been keeping well' and 'Relationship with partner was good'.

Thus, the various studies of precipitating factors and depression have used different methods and ended up with different classifications. But none of the findings actually contradicts the results that emerged from our questions about dominating problems. Brown and Harris (1978) concluded that 'separation from either a husband, boy-friend, confidante or child' was a loss common to many of those who developed clinical depression. They emphasized 'that loss and disappointment are the central features of most events bringing about clinical depression and these are, of course, just the kind of events that would be expected to produce feelings of depression' (p. 103). In this they agree with Stenback (1975), who found that the most common major problem underlying depression was 'external losses' and in particular 'loss problems related to nuclear family'. Leff *et al.* (1970) found that 'threat to sexual identity and changes in marital relationship were the most important stressful environmental events within one year prior to the point of breakdown in functioning'. Paykel *et al.* (1969)

compared life events that occurred six months before a psychiatric contact in a depressive group and a control group. The depressive group proved to have suffered many more events which could be described as 'exits', i.e. death, divorce, geographical separation, and so on had caused departures from the social field of the subject. It also appeared that a very high proportion of the events were connected with marital relationships, in particular divorce or 'an increase in arguments with the spouse'. Thus these and other studies show that many factors which often precipitate a depression can be traced to family relationships. The corresponding categories in my classification are separation, problems in partner relationship, and family problems. It is less usual for the predominant precipitating problems to be connected with working life or the subject's physical health. My own study suggested, however, that the situation at work can often be the direct cause of depression among people who do not seek psychiatric help. Factors connected with friends and leisure activities are very rarely mentioned as a major problem in connection with depression.

3.1 DOMINATING PROBLEMS AND WHY PEOPLE BECOME DEPRESSED

Why and how do the dominating problems discussed here constitute so serious a threat to self-esteem that depression can result? In discussing this question I shall refer to Becker's theory and to the findings presented in Table 2.

3.1.1 Loss of close relative

The loss of a close relative is something which we almost all have to suffer at some time or another. But the risk of losing a close relative becomes greater as we grow older. One reason for the comparative rarity of this particular problem in my data was the age of the interview subjects who were all between 25 and 50 years old. The difficulty of deciding where to draw the line between grief and depression has already been mentioned (see pp. 4–5). Why can a natural grief so easily develop into depression? Benton (1972) points out that dependence on the lost one is more important in this context than, for example, how much he may have been loved. Ramsay (1978) studied grief in terms of behavioural psychology and came to the same conclusion. Most vulnerable were people who had an ambivalent love–hate relationship with the lost one, or who had been passively dependent upon him. What is crucial in these cases is 'the feeling of release from a difficult partnership, with the accompanying guilt for not feeling sad'. Not being sad about the deceased although one should be, hating him although one ought not to, and thinking more about oneself than about the deceased—all these reactions can generate terrible feelings of guilt. And such feelings will be reinforced by guilt about the actual death: at certain moments the bereaved may have wished for the other's death, and he now thinks that if he had treated the lost one more kindly he would not have died (Arieti, 1978). Guilt easily turns into self-hate, with resulting depression.

Thus the important point is how dependent we were on the one who has died. But the reverse relationship is also important: how dependent on us was the one who has gone, endowing us in this way with a sense of value? Now we have lost the self-esteem we acquired simply by 'being there' for someone else, by being and feeling needed. And the threat to self-esteem must be even greater if the hopes that we consciously, or unconsciously, invest in other survivors are dashed, if our children, for example, do not appear to want us.

Loss of the spouse through death is also more likely to lead to depression if the dead partner was involved in most of the possible actions available to the surviving partner. If you have lived with someone for a long time he is obviously likely to be a part of most of the things you do. And the more complete the world you have built up together, the more difficult it will be to find new openings, new opportunities for action. You have become familiar with a certain definite 'world', inextricably linked with the presence of your life partner. 'We did so much together; now he's gone there's nothing left to live for.' As Emmy Gut (1974) puts it, the mourner may be at a disadvantage if she has always before adapted herself to the needs and habits of the deceased. She has refrained from satisfying some of her own needs and thus ignored opportunities for developing her own talents and interests. 'Doors have been closed, bridges have been burnt, perhaps a long time ago.'

Gut also discusses another quite different aspect of the problem: namely, the death of a close relative reminds us of our own death. And this arouses feelings which our culture seldom allows us to express. Such feelings smother our possible action outlets from within, by arousing in us the strong fear of our own death, and above all the fear of having to die.

3.1.2 Loss of work

Loss of work might have been expected to prove a common problem underlying depression. One reason why it was not so common in our study was presumably that 80 per cent of our interview subjects were women. About one-third were housewives or students and were therefore excluded from the possibility of being officially 'unemployed'. The question we asked about stressful events also showed that since they became adult less than 10 per cent of all those interviewed had ever had to leave a job. And of the five stressful events discussed in the interviews (see p. 37), loss of work seemed to be regarded as the least serious. Here, too, the explanation is probably to be found in the high proportion of women among the respondents. I have already referred in several contexts to the relative importance to women of the life of the family. The argument can also be turned round: events outside the family do not generally mean as much to women as they do to men. The loss of an occupational position would not therefore be such a disaster to a woman's self-esteem as it would be to a man's. There are, of course, many reasons for this situation connected with traditional sexual roles, economic dependence, political resources, and so on.

In what situations can unemployment lead to depression? Our study suggested that depression in which the dominating problem has been unemployment will also be connected with limited access to leisure interests and a restricted range of intimate relationships. In such cases work is the only thing that means anything. Unwanted job loss cannot therefore be remedied in any other sphere and there is nobody to discuss the disappointment with; the range of possible actions is thus sharply restricted. Any hopes that had been invested in the lost job are also naturally important, and so are the opportunities for finding other work. If a man has staked almost his whole self on a particular job, and if the chances of finding a similar occupation are small, he will obviously be very vulnerable to depression if he is compelled to leave his job.

3.1.3 Problems at work

In our investigation, difficulties at work or in connection with studies were a common problem in the control group, both for those who admitted to a depressive period and to those who merely admitted to a negative one. On the other hand, this kind of problem was far less common in the patient group. This does not mean that difficulties at work were unimportant in the depressive context, simply that in the patient group they were seldom the *dominating* problem. It was much more usual for this to be the dominating problem among men than among women. Stenback (1965) came to a similar result in a study undertaken in the USA. He also reached a classification based on the dominating problems (what he called 'main factors with crucial etiological importance'). Of the 86 hospitalized patients with a diagnosis of depression, loss of partner was the most common problem among the women, and difficulties at work the most common among the men.

There can, of course, be different kinds of problems at work. Those most often mentioned in my study were conflicts with superiors or with colleagues, and underlying most of these seemed to be a loss of control over one's own actions. Jobs that had previously been accepted without any complaints were now perhaps no longer approved. The sense of security connected with knowing what one could and should be doing had been lost and so, too, had the sense of being in control.

What can this mean in more concrete terms? It is quite common for people to feel that conflicts at work are insoluble. For both rational and irrational reasons they can see no way out. At the same time they regard their jobs as meaningless. If they receive no appreciation from superiors or colleagues, and can see no point in the tasks that absorb so much of their time, they will naturally feel unsuccessful and soon nothing seems to have any meaning any more. The sense of personal loss will be particularly strong in people who have adopted what Weber calls the Protestant ethic, i.e. people who believe that work is what chiefly gives meaning to life. This ideal and this attitude are certainly very common among men in Western societies.

3.1.4 Somatic illness

A physical illness is sometimes a serious underlying factor in depression. Physical illnesses vary very much in their nature and severity, and the crucial question in the present context will be: how much does a severe illness or disability affect the patient's previous way of life. How much of what he used to enjoy doing must he now give up?

Why is it that despite their obvious unpleasantness somatic disorders are not a particularly common precipitating factor in depressions? One reason why the respondents in my study so rarely mentioned this as a dominating problem prior to depression was simply that they were comparatively young (25–50). Stenback (1965) has shown that physical disease is a much more common and more important factor in depression among people over 65. But even in this age group it is not the most common. And in the lower age groups, physical illness comes low on the list of important factors.

Perhaps somatic illness rarely leads to depression mainly because it does not generally have much effect on our actual *control* over the range of possible actions: either we can do what we used to, or we cannot. The element of uncertainly, of continually having to wonder whether we can cope, is not so common. This last point suggests another important aspect: when we are physically ill, it is not our value as human beings that is primarily in doubt. Nor need there necessarily be any drastic change in our contacts—in the first place our verbal contacts—with other people. The assumption that somatic disease constitutes little threat to self-esteem receives some support from the fact that only the outpatient group in my study—i.e. those whose depression was less acute—ever mentioned this as a dominating problem.

Thus in cases of physical illness depression is more likely if there is uncertainty as to the seriousness of the illness or if there is some uncertainty in the patient's personal relationships: how will his family react or act in the new situation? There will naturally also be a greater risk if the physical disorder radically changes the whole of the patient's life and he is faced with the loss of a great many possible actions, as in the case of severe disability or blindness. In such situations the patient often finds himself—or prefers to be—alone; he is unable to take part in normal social life any longer. This element of ambivalence, of uncertainty, of not knowing where to turn, has also proved to be the critical factor in cases of bereavement and grief, problems at work and difficulties in personal re-lationships. And this in turn goes back to a characteristic feature of the depressive personality, namely, rigid action patterns. Those who are not flexible, those who are anxious to have clear lines to follow in life, are more likely to react to trouble with depression.

The concept of the depressive personality also helps to explain why somatic illness does not more often lead to depression. As in the case of 'Loss of a close relative' and 'Loss of work', nothing suggests that a serious illness is likely to have been preceded by the development of a depressive personality. We cannot, in other words, assume that people with depressive personalities are more likely to be afflicted by severe illness, whereas we can assume that such people are at greater risk of having problems in their families, for example. But a person who is suffering from a serious illness *and* has a depressive personality will, of course, be in a difficult position; the combination will make it difficult for the sufferer to envisage any new possibilities in life or to understand the reactions of those around him.

3.1.5 Separation

Separation from the partner is in my view the most important of the factors which can precipitate a depression. Separation is particularly likely to mean the loss of many previous opportunities for action, while at the same time the threat to self-esteem is very great.

What action opportunities are lost? Separation generally involves radical changes on many levels. On the purely practical level, life often becomes more difficult; the economic situation deteriorates, housing is difficult, and many practical everyday tasks which were previously shared now have to be tackled alone.

More important than this, however, separation means the loss of the person who has presumably been most important to self-esteem in both a positive and a negative sense. The partners both lose a bit of themselves. It may be a bit which they dislike as well as like, but it is still something which confirmed them in their knowledge of who they were. Many newly divorced people say that they feel as though they have been thrown out into the unknown, into the darkness. They have often lost someone with whom they have lived for many years, someone who was constantly present. This results in what Becker would describe as 'object-loss resulting in loss of many meanings'. In their therapeutic work with divorced families Öberg and Öberg (1979) found that divorce can often be compared with grief. 'One may grieve for lost companionship, because nothing has turned out as expected. . . . One woman we met said bitterly: "it would have been better if my husband had died—then I could have kept my good feelings about him. Now he is dragging all our wonderful years down into the dirt"' (p. 288). Öberg and Öberg refer to Parkes (1972). Parkes studied the reactions of widows on the death of their husbands and found that the loss of identity and roles was a very important factor. The same applies to divorce: we suffer from the loss of the roles which the other person provided us with. None of the things the partners are used to doing together is available in the same way any longer. Many women who separate from their husbands lose friends at the same time, since many of them were connected with the ex-partner (see, for example, case P, p. 174). Thus there is not only the loss of action opportunities connected with the partner, but also the loss of opportunities that the partner made available. Where there are children, one partner is probably also going to lose the action opportunities that the children used to provide.

So far we have only looked at the loss of action opportunities in the external or social sphere. As part of our interior life we all build up a number of definite ideas around out partners, and these become part of the way we see the world. It is probably in connection with our partners that we are most likely to develop very rigid action patterns. The separation is in itself a sign that our previously definite ideas have collapsed. As a result of the separation we lose a conceptual base, that base which previously consisted of the rigid action pattern.

Öberg and Öberg's study confirms the view that people who are emotionally and cognitively fixated on their partners are affected more severely by divorce. Paradoxically, it is the people who do not dare to *express* their despair at having been rejected, at having been found wanting, who have the greatest difficulty in coping with divorce. The grief has to be worked through just as in bereavement, otherwise the loss will weigh increasingly on the mind, and the sufferer will not understand why. This introversion, this paralysis, lays the foundations for future depression. We should be able to express not only our loss but also the aggression that we feel towards our partner. People who are 'sensible', who are 'brave', who do not give vent to their sense of loss, disappointment, and rage—they are the ones who in the end run the greatest risk of becoming depressed. As Becker would put it, they are the frightened people, who are terrified of anxiety, who try to put a brave face on it. But brave faces can become impossible to keep up if the pain and disappointment are too great.

3.1.6 Problems in the partner relationship

Problems in a partner relationship will naturally often precede a separation. The decisive difference between these problems and an actual separation is that they do not constitute an irretrievable loss, and this is certainly one reason why relationship problems did not appear as often in our investigations as we might have expected. The analysis of non-responses also suggested that many people prefer to cover up problems of this kind. Several people whose medical records, for instance, revealed problems in their partner relationships, refused to take part in the study. I have also discovered subsequently that one or two respondents failed to mention this problem when they were interviewed. I conclude from all this that problems in the partner relationship are a more common underlying factor in depression than our study showed.

What kind of problem in the relationship between two people may represent so great a threat to self-esteem as to lead to depression? According to my results it seems to be mainly a question of conflict and difficulty in getting through to one another. Conflict is an expression of disappointment; the couple fail to live up to one another's expectations. If they are also unable to communicate their expectations to one another, they may soon draw back, letting the space between them stretch to almost unbridgeable proportions. When people sense a great distance of this sort, they want to shout or express themselves in some other exaggerated way in order to make themselves heard. And this leads to feelings of guilt and failure. They feel worthless; their self-esteem is threatned. If their common platform threatens to fall apart, they begin to suffer from the same losses as the separated couple: they miss the actions they previously shared, and their definite picture of reality, in which the other partner has always represented an integral part, begins to dissolve. If the situation gets as bad as this there will naturally be a great threat to self-esteem.

3.1.7 Family problems

Family problems as defined in my study often include an element of partner-relationship problems, but not of such a serious kind as those just described. The fundamental difference, however, was that this category included cases in which we judged the whole family situation to be difficult. The parent–child relationship was often one element in a more complex whole. Moreover, depression cannot always be explained solely on grounds of the *relationship* between husband and wife; it is often a question of one of them having difficulties which then affect the whole family. One woman whose husband did a lot of overtime provided an example of this. The man had no time to spare for family life; he bacame over-tired and, in the end, so depressed that he sought psychiatric help. At about this time one of his brothers committed suicide, which added to the overall difficulties. His wife—our respondent—had no help with the children; she was anxious about her husband and the family. The woman in this example did not become depressed, but she described this period in her life as a negative one. The couple apparently had an open and trusting relationship. She was affected by the situation and she worried about it, but she did not feel *let down*.

It is when the common problems cannot be discussed openly that depression may follow. People wonder: 'Have *I* done something wrong?' They turn their reproaches in on themselves, and find it impossible to change the situation by making a common effort. Guilt feelings and passivity are a threat to self-esteem. There are also cases in which great hopes are invested in the family, particularly in the children. If the parents believe their children have failed, they only too readily blame themselves, since the children have been the crucial interest in their lives. And in fact a feature common to people in our study whose family problems led to depression was just this: that they had devoted most of their lives to the family, and the hopes they had invested in it had come to nothing.

3.1.8 Nothing special

'Nothing special' was registered when respondents could not point to any particular events or problems which might have been connected with their depression. Possible explanations of this inability will be discussed in Chapter 9. I agree here with Leff *et al.* (1970) and others that a closer investigation of the lives of the depressed nearly always reveals perfectly understandable reasons for the depression. Why, then, can they not see the explanation themselves? The answer is probably to be found in the inadequate self-insight that is typical of the depressive individual. Over the years he has increasingly organized his experience and his picture of life in line with what he feels sure of, what he can predict with certainty. His view of life and of himself is thus very narrow. If some event falls outside his rigid patterns, he finds it very difficult to explain it to himself and even more difficult to explain it to other people. Searching for explanations means looking at things from *different* viewpoints; for a person who has only one viewpoint, which for some reason has become invalid, no alternative viewpoints are available from which to take a look at himself. This must be particularly difficult when, as is often the case, the underlying problems are very complex and have their roots in early childhood.

3.1.9 Other problems

If we now look again at Table 2, we see that a large proportion of the patient group have a dominating problem that is assigned to the residual category 'Other problems'. The most common problems under this heading were: a feeling of isolation and unsuccessful attempts to break out of isolation, major financial problems, and difficulties during or immediately following pregnancy. The following is an interesting case in which it seems to me that the predominant problem was isolation and loneliness.

N was a fairly young, single woman who had been attending the psychiatric clinic as an outpatient the same year that she was interviewed by us. She was still feeling pretty low when we met her, and since our questions refered to a fairly recent period she had good recall. The interview was a long one, since N obviously greatly needed to talk about her feelings.

In the period prior to the onset of depression N had been working for a year in nursing. She enjoyed her work, but still sometimes found it difficult to cope with all the strain and responsibility. She lived with her sister, but did not feel that they were very close to one another. She was much closer to a friend she didn't see very often, because they lived about 60 miles from one another. Otherwise she spent her leisure time with a colleague, and less often with her two brothers. At the beginning of 1975 she began to spend more time alone; she didn't find any of her interests enjoyable any more. She didn't feel that she could ever be herself but was simply putting on an act. There was no one she could talk to about it.

N grew up in a working-class home in a town in northern Sweden. Her father worked at the sawmill and her mother stayed at home. Her mother was very nervous; among other things she chain-smoked and chewed rice. N does not have very much contact with her parents now, and what contact she has is unrewarding; her parents make heavy demands on her.

We also interviewed N's sister. She seemed rather uncertain about the nature of N's relationships. But N's sister found it a relief to talk about things with somebody, since she was having rather a difficult time herself. She gave much the same explanation of the depression as N herself, i.e. that N felt lonely and found it difficult to communicate with other people. N wasn't good at superficial contacts; she wouldn't pretend, but wanted to be herself. According to her sister, N was too wrapped up in her job. She showed her feelings, with the result that the patients made heavy demands on her. N quite often went out dancing with her sister, but regarded the whole undertaking as pointless. Sometimes she was unhappy because she wasn't asked to dance often enough.

A dominating problem for N, although it was never mentioned openly, seems to have been the lack of a close boy-friend in whom she could confide. The sister mentioned that N was once deserted by a boy-friend, and that she had been depressed afterwards. N did not mention this herself.

Loneliness can be particularly difficult to bear when, as in this example, it is involuntary and occurs at a time when the pressure of work is great. Minor failures become exaggerated if there is no chance of talking them over with somebody close. It is easy to lose faith in oneself if gallant efforts to make human contact all fail. This must be particularly threatening to someone whose earlier social environment was very different from the present one, someone who perhaps set great store by acquiring social contacts. If an individual has weak roots in the past (and therefore little support for self-esteem), and these fragile roots anyway prove irrelevant in the new social setting, it is hardly surprising if she (or he) begins to feel worthless as a human being.

Respondents who mentioned financial problems as grounds for depression were almost all men. Men generally expect to have to cope with the economic side of life, and if they do not succeed they feel they have failed both as men and as human beings. It is probably not the economic poverty as such that is critical in a depressive context, so much as the anxiety about what may happen, the self-reproaches and criticism from the immediate family, all of which in different ways can help to destroy self-esteem.

Finally, let us look at those who mentioned pregnancy and the period immediately following it as the cause of depression. It is not unusual to hear this type of depression explained in terms of biological changes in the body. Major physical readjustments and hormonal changes are often mentioned. It seems to me that we are dealing with a phenomenon similar to the depressions arising at the menopause (known as involutional depressions, see p. 60f), but that in the present case the social–psychological factors can be even more clearly distinguished. The pregnant woman is abandoning, or is about to abandon, her life as one of a pair, and to embark on a completely new relationship with the baby. Expectations are vested in both husband and child. If the happiness she has envisaged is not realized, everyday problems are going to seem overwhelming. Neither husband nor wife give each other strength as before: they feel alone, missing the old confirmation of their own value. Another factor that certainly helps to reduce self-esteem at this time is the new obstacle to social activities; the couple are suddenly tied to the domestic hearth. For a woman (or man) who has enjoyed many interests outside the home, this is an obvious loss of possible action alternatives. And all these problems are naturally aggravated by the fact that during this period the woman is not as physically strong as she was before.

CHAPTER 4

Personal history—trauma and previous depression

In this chapter we will look at life events in adulthood as factors predisposing to depression. Events in childhood will be examined in more detail in Chapter 5. The present discussion will be limited to stressful events, since these have been the subject of most previous empirical investigations. In particular I shall examine the importance of an earlier depressive disorder.

4.1 HAVE THE DEPRESSED SUFFERED MORE STRESSFUL EVENTS THAN OTHER PEOPLE?

One question in our empirical investigation concerned events in adult life (18 years or older): had the respondent suffered any such events and if so how serious were they felt to have been? In order to counteract as much as possible the effects of memory, we suggested a number of specific stressful events that might have occurred. If the same type of event had occurred more than once, it was registered as two events. The following stressful events were included in our lists:

(1) Involuntary cessation of work
(2) Death of a loved one
(3) Rejection in an important relationship
(4) A serious accident or illness
(5) An event that interfered with important plans.

The list was composed after consulting psychiatric literature and discussing the various items with psychiatrists and sociologists. The headings probably cover most of the events that are regarded as serious by members of modern Western societies. By limiting ourselves to such specific, isolated events we naturally risk missing other long-lasting 'events', i.e. processes that may be difficult to identify but which can be every bit as destructive in their impact.

Our results suggested that depressed people will have been exposed to a far greater number of stressful events than the non-depressed. The event most often mentioned was 'death of a loved one' (68 per cent), followed by 'rejection in an important relationship' (28 per cent). More people in the depressed group than in the non-depressed group had experienced all the listed events except for one: the death of a loved one was mentioned equally often by both groups. The interesting point here is that 'death of a loved one' is the only event over which we as human beings have absolutely no control. In the case of other events which are extremely difficult to control, namely 'involuntary cessation of work' and 'serious accident or illness', the difference between the two groups was also slight.

This result seemed to suggest that the predominance of stressful events in the lives of those who later became depressed may have been a retrospective construction rather than a reality. In other words, the depressed turned to such events to explain their depression. However, our interviews with the close relatives of the depressed provided no support for this suspicion. The relatives of the respondents mentioned a somewhat lower number of events, but this was as true of the non-depressed as of the depressed group. Moreover, the respondents and their relatives both mentioned the *same* events and were equally able to state clearly when they had occurred. Thus it seems reasonably likely that the events really happened and that the depressed subjects were not showing any particular tendency to rewrite the past.

4.2 WHY HAVE THE DEPRESSED EXPERIENCED A GREATER NUMBER OF STRESSFUL EVENTS IN THEIR ADULT LIVES THAN OTHER PEOPLE?

The explanation that immediately suggests itself in answer to the question introducing this section is that the stressful events are in some way an underlying cause of the depression. Most researchers who have studied the depressive implications of stressful events have restricted themselves to the time immediately preceding onset. However, a methodically stringent study to which I have already referred in several contexts, namely Brown *et al.* (1973b), shows that 'markedly threatening events may well play a part in the development of a disorder whose onset occurs more than a year later' (p. 168). An interesting aspect of this investigation is that the authors ask a depressed group and a control group to say how many stressful events of varying degrees of severity they had experienced over a period of twelve months. The difference between the two groups was fairly small with regard to the less severe events, but was slightly greater for events of moderate severity experienced immediately before the onset of depression. But when it came to the very severe events, the depressed groups had experienced more of them *throughout the whole period.* The authors suggest that these events may thus have had a causal significance, and that they were not simply precipitating factors. I suggest that the events included in our investigation can be ranked as serious. Perhaps the traumatic event triggers off a long process which ultimately leaves the individual unable to cope and ready to retreat into depression. This hypothesis fits the findings of crisis therapy and crisis research (Cullberg, 1975; Caplan, 1964), namely that unless a crisis or a traumatic event can somehow be 'handled', it will sooner or later lead to psychological breakdown. This was exactly what had happened to most of the depressed people in my study. In many cases severe events from earlier periods in their personal history had also caused previous depression. It was thus impossible to say whether the earlier events as such or the earlier depression lay at the root of the present depression. Why earlier depression can contribute to the development of further depression will be discussed later in this chapter. Thus my first answer to the question at the head of this section is that directly or indirectly traumatic events lead to depression, from which it can be concluded that the depressed have been involved in more stressful events than the non-depressed.

Or, secondly, we could reverse the causal sequence and assume that a depressive personality (with low self-esteem, a narrow range of possible actions, and so on) has a predispostion to become involved in stressful events. In part they actually cause the severe events to happen. There was some support for this hypothesis in our findings. The events which revealed the least difference between the groups were those over which people had hardly any control. On the other hand, the depressed group had been involved in considerably more events in the categories 'rejection in an important relationship' and 'an event that interfered with important plans'. People are, of course, predisposed to events of this kind if they nurse unrealistic aspirations, persuading themselves, perhaps, that a relationship characterized by inequality and mutual misunderstanding can evolve into an equitable and satisfactory partnership, or even convincing themselves that this has happened. And then, suddenly, the unimaginable happens and they are rejected. Others may be equally unrealistic about their occupational or educational goals; with very poor grades they perhaps expect to be accepted for a university course demanding high entrance qualifications. According to Becker's theory (see p. 144) it is just this unrealistic view of the self and the world that is typical of the depressive personality. Another noticeable feature of the typical depressive is lack of confidence in his own resources and over-reliance on other people. This makes it difficult for him to predict what is likely to happen, since someone else is the agent of his actions. At the same time, he is likely to lay himself open to oppression, to control by other people. All this leaves the depressive personality vulnerable to situations that threaten his self-esteem.

A third answer, stemming from psychodynamic theory rather than from Becker, is that some new sequence of events reactivates earlier stressful happenings, thus traumatizing the new events in a way that is difficult for an observer to understand. There is fairly clear evidence that people who develop depressions in adult life will have been involved in more traumatic events than other people during childhood. White (1977) emphasizes that loss of the mother during the first year of life creates a greater than ordinary vulnerability in later life to loss of people. He refers to loss in a very wide sense, including the physical absence of the mother as well as an emotional absence resulting from her inability to fulfil her child's emotional needs. What I regard as important, and what White also emphasizes, is that these earlier losses are connected with a basic human need for security. And they leave us particularly vulnerable to any later threat to our sources of security.

It is very difficult to *prove* such a connection between earlier and later trauma empirically, since we are now dealing with a subjective dimension (the *perception* of both the earlier and later stressful events). Leff *et al.* (1970) noted a frequent interaction between an event and a specific core sensitivity in a patient.

For example, one patient had as a child been fearful of losing her father, had become quite upset at his death when she was sixteen, and had subsequently married a man thirty years older than she was. Her renewed fear now was that her husband would die, and every time he went on a trip, she was completely unable to sleep. She became psychotically depressed on the date of the anniversary of her father's death, while her husband was out of town. Thus, we see the interaction of a specific event with what is probably a past core-conflict area in this patient. (p. 303)

It may also be a question of some event which in a more subliminal or unconscious way reawakens memories of an earlier severe loss and thus causes depression. This is part of the explanation that Alvarez (1971) suggests to explain why a woman as rich in resources as Sylvia Plath could take her own life. Although she and her husband were in full agreement about their divorce, she suffered a piercing sense of grief and loss; her feelings were the same as those aroused in her as a child when her father 'abandoned' her by dying. As an artist she had continued to play upon these memories and feelings; she gave free rein to them in her imagination. When she separated from her husband, it was as if she had lost her father all over again and the unbearable grief was revived.

The fourth and last answer to our question why the depressed have been involved as adults in disproportionately many severe events can best be described as a combination of the last two explanations. People are more likely to perceive negative events as *severe* or even traumatic if they have a depressive personality or have suffered some severe event earlier in life. What distinguishes this from the third explanation, however, is that the present event need have no direct connection with earlier stressful happenings. My own study provided some support for this fourth explanation. All five types of stressful events were perceived as more negative by the depressed than by the non-depressed group, and in all five cases the difference was significant. Schless *et al.* (1974) studied the assessment of various events by a group of hospital patients (mostly with a diagnosis of neurotic depression) and by a control group. The patient group gave all the events that we included in our study (and several others) a more serious rating than the control group did, regardless in most cases of whether or not they had actually been involved in the type of event concerned. It is also interesting to note that the assessments were more or less the same at the time of admission and discharge, regardless in many cases of considerable symptomatic improvement. Moreover, the depressed group's *ranking* of the events was consistent with that of a normal population, which suggests that the relative perception of these events has no special connection with depression. It is simply that people who tend to become depressed are also more sensitive and vulnerable to change, or at least (as Schless *et al.* have shown) that they find it difficult to *envisage* change and that their perception of events as severe is greater than that of a normal population.

4.3 EARLIER DEPRESSION—A STRESSFUL EVENT

A stressful event which is hardly ever registered or discussed in a research context is depression itself. If anything represents a period of extreme difficulty in a person's past, a previous depression must surely do so. How, then, does the fact of a previous depression affect that person's future? (And let us not forget that it is very common for depressions to recur.)

One of the selection criteria in my investigation was that the respondent should have been in contact with a psychiatrist for the first time on account of depression more recently than 1971. Two of every three respondents, however, had in fact suffered from depression previously in their adult lives, but without then having sought psychiatric treatment. Half of those in the depressed population had been depressed before the studied period (1971). Patients with a diagnosis of neurotic depression, and endogenous depression in particular, had been depressed before, which was hardly surprising since this diagnosis is often given on the grounds of an earlier depressive disorder.

We found among other things that women working at home had suffered depression prior to 1971 much less often than others (about 25 per cent in all three groups). This may be because women working at home are not exposed to as many risks of a kind that threaten their self-esteem as those in paid employment or following courses of study. It is another question altogether that when something untoward does happen, the housebound woman is at least equally at risk since her self-esteem depends to such a great extent on the home and the family. The proportion of those who have been depressed at some point during the last five years is about the same among women in paid employment and women working in the home.

That such a large proportion of the depressed population had previously been depressed leads me to the same general conclusion that I reported in the previous section, namely that these people have what we can call depressive personalities, i.e. an unrealistic view of themselves and other people, low self-esteem, and a limited range of solutions to turn to in difficult situations. When their self-esteem is threatened they become depressed much more easily than other people. Furthermore, they have a certain predisposition to find themselves threatened, because of their rigid and unrealistic view of themselves and other people. How, then, are they to solve their difficulties? They have learnt that depression is a possible solution, and that it has a special language which they have discovered how to master. To be in control of the situation—that is just what the depressive subject longs for. The 'choice' of depression as a way out may also be inspired by an earlier 'success' in a similar situation: for once the depressed individual is at the centre of interest, for once people bother about him, perhaps even sympathize with him. In his present state, like a hysteric, he can control his surroundings. Another explanation of his repeated bouts of depression is that the very fact of believing he has a recurrent illness (depression) causes further outbreaks by self-suggestion. 'Everything seems so difficult; I must be getting one of my depressions.' And so the depression, a kind of self-fulfilling prophecy, does indeed develop. I suggest that this type of self-fulfilling prophecy is much more likely to be found in people who already have a depressive personality. They cannot see any other way of influencing the world or their own situation in it.

Thus a negative cycle develops consisting of trauma, depression, depressive personality, trauma, etc. The point I would like to emphasize here is that depression in itself can help to forge a depressive personality. Drake and Price (1975) describe the process by which depression can set off such negative cycles. They base their analysis on manifest depression, but their argument seems to me to apply equally well to what I have called the depressive personality. We have the type of person who expresses his helplessness or loss in uncontrolled rage, his behaviour becomes destructive, and he suffers from guilt feelings. He has tried to resolve his depression but has failed. Those close to him, who could have tried to help him, can hardly do so after being shouted at and told how stupid and useless they are. Guilt feelings and social isolation follow, restricting further his scope for action and cutting him off from possible resolutions of the depression. A depressive personality is in the making. The second negative cycle described by Drake and Price seems to me to be very much more common. It starts when anger and agression are turned inwards on the self. This reinforces the subject's feeling of being in the wrong; he feels worthless and sees no point in any of his actions. He cannot, or so he believes, exercise any control over events; he is left to his own gloomy feelings and other people's mercy. Such an experience must leave a scar similar to that left by a trauma, at least if the subject fails to resolve the underlying problem constructively. He remains convinced that if he becomes depressed his feelings will take over; he will not be able to do anything about them. He is trapped.

4.4 WHY CAN EARLIER TRAUMA LEAD TO SUBSEQUENT DEPRESSION?

I have suggested above that people who become depressed have been involved in a greater number of stressful events than other people, and we have tried to find out why this may be so. At the same time we have discussed the process by means of which events from an earlier period may lead to depression a long time afterwards, perhaps because a severe event triggers off a negative reaction and engenders extreme vulnerability. The subject will be specifically vulnerable to events that remind him of the original stressful situation; it is also possible that he becomes generally vulnerable as a result of the uncertainty and, perhaps, low self-esteem engendered by the earlier event.

At the same time we all know, perhaps from our own experience, that stress can sometimes be constructive, that it can strengthen a person's capacity to cope. Why, instead of leading to this positive outcome, does it sometimes pave the way for a later depression? A decisive factor is the manner in which we deal with the stressful event, i.e. whether or not we have been able to give it a content and a constructive meaning. According to Becker, we very often fail to process traumatic events to which we have been exposed, fail to incorporate them satisfactorily into our picture of ourselves and the world. Instead, we thrust the events away out of sight, often into the subconscious, without ever acknowledging and accepting them as part of our fund of experiences. Such events are thus very painful (= traumatic) and we find them difficult to exploit constructively.

Moreover, we cannot place them in any acceptable context; we cannot or do not want to explain them; we conceal them as well as we can and set up defence mechanisms around them. But, as Becker emphasizes, a stressful event of this kind can easily rise to the surface, since we always try to impose some sort of order on our experiences. But it is very difficult to incorporate the stressful events into our experiential scheme at a later stage, since the relevant external situation no longer exists. As time passes we create new experiential schemes which make it more difficult to suppress the traumatic events: the old defences may not be relevant any longer—perhaps, for instance, we can no longer project all our failures on to a sister or brother. Another and possibly more common reason for our failure to repress former stressful events, is that simply by remaining alive we are exposing ourselves to difficulties; sooner or later something will happen to reactivate that 'forgotten' event. Naturally, too, the younger we are, the more difficult it is to process and come to terms with a stressful event; neither our language nor our experience is sufficient. And yet later, in adult life, it is very difficult to recognize what really happened.

We have already seen that, by triggering off the development of a depressive personality, stressful events may also pave the way for subsequent depression. All the events mentioned in my study, except possibly interference with important plans, probably result in the loss of action opportunities of a kind that have helped to build up self-esteem. Thus we can see the connection between the number of stressful events a person has experienced and his perception of their severity. Stressful events, in particular those which have greatly affected self-esteem and those that have not been adequately worked through, can set off a negative cycle. A traumatic event impairs self-esteem, and this means that subsequent negative happenings are more likely to be perceived as traumatic events.

We can also assume that a reduction in self-esteem, which need not in itself have led to a depression, encourages the fear that coming events may threaten self-esteem even more severely. People 'solve' this problem by restricting the scope of their lives and by relying on other people, thus hoping to preserve the little drop of self-esteem that remains. This last point suggests that people who are afraid (of themselves, of others, and of change) will have the greatest trouble in transforming a personal crisis into a positive and constructive experience. A difficult problem or crisis can teach us a great deal about ourselves and help us to understand other people, if only we dare to grasp its possibilities and if we are supported by other people in the radical changes involved (see, for example, case A, p. 76).

CHAPTER 5

Parents—present and previous relationships

Of all the people around us our parents have the greatest impact on our self-image and on the way that we live our lives. Up to a point this is probably also true of those of us who have grown up without the physical presence of parents. We still have fantasy parents, perhaps as unattainable ideals or as objects of (unconscious) hatred because they have abandoned us. Our parents are the cause of our very existence. What right have I to exist? What is the meaning of my life? These questions assume exaggerated importance for the depressed. Thus parents are important in the ultimate context of life and death. Parents are also the first people to give me a picture of myself: Am I good? Can I control my surroundings? Am I clever? Where is the borderline between self and other (am I part of my mother)? The answers we absorb to such questions during the first years of our lives will remain an integral part of our life view, but by making them conscious we can reduce them to manageable proportions. The influence of our parents continues as we grow up. We generally have more contact with them than with anyone else; above all they assume the role of authority, they show us what is right and wrong. In adult life they remind us of what we should be, but perhaps are not. Or they may remind us of what we do not want to become, but perhaps are. Both these parent-inspired self-views are common in the development of depression. Are we free, are we mature enough to take responsibility for our own lives, or are we trapped in a state of dependence with its roots in the distant past, conducting a continual internal dialogue with our superegos—superegos which tell us what we *ought* to be like?

These are some of the ideas I shall be examining in this chapter. In doing so I shall consider the implications of the loss of a parent during childhood, the pattern in the childhood family, the depressive social heritage, and the present-day relationship with parents. The concept of domination is of key importance in this last connection; it is also something which can give us an idea about early-life conditions.

5.1 LOSS OF MOTHER OR FATHER IN CHILDHOOD

There is no clear proof that depressed people have suffered childhood separation from a parent to any greater extent than a normal population. Cadoret *et al.* (1972) found that of 100 depressed patients at the Renard Hospital in the USA, only 27 had lost one of their parents by death, separation, and/or divorce before tha age of 16. However, since these results were not tested against a control group, it is difficult to draw any conclusions from them. Munro (1966a, 1966b) compared depressed patients and a group of the physically ill and found that cases of parental death before the patient was 16 occurred equally often in the two groups. Both these studies can be criticized on methodological grounds, but their findings on this point are supported by Jacobson *et al.* (1975), who found no connection between depression in the adult woman and overt childhood loss events, and who did test their results against a control group. Brown and Harris (1978), however, obtained quite different results in their methodologically stringent investigation. Among 458 women in Camberwell diagnosed as chronic or onset cases, 22 per cent had lost their mothers before the age of 11, compared with only 6 per cent in the normal group. 'Loss' referred here to death or separation of at least one year's duration. No difference was found in the case of loss of father, loss of a child at any age through death or adoption, or loss of a husband by death. There was, moreover, a very close association between past loss and the severity of the depressive symptoms.

The point that has been neglected in all these studies is that parental loss can assume forms other than actual physical separation. At least as important is the emotional loss or absence of the mother during the first years of life (White, 1977). This is, of course, difficult to measure, but even a traditional psychiatrist such as Munro finds that the most severely depressed manifest a 'highly significant excess of disturbed relationships with both mother and father during childhood'. Jacobson *et al.* (1975) also found that the depressed patients had scored higher on negative child-rearing experiences (e.g. parental abuse, maternal rejection or overprotection) than the control group. On a basis of clinical examinations Bemporad (1978) emphasizes the important negative effect of realizing that love can be abruptly withdrawn if parental expectations are not met. Love is conditional. It is not particularly common that actual loss predisposes the individual to depression; the most crucial factor is whether the child continuously suffers from a fear of losing his parents if he does not behave himself. (See also p. 39.)

In psychodynamic theory particular importance is ascribed to the physical and psychological loss of the mother, especially during the first three years of life. This agrees with Brown and Harris's results: it is the loss of the mother in early life which can pave the way for a future depression. Why is there a difference in the importance of the mother and the father in this connection? It is almost always the mother who is closest to the child, who cares for it during its first years of life. She represents security in the child's external world; she is always there to satisfy its fundamental needs. In this way she represents an extension of the child itself during its first year. At this time the child can only identify fully with one 'other' (Mangs and Martell, 1977), generally the mother. It is thus the mother on whom the child depends for acquiring a basic sense of trust. A trust that later permits him (or her) to stand on his own feet and to build up his self-esteem. If he lacks this basic trust as a result of his mother's psychological or physical absence and the lack of an adequate mother substitute, there is a risk of his becoming a leaf blown hither and thither by the wind, always dependent on other people. The whole of this argument is, of course, based on conditions in our present society and on the division of labour between the sexes that generally obtains. As an increasing number of couples are now making adjustments in the traditional male–female roles within the family, it will be interesting to follow the development of children who have two parents actively involved in their life picture from the earliest years.

Brown and Harris discuss some of the possible social effects on a girl who loses her mother before the age of 11. Their results are perhaps most typical in the case of working-class women. '... she may leave school earlier, make a hurried marriage, have her first child at an early age, fail to find satisfying work when she first leaves school just because she has no mother; and all this will mean that later in life she has fewer alternatives available to her when faced with loss' (p. 287).

Generally speaking, a relationship with a *single* parent provides fewer action opportunities than a relationship with both a mother and a father. The child becomes dependent on one person's way of being and communicating. And the narrowing of the range of possible actions must be particularly marked if the child has to assume the mother's place as the family member who lives for other people. Nor is it much better, it seems to me, if another woman takes over the mother's role: family life will then revolve round her, and the child's own ideas and earlier gleanings about what life is all about may not be relevant or even permissible any longer.

5.2 THE CHILDHOOD FAMILY PATTERN OF DEPRESSED ADULTS

The following description of family relationships in the childhood families of depressive adults is based mainly on two studies: Cohen *et al.* (1954), which describes the intensive psychoanalytic psychotherapy given to a number of manic-depressive patients, and Gibson's 'The family background and early life experience of the manic-depressive patient' (1958). Both studies are thus restricted to manic-depressive patients. Furthermore, their material is limited (12 and 22 patients respectively) and there were no scientifically acceptable control groups. Nevertheless, these studies seem to me to provide an insight into the early-life experiences of the depressed which is at least as good as other, more systematically controlled investigations. Why? The studies are based on a theory that allows for the complex inner life of the individual and the analysis calls on an impressive body of clinical experience. The aim was to identify constellations of experiences in early years that predisposed to subsequent depression, and the results obtained accord fully with the conclusions of other, more comprehensive research undertakings about the adult lives of the depressed. It was thus found that the depressive personality has high and therefore often unrealistic ambitions about what he wants to achieve. Furthermore, his social and psychological life is greatly circumscribed; he has what I have called rigid action patterns. The first of these personality traits is probably most typical of the manic-depressive, but both traits seem to me to apply in general to those with a predisposition to develop depression. And what Cohen, Gibson, and their colleagues show is how these personality traits are formed by family conditions in early life.

Let us first see how the importance of high aspirations was impressed on the child's mind. He was firmly expected to do well at school, mostly in order to compensate for the family's lack of success. Cohen *et al.* point out that the mother was generally the stronger parent; the father, who should really have promoted the cherished family prestige, was regarded more or less as a failure. The children were going to give back to the family the status it really deserved. Most of the patients preferred their fathers to their mothers and often tried to defend the father's unsuccessful career; but in this very defence of the father the patient was demonstrating his acceptance of the mother's standards. Gibson was not able to confirm this last point, but otherwise the two studies agreed. Gibson found that the childhood family of the manic-depressive had been characterized by a striving for prestige, and that as a child the patient had borne the brunt of this. The heavy pressure on him to succeed in social life stemmed from one or both of his parents.

The high ambitions, the need to succeed, are also manifest in keen competition between siblings. But only the non-depressed siblings seem to be aware of the existence of this competition. The patient, on the other hand, is rarely aware of any feelings of envy, since he has adopted his parents' viewpoint in full, and this includes an envy-excluding belief in the 'togetherness' of the family, in the importance of sticking together in an adverse world. Why is it that certain children become trapped in this harshly demanding world and others in the same family do not? One child is usually chosen to be the main carrier of the parents' hopes. It may be the child who happened to be born just when the need to enhance family prestige was greatest; or one child may have shown special abilities in advance of his siblings at an early age; or the child may be the only boy or possibly the only girl.

These children are not only expected to attain greater prestige than their parents; they are also to be well adjusted socially and to conform to the expectations of the community. Once again, this is something that the parents have partly failed to achieve, since most of the families in which the depressive patients grew up can be described as socially isolated. The family had felt itself to be socially inferior to other families and the overriding goal thus became to *be like other people*, to be successful and respected, to conform to the supposed life style of the neighbours. (Could this, perhaps, be a typically American reaction?)

To become like other people the child will have to suppress his own needs and strive to adapt his behaviour to other people's patterns. This brings us to the second typical aspect of the depressive's early-life experience, namely the circumscribed world into which he was forced. The family showed little interest in the child in his own right, but only in his role as the carrier of prestige. Parental approval depended not on 'who you are' but on 'what you do'. There was heavy pressure to conform to the parents' attitudes, and the parents in turn were strongly attached to certain strict moral standards, showing a high degree of concern about social approval. Both parents and children seem to have upheld extremely stereotyped values and beliefs: a person could not in their view be a mixture of good and bad; if he was not good then he was bad. Only one moral posture can be right, and that is the one that the recognized authority in the family's present social setting is thought to represent. This helps to explain the guilt feelings which are so common in these patients: if they fail to live up to all that they 'ought' to be or to do, they have only themselves to blame. They *are* bad.

A third trait that is typical of the depressive's family is a lack of reciprocity. Family members are unaware of the needs of the others; they strive to satisfy only their own need for love and attention and possessions. Tragically, this pattern of behaviour follows the child into adult life. He finds it difficult to give and take. Living in his circumscribed world, unable to show reciprocity, he becomes emotionally isolated and empty. As a child he was expected to remember all the time that 'we—the family—belong together'; and yet family life was full of competitiveness and was strongly dominated by authoritarian elements (mother, grandparent, uncle, aunt, and so on). The child had no opportunity to develop a confiding one-to-one relationship.

5.3 DEPRESSED PARENTS

A child can also be affected by the depressive history of its parents. Weissman and Paykel (1974) compared the behaviour of depressed women and other women towards their children. The general impression was that the depressed women took very little part in their children's daily activities; they found it difficult to talk to their children and were aware of a lack of affection for them. Such contact as they did have with the children was marked by considerable friction. It is only to be expected that such a reaction pattern will affect the child. There are many studies in the sociological tradition (particularly symbolic interactionism) which reveal the importance of parental attention in helping to build a child's self-esteem. Gecas (1971), for example, draws the following conclusion from an empirical study of parental behaviour and adolescent self-evaluation: 'Among the most important significant others for the developing child are his parents. If the child perceives his parents' behaviour toward him as expressing positive evaluation, such as love, concern, attention, support, and direction he will evaluate himself positively' (p. 478).

The reverse is also likely to apply, particularly to the children of depressed parents or of parents whose behaviour follows a generally depressive pattern. Gecas is particularly interested in the direct negative effect on self-esteem of the lack of attention. In the long run, however, the indirect effect can be more dangerous: the children of depressed, passive, non-supportive parents can so easily become passive themselves. They dare not test or confront the world around them. The passive and frightened child becomes an adult who finds it difficult to acquire self-esteem.

Drake and Price (1975) examine the problems of those whose parents suffered depression while their child was growing up.

Predisposition to depression can generally be related to development in early childhood and the presence of parents struggling with their own depression and dependency. Such parents tend to overprotect and do for the child in the passive and more active stages of infancy in order to meet their own needs to feel worthwhile and necessary. The child is a primary vehicle through which parents meet their dependency needs. Ironically, he seems to be in the role of being a parent to his parents. (p. 164)

Another way of putting this last point is that the child is being forced into *doing instead of being*—something which characterizes the situation of the depressive personality. The child thus has no chance to develop his own needs and resources. He 'overtrusts' others and 'undertrusts' himself and his ability to cope with life. This can easily lead him into a vicious circle. He develops more slowly than other children; his parents are frustrated because he does not fulfil their need to feel worthwhile and needed, and so they put increasing pressure on him to perform well, and so on, and so on. The child learns that happiness comes only through satisfying the needs of his parents (other people). The parents transfer their own low self-esteem to the child; they see their own problems and their own low self-esteem reflected in their child and are constantly 'putting him down'. A third important factor which the authors mention is that such parents teach their children to judge themselves according to extrinsic standards: a beautiful home, fine clothes, academic qualifications—these are the sort of thing that are important. The parents often compare their own child with some other or measure him against some external standard. And so the child comes to rely on conventional standards, on demonstrations of outword show, at the cost of his inner life and his own real needs, wishes, experiences and opportunities.

In our study we found that the depressed had more often than the non-depressed also had depressed parents. This result, which agrees with the findings of other studies, is generally ascribed to biological heredity. I would like to suggest, however, that it is at least as likely to be a question of social heredity, and this view has considerable support in the arguments we have just been examining. Thus when parents are often depressed it can be assumed that their children will become very dependent upon them. An interaction pattern develops in such families, whereby the children's opportunities for influencing events are reduced. In other words, the foundations are laid for the development of a depressive personality. Drake and Price noted the possible negative effect of depressed parents on their children and mentioned the transmission of passive postures, low self-esteem, and conformist attitudes to supposed community values. The first of these legacies seems to me to be particularly important: a depressed mother is obviously not going to be easy to influence; it is easier to withdraw. A family in which one or more members suffers from depression can easily become a passive family: 'We do what we can, but nothing seems to help.' And this is not an attitude likely to broaden the range of action opportunities.

A rather different reason why depressed people are more likely than others to have had depressed parents is that the parental model has presented depression as a socially acceptable way of reacting to personal problems, an acceptable way of relieving oneself of responsibility. The depressed subject makes himself entirely dependent upon others, just as he saw his mother or father doing. Nor does it seem necessary to struggle against the depression. The depressed mother had shown by her example how it is possible to become dependent on other people and thus to avoid responsibility. The child understood this mechanism and grew up believing that depression is a socially acceptable way of dealing with a difficult situation.

In the following case study we get some idea of B's difficulties in acquiring an adequate range of possible actions during her childhood, hemmed in as she was by her parents' uncommunicative egocentricity. And we can see the effect this had on her development.

B is 25 years old and works part time in one of the welfare departments of a fairly large hospital. She also studies part time. She has often been depressed, and about a year ago, after her father had committed suicide, she went to see the students' psychiatrist. She spent several months brooding upon death; she could not cry. During this same period there were difficulties at work: several patients threatened to commit suicide and some of them even did so. B could not get free of thoughts about death; among other things she had great difficulty in sleeping.

Both her parents had suffered several periods of depression. Her father was a silent man, self-destructive and egocentric. These traits became more marked as he got older. Her mother was also egocentric and full of self-pity over her husband's periods of depression. B claimed that her relationship with her parents was very poor. During this critical period B tried to discuss her problems with her husband, but he found it very difficult to cope with her confidences as he, too, is rather a reserved person.

B has a physical handicap, the result of an accident when she was 8 years old. She has now accepted this, but during the 1960s it used to trouble her and she was frequently depressed because of it. Since leaving school she has applied for a great many jobs but without much success. She has also applied several times for a particular course of studies. There are a limited number of places and so far she has not been accepted.

She has had some talks with the students' psychiatrist, and obviously badly needs to talk to someone 'outside'. Our interviewer regards B as an open and capable woman, with a very strong will. According to B, and also her husband, she often puts up a happy front in company, even when she is most depressed. During the interview, however, she was rather serious and thoughtful.

B's husband says he is sure that a lot of her problems depend on her failure to be accepted for the profession she has set her heart on. He seems unaccustomed to thinking along the kind of lines that our questions presuppose. He is taciturn and uncommunicative; he interprets our questions as performance-oriented. They find it difficult to talk to each other about B's problems. Husband and wife seem to live in separate worlds and find it difficult to get through to one another, although they appear to feel affection for one another.

One wonders whether B is doing what she really wants to, or whether her actions are still dependent on her parents' (probably unexpressed) expectations. It is tragic that she seems to have chosen a husband who greatly resembles her parents. As a child she had to be prepared to support her parents; in her job she deals with people in dire need of help. And yet there seems little chance of anyone giving her the sort of support or help she needs. Generally speaking, people with depressive personalities, people who are afraid of the uncertain, seem to choose as their life partner someone who resembles their parent of the opposite sex, since this recalls a relationship with the opposite sex that they had once been able to master.

5.4 POOR PRESENT-DAY CONTACT WITH PARENTS

When we asked the patients and others in our study to assess their present relationship with their parents ('Can you talk to your parents about almost anything?'), we found the answers of the depressed and the non-depressed differed considerably, as they had with reference to the partner relationship. It is interesting to note that the statistical relation between 'Depth in partner relationship' and 'Depth in parent relationship' is relatively slight in all three of our main groups (depressed who had sought psychiatric treatment, depressed in the control group, and non-depressed in the control group). And the same applied when we asked the same question about relationships with other people besides partners and parents. These results suggest that the ability to achieve deep contact with other people is not a gift that we either possess or lack. Instead, it suggests the existence of problems in certain *specific relationships*. The only other variable with which 'Depth in parent relationship' show a significant statistical correlation is 'Demand in parent relationship'.

Before discussing the results as presented in Table 3, I should point out that almost 20 per cent of the control group and almost 30 per cent of the patient group declared that what their parents thought of them was *not* important. These people were not asked to describe their relationship with their parents as the others were, and I wish now that they had been. I assume, however, that people who do not regard their parents as important will tend not to have any deep

Table 3   Depth in parent relationship

	Non-depressed (%)	Depressed controls (%)	Patients (%)
'Lack of depth' in parent relationship	31	44	59
'Depth' in parent relationship	69	56	42
	100	100	101
	$n = 83$	$n = 34$	$n = 41$

contact with them either. Moreover, the frequency of contact between parents and children appears to be lower in the patient group than in the control group. This alone can indicate an absence of deeper communication. The differences shown in the table are thus likely to be slightly greater in reality than they appear to be here.

It seems to me that a 'lack of depth' in the parent relationship, to which so many of the depressed admitted, is a manifestation of a narrow range of possible actions, as well as actually causing a reduction in the range of action, thus leading to difficulties in coping with problems. Why should this be? To begin with, it is reasonable to assume that if the relationship is poor now, it is unlikely to have been much better during childhood. The flexibility and maturity of the child's language may have suffered, and if he later finds it difficult to tackle problems verbally, it will also be difficult for other people to understand him and help him when he needs it. A further restriction may be laid on him if he develops a fear of older people, an inability to deal confidently with authority. Anyone 'senior' to him becomes inaccessible, frightening; there is a linguistic barrier between him and them. He turns instead to his contemporaries, his equals, as the results of our study also show: subjects who had poor relationships with their parents enjoyed comparatively good contact with their partners or their colleagues.

Naturally, a poor present-day relationship with parents involves a certain reduction in action opportunities. Although several people claimed the contrary in our study, parents are among those who have the greatest effect on our self-esteem. People who cannot talk openly with their parents probably also have less insight into their own natures. Parents represent our past selves, which in part determine our present selves. If we lack this link with our own past, it seems likely that our range of possible actions today will be limited.

As I mentioned above, the lack of depth in the relationship with parents is in itself a manifestation of a narrow range of action opportunities. This restricted range of action need not necessarily have been caused by an earlier lack of close contact with parents. Let us turn for a moment to the group where the number of those who claimed to be able to talk to their parents about almost anything was highest, namely the non-depressed group. If these respondents were speaking the truth they were showing evidence of considerable inner resources. There are, after all, certain inevitable circumstances that make for difficulties in the interaction between adult children and their parents. The opportunities available to the now adult child were either unheard of or at least very unusual when the parents were the same age. The two generations necessarily start from different frames of reference, which makes it difficult for them to speak to one another in the same language. The parents, moreover, have reached a stage in life at which the loss of certain roles becomes more common (the spouse role, the parent role, the occupational role) and death increasingly forces itself upon their notice. The problems facing the adult child are often quite different. In view of all these natural obstacles to contact with ageing parents, a good relationship with them surely shows that the child is able to view life situations from many angles (and naturally communication will be easier still if the parents also have this ability).

There are, of course, many people who enjoy close contact with one another but who are nevertheless confined in their own worlds. Conversely, it is possible to enjoy a wide range of possible actions and still lack the ability to talk openly with other people. But I think that in our society, in which people live far removed from one another (both geographically and in their daily activities), we can assume that a deep and close relationship between parents and adult children is *generally* evidence of the possession of a wide range of action opportunities.

5.5 SUBMISSION

The title of this section could equally well have been 'Dominating parents', 'Fear of parents' or 'The dominant other'. This last term was coined by Arieti and Bemporad (1978). They postulate that a child who experiences a sudden loss of attention and love from its parents at an early age, will seek perpetually to regain the lost love by submitting to a 'dominant other' or achieving a 'dominant goal'. But it may also be a generalized fear that parents have impressed on the child, which makes him anxious later to adapt himself to other people. (See, for example, the cases described in Rowe, 1978.) To try to discover how far our respondents submitted (as adults) to their parents, we asked them who seemed to them to have been the dominant party in the period preceding the depression, they or their parents. Generally speaking, respondents appeared to find this one of the easiest questions to answer on the subject of their relationships.

The difference between the non-depressed and the depressed is significant. (See Table 4.) The category 'No parental dominance' includes respondents who declared that they dominated over their parents (2 per cent of the patient group and 15 per cent of the control group).

What effect can parental dominance have on the development of a depressive disorder? There are probably two mechanisms at work. The dominated individual has less opportunity to devote himself to what he naturally finds most satisfying. And the discovery that one cannot always be in command of one's own actions in turn has a negative effect on self-esteem. Self-doubt about being able to achieve the goals prescribed by the parents. The relation with other variables is interesting here. Dominance in the parental relationship is connected with parental demands, a high level of education, and job dissatisfaction—which seems to support the assumption that dominating parents make it more difficult for a child to 'do his own thing', to act in a way that answers his own needs.

Table 4   Dominance in parent relationship

	Non-depressed (%)	Depressed controls (%)	Patients (%)
No parental dominance	86	62	71
Parental dominance	15	38	29
	101	100	100
	$n = 83$	$n = 34$	$n = 41$

We have thus seen that subjection to a dominating parent probably tends to restrict the range of possible actions and to produce low self-esteem in the child. But I would also suggest that dominance on the part of a parent can lead to the establishment of rigid action patterns. The case of D provides an example of the way in which an adult's behaviour can become fixed in rigid patterns as a result of the parental relationship.

D is 33 years old and has been diagnosed as a manic-depressive. She is studying at the university and lives at home with her mother. D admits to violent swings in mood, but only when something happens that affects and, above all, upsets her. A few years ago she finished with her boy-friend. It was not a good relationship; she felt that he made heavy demands on her and they had difficulty in talking to one another about their problems. Just at that time D was starting her first courses at the university, but because of the problems with her boy-friend she found it very difficult to concentrate on her studies. Furthermore, she found her relationship with her mother difficult, and this added to her depression.

After the interview D's mother invited the interviewer to have some coffee. The mother treated her daughter like a dependent child incapable of looking after herself. The daughter played her part in this game, behaving like a giggling 10-year-old who hardly dared to contradict her mother. The mother told the interviewer about her daughter's inability to look after herself. Throughout the conversation she referred to her daughter as 'she', although D was sitting only a few feet away from her. The mother exhibited an amazing ability to manipulate her daughter, to bind the girl to her, to emit ambivalent messages, and so on. The interviewer declared that never before had she seen so many games of such a destructive kind, and so many harmful manipulations, in such a short time.

The case of D provides a classic example of the extremely dominating parent who denies her child the opportunity to grow up. Despite her 33 years, D is still a little girl in her mother's eyes and so, naturally, she continues to behave like one. It is probable that parents like D's and the others who were stamped as dominating by their adult children were *at least* as dominating when the children were growing up. These children have had to learn to adapt to their parents' way of looking at things, to their way of being. And people whose frame of reference has been largely determined in this way by their parents' earlier behaviour will be more vulnerable to subsequent threats to their self-esteem. From their parents they have learnt ways of achieving self-esteem which may no longer be viable. The adult child does not live in the world that his parents knew. He finds it difficult to cope with problems, difficult to look at situations from different angles, because his expectations of the way the real world should look are so very definite. We can also see from the cases such as D's that the parental dominance may not always be obvious to the child: the passive state induced by the parent's *manipulations* must make it difficult to grasp what is happening and even more difficult to do anything about it.

Rowe (1978) describes in considerable detail the cases of nine depressive patients who came to her for psychotherapeutic treatment. Her book, 'The Experience of Depression', is very aptly named, since she starts from these people's unique experience of their own depressions and their own lives. A trait that emerges very clearly as being common to all patients is their sense of having adapted themselves to the needs of other people and of having repressed their own feelings. They measure their own worth by what they do—or think they do—to satisfy other people's needs and interests, but tragically they fail to recognize what needs other people actually have. At the same time they have great difficulty in standing on their own feet. They have, in most cases, submitted to their parents' will. They declared that their parents had been dominating but, unlike the patients described in Cohen *et al.* (1954), they generally mentioned their fathers as being the most dominating parent: taciturn, demanding, and imposing strict rules of conduct. Many parents succeed in keeping a hold on their children even in adult life by rousing in them feelings of guilt for going against their mother's (or father's) wishes. One female patient, Kay, complained that her mother loved her too much. 'She puts me on a pedestal all the time.' But there was no openness, trust, or reciprocity in this 'love'. As a result Kay became dependent on praise without being able to praise others in return. Kay also lived with a feeling of not being such a marvellous daughter as her mother was always telling people she was. Because of the narrow-minded, conditional love that Kay's mother and father poured over her, she never dared to contradict them. 'They've spoilt me absolutely, but not to make me nasty. Even to this day I would not answer my mum and dad back, even if I thought they were in the wrong' (p. 182). To respond to her mother's love, she always tried to act in order to satisfy her mother's needs. For example, she could never bring herself to read or knit when she visited her mother, in case she might appear uninterested in her mother's never-ending flow of talk. ' . . . all the time I am wanting to say "Shut up!" But I can't be nasty to her.'

In the families described by Rowe there was very little scope for play. The parents rarely had time to play with their children, which seems to substantiate the claim that the children adjusted to their parents' needs rather than the other way round. Playing with children means accepting their conditions, their needs, their terms. In role games, particularly, people learn how to tackle life from several angles; sometimes they can act as the one who controls and sometimes as the one who submits. If children see that their parents, too, can assume different roles—that it is possible to influence them—then there is less risk of these children adjusting exclusively to a single way of being and living that matches their parents' ideal. In adult life games pose problems for the depressed: games ignore the element of 'use'; they mean that people have to take themselves a little less seriously.

What has forced the patients whom Rowe describes to submit first to the will of their parents and later to that of their partners?

Throughout the accounts of the people here runs a theme of fear, fear of being angry, fear of making others angry, fear of being rejected, fear of losing control, fear of death, fear of ordinary places, things, activities. They fear the future, their memories are of being frightened, their images are those of fear . . . . So long as we bring children up in conditions that make them afraid, so much of the experience of human beings will be the experience of depression. (p. 268)

Instead we should try to bring out what is good in the child. And it is important that the child learns to control its environment by its own efforts. If the adults exercise too much control over the child's *doing*, they pave the way for uncertainty and fear. It is frightened people who submit, who do not trust themselves but rely on 'the power of the dominant other'. To Arieti and Bemporad (1978) this is a key concept in the understanding of depression. The depression-prone individual tends to subject himself to others, lets other people dominate him, and directs his life towards satisfying their needs. The seeds of this strong submissive tendency are to be found in deprivation of the mother during the first years of life, and according to Bemporad this applies to both the severely and the mildly depressed. The difference is that severe depressives appear to derive their *total* sense of self—in particular what they regard as bad about themselves—from the dominant other. Mild depressives, on the other hand, depend mainly on the dominant other for the acquisition of a certain amount of pleasure and meaning.

Those who become severely depressed as adults have generally been born into homes where everything is done to satisfy their needs. The mother is very willing to accept the child and this willingness is in turn quickly accepted by the child. Arieti emphasizes that the child thus soon becomes very receptive to the influence (or giving) of its mother. But then there is a change in the child's environment and, paradoxically, the two first years of comfort and need-satisfaction become a handicap to the child.

. . . perhaps a new sibling is born, and the mother begins to give all her love to the new baby and neglect the other child. Or perhaps because the mother and the other family members were raised in a culture in which duty and responsibility were expected very early in life, the older child is now expected to be on his own, to be like a little grown-up. From the bliss of the first years, the child thus enters an entirely different climate. He experiences his new situation as a sort of 'Paradise Lost'. (Arieti, 1979, p. 57)

This total reversal in the attitude to the child is generally the result of the parents' dissatisfaction with their *own* lives, partly perhaps because the child has demanded much more work and responsibility than expected. The parents often conceal their hostility towards the child while at the same time they continually increase the demands they make upon him. The only way in which the child can hope to regain the lost ground, in particular the mother's love, is by trying to live up to her expectations, however heavy the burden may be. He develops a strong sense of duty and is prone to feelings of guilt whenever he has apparently failed to live up to her expectations. Later in life a partner or colleague will generally become the dominant other whose love and appreciation he has to have. Arieti says that this appreciation is as 'essential to his well-being as the oxygen he breathes'. The depressed person may even become so 'anchored to the dominant other that he cannot establish a deep or complete relation to any other person'. The striving to satisfy the dominant other may be transformed in adult life into a wish to regain the love of the mother by achieving some great success, perhaps becoming a famous film-star, getting to the top of the company, or rearing a large family of children. The way in which the dominant other is to be satisfied has become an end in itself: the adult child is totally absorbed in the dominant other or the dominant goal and blind to the possibility of alternatives. 'Their lives are like a tunnel with no escape', as Arieti puts it. If a serious crisis occurs, they can see no way out; they become paralysed, helpless, and in the end depressed. The precipitating crisis may be the patient's realization that he can no longer keep the dominant other on a pedestal, that the relationship has failed. When the illusions collapse and the falsity is revealed, the patient finds himself in a vacuum, unable to conceive of any alternatives of his own.

Let us now examine this situation in the light of Becker's theory. We find that the absence of action alternatives lies at the core of the problem. It is the most serious consequence of the relationship that the depressed patients once had—and often still have—with their parents. And there are two completely different ways in which parents can lay the foundations of a depressive personality in their child by limiting the range of his possible actions, namely by being passive or by exerting a powerful dominance over their child.

In this chapter we have discussed passive parents mainly in connection with cases of people who had depressed parents or who lacked depth in their relationship with their parents. A parent who is depressed is very difficult to influence; the child of such a parent easily becomes withdrawn and passive, prone to give up. The parents provide the child's closest contact at the time of his life when he is expanding his range of possible actions or meanings. If he finds from the beginning that his own world is difficult to master, that 'I' am unable to take over and guide my own life, then the foundations are being laid for a lack of self-trust (self-esteem). The child has learnt from his models (his parents) that he cannot exert any influence over them. They are statues of stone.

The child of dominating parents, on the other hand, has no chance at all to develop his own range of possible actions or meanings; he is more or less forced into a submissive role. In fact, it is only too likely that both these types—one strong and dominating partner and one who submits and becomes passive—may have been present in the childhood family of the depressed person. The model absorbed by the child is necessarily circumscribed: neither the oppressor nor the oppressed provides a desirable model, and the child will often, albeit unconsciously, despise both the parents. This circumscribed view, these limited ideals, this difficulty in identifying with a parent who is either strong or good, will greatly reduce the range of action alternatives and meanings available to the child.

It is probably by a similar mechanism that a socially or psychologically abandoned child becomes susceptible to depression. Such a child loses contact with an adult who could have helped to extend his repertoire of actions, who could have taught him what life and reality can be like. The child often feels betrayed by the lost one—lost, perhaps, because of death or divorce—but he may feel even more let down by the parent who is left, the one who let the loss happen. The dependence on a single parent, combined with disappointment in this same parent, is not likely to provide the most fertile ground in which a wide and varied range of meanings can grow.

A recurring theme in any study of the relationship between the depressed person and his parents is *dependence*. (a) The child is compelled to become dependent on the dominant other, perhaps (b) on a depressed parent; (c) the confined and circumscribed family pattern leads to dependence; (d) there is only one parent to satisfy the need and the dependence is thus reinforced; (e) the child learns to strive for certain limited goals, thus becoming dependent on a particular way of being. But it is not the dependence in itself that paves the way for a future depression; it is rather the fact that this kind of dependence narrows the range of possible actions or meanings. If the child does not learn to rely on himself as he follows the path laid down by his parents, how will he be able to do so when he discovers that the signposts along the road have been removed? He will feel abandoned and helpless, and depression may seem the only way out.

CHAPTER 6

Sex and marital relations

The sex you happen to have been born into greatly affects the likelihood of your suffering a depressive disorder. With a degree of empirical agreement that is unusual in psychiatric contexts innumerable studies have shown a high proportion of women among the depressed. The ratio most often arrived at is 2:1; in other words, of 75 depressed people 50 are women (Weissman and Klerman, 1977). Naturally, the difference varies, depending on the social context in which the comparison has been made. There is also a clear tendency, to which I will return, for the sex differences to apply on the whole to married or cohabiting people only. There is thus considerable agreement about the facts; on the other hand, a great many different explanations of the preponderance of women among the depressed have been suggested. In this chapter I shall try to demonstrate how the different explanations hang together.

6.1 SEX AND DEPRESSION—SOME EMPIRICAL FINDINGS

The following results are drawn mainly from Weissman and Klerman's excellent and comprehensive survey 'Sex differences and the epidemiology of depression' (1977). This study includes an international comparison from which it can be seen that in the USA, England, and Sweden, for instance, women outnumber men by two to one among *treated depressives*.

The ratio is much the same in the rest of Western Europe, with three exceptions. In Finland and Norway the preponderance of women is very slight, while in Denmark it is at least three times as common that a depressed subject (in this case patient or other) would be a woman (Sörensen and Strömgren, 1961). What could explain this difference between the Nordic countries? Finland and Norway differ from Sweden, and even more from Denmark, in being more close-knit and family-oriented. The local community is more culturally isolated from the rest of society. Sex roles in Finland and Norway are more rigid and traditional than in the rest of Scandinavia. Ten years or so ago the rate of industrialization and migration to the towns was still some way behind that in Sweden and Denmark. Industrialization and migration break many of the social bands which are particularly important to women, and only now are Norway and Finland beginning to undergo big changes in these dimensions. Perhaps the preponderance of women among the depressed will become more marked.

Weissman and Klerman found two non-industrialized countries, namely New Guinea (Dakar) and India, which showed the same picture in reverse: in these countries men outnumbered women by two to one among *treated depressives*. This result may, of course, depend on what the authors call 'a national pattern of help-seeking', but it may also tie up with the argument I have just proposed. In both India and New Guinea the women probably have a greater number of significant emotional relationships than the women in the industrialized world. The same will certainly be true of the men, but in their case work is perhaps the most important source of self-esteem.

Can the age factor help to explain why women are more depressed than men? In a nationwide community survey of the Swedish people which included a survey of their health, Johansson (1970) found that 2.4 per cent of the men and 4.8 per cent of the women had been depressed during the preceding twelve months. Women were clearly over-represented in all age groups. A Danish survey (1977) shows roughly the same results as the Swedish study. Among hospital patients with a diagnosis of manic-depressive psychosis (a diagnosis based on biological changes) in 1970–1973, the ratio of women to men was very high in the 45–64 age group; a diagnosis of psychogenic psychosis was most common between the ages of 35 and 49, and neuroses dominated among women between the ages of 25 and 54. Charlotte Silverman (1968) concludes from epidemiological material that depression 'reaches its greatest frequency in the middle years'. To anyone with a medical orientation the menopause will certainly come to mind as a probable explanation of this phenomenon.

In a clinical investigation of more than 800 Swedish women between the ages of 38 and 60 (Hällström, 1973) no connection was found between depressions and the menopause itself. After controlling other possible causes of mental illness, it was concluded that 'the most probable explanation for the negative outcome of the testing of these hypotheses would appear to be that there are in fact no causal relations between the particular climacteric phase and the development of mental illness' (p. 143). What did emerge, however, was that 'the following factors showed significant relations with mental illness occurring during the years preceding examination: marriage disrupted by reason of separation, divorce or death of the husband, serious problem with the children, unhappiness at work and large number of psycho-social stress factors in general' (pp. 145–146).

Pauline Bart (1974), an American sociologist whose work I will return to later, points to major social changes in the lives of women in middle age which may explain the preponderance of female depressions.

Weissman and Klerman (1977) found that the preponderance of women was least among the manic-depressives and highest among the neurotic depressives. This may, of course, indicate that there is a genetic or hormonal cause of manic-depression, and that socio-cultural factors (sex role patterns) do not have the same impact in connection with this type of depression. We could equally well conclude that there is something typically masculine about manic-depression. The manic-depressive is typically a conformist who finds it difficult to look at himself in the light of earlier events, and who lacks emotional openness. The opposite personality traits, which could be said to be more 'typical' of women, occur more often in the neurotically depressed.

Are women under more stress than men? In the case of discrete life events, rather than chronic conditions such as poverty or ill-health, Weissman and Klerman conclude that 'the available evidence is that women do not experience or report more stressful events' (1977, p. 102). But as Brown and Harris (1978) among others have shown, the context in which the difficult events occur is important. Unfortunately Brown and Harris's study is restricted to women, so it is not possible to draw any conclusions about possible sex differences. But one of thier conclusions, namely that a large family could constitute a major negative factor in the lives of working women, suggests that there are certain special circumstances that affect women more than men: role conflicts (wife, mother, worker, economic responsibility in the home, etc.), and the generally heavy psychological pressure to which working women are subjected.

6.2 WHY ARE WOMEN MORE SUSCEPTIBLE TO DEPRESSION THAN MEN?

6.2.1 Inturned aggression

Depression has traditionally been regarded by the psychoanalytical school as inturned aggression (see pp. 3–4). Drake and Price (1975) suggest that an aggressive reaction to helplessness can serve to direct a person towards constructive solutions. (They add that in some cases aggression can also lead to destructive action which in turn rouses feelings of guilt, thus confirming the sense of helplessness.) I would argue that in our culture it is much more permissible for men to react aggressively than it is for women; indeed men are even trained to react in this way. It is probably easier for them to deal with anger without acquiring feelings of guilt. Thus *one* explanation of the lower incidence of male depression could be that they have more opportunity to act out their disappointments; they do not blame themselves; others—perhaps their women—have to assume the burden of guilt.

Howard Kaplan (1977) has tried to discover why depression is more prevalent among women. He assumes that depression is a result of the loss of self-esteem, and that this is connected with an inability to avoid self-blame. He points out that many studies, regardless of the research design, have shown that women find it more difficult to give vent to their aggressions. 'Since the blaming of others is a major mechanism for avoiding self-blame, and since this mechanism involves expression of some degree of hostility, this finding is consistent with the assertion that females are less likely to be trained to deflect blame from self'(p. 85).

But why is this so? Women react to aggression, both their own and other people's, with greater anxiety. Women, and above all those with depressive personalities, are eager to avoid anxiety, partly because their range of alternative actions is smaller than men's. In our culture there is also a negative reaction to a woman who is aggressive in a situation where the same reaction would be accepted in a man. Women are also more eager for approval, and are afraid of losing people by showing anger. Kaplan provides plentiful empirical support for these ideas from many sources. He also describes an empirical study of his own which provides a social explanation of women's tendency to turn guilt inwards on themselves. Summarizing these results in Becker's terms, I would suggest that it is once again a question of rigid action patterns. The woman whose upbringing and adult life has trapped her in set routines, the woman who is mainly expected to satisfy the needs of others, she is the one most susceptible to depression. I will develop this explanation below (pp. 66–70).

6.2.2 Male depression manifests itself in the abuse of alcohol

There is much to suggest that alcohol abuse and depression have similar roots: a lack of adequate action alternatives, low self-esteem, fear of anxiety, and difficulties outside the self that threaten self-esteem. Alcohol abuse and depression may be related in various ways: faced by a difficult situation a person may 'choose' between depression or recourse to excessive alcohol; or the person abusing alcohol may really be depressed, but his depressed state is partly concealed by the alcoholism (this group includes people whose depression has led to the abuse of alcohol—the alcohol is the medicine the person has prescribed for himself). Or there may be no question of choice. The cultural setting and the social environment more or less force a 'solution' upon the powerless individual. A woman may be told: 'You really have got problems, you are to be pitied; but pull yourself together, it will be better in time'—in other words, she gets no help but is forced further and further into self-pity. Meanwhile, a man is perhaps told instead: 'You really have got problems—why not have a quick one and you're sure to feel better.'

In the case of alcoholism and depression, it seems to me that the picture contains elements of both compulsion *and* choice. Naturally, 'choosing' depression or alcoholism isn't like choosing where to go for your holiday. Nor can it be compared with the choice of suicide, a grave and irrevocable choice between being and not being which may have to be taken in an insoluble situation. The choice between depression and alcoholism is hardly likely to be made on the same conscious plane.

How have alcohol and depression come to function as 'solutions', the first mainly for men and the second mainly for women? In our culture depression is more acceptable in women, who are allowed to show their feelings and who do not always have to appear controlled. For historical reasons, connected with the division of labour and the distribution of power, women have not always had to strive to remain cool. The only forbidden display of emotion concerns anger, which as an instrument and expression of power has been man's prerogative. One reason why men put up less resistance to drink may be that aggression is permitted to them, and alcohol usually renders people more uninhibited in their behaviour and more liable to express anger.

On the other hand, women are probably more readily 'allowed' to be depressed; it is thus also easier for them to obtain secondary benefits such as sympathy and attention. Depression can be regarded as a solution to which a woman may turn in an intolerable situation. 'Choosing' depression may be the only way of making the situation comprehensible to herself and/or to other people. Another possible solution could be drink, but to a woman this probably brings few if any secondary advantages. Perhaps, then, similar problems underlie both alcoholism and depressive disorders, but our culture 'steers' the choice of solution. Such an assumption appears to be supported by the preponderance of male alcoholics. (However, the proportion of *younger* female alcoholics seems to be increasing. I have not yet found any confirmation of a corresponding shift in the sex ratio as regards depression. But it seems that our common role as human beings is perhaps taking over from our respective sexual roles, and that this is therefore also levelling out the risk of depression between the sexes.)

My second assumption was that men conceal depression behind their alcoholism. That depressives and alcoholics share certain personality traits has been shown by Shaw *et al.* (1975). Both groups can be described as 'sub-valid', by which is meant lacking in energy, bound to routine, cautious, and tense. Tyndel (1974) studied 1000 alcoholic patients and found that about 35 per cent had serious depressive symptoms either at the time of the interview or earlier. In another group of outpatients in New Haven, Connecticut, over 50 per cent were found to suffer from depressive disorders (Weissman and Klerman, 1977). As these last authors quite rightly point out, we must be cautious about drawing conclusions from these studies, since people with two serious conditions (in this case alcoholism and depression) are more likely to seek treatment. It is also difficult to sort out cause and effect. It is always possible that alcoholism leads to depression, and it certainly often does so. Nevertheless, I hold to my main argument, namely that the underlying social–psychological process is much the same in depression and alcoholism, and that the cultural context determines which 'solution' is chosen.

6.2.3 Childhood and upbringing

The female role, which we will study later in the adult, is formed to a great extent during childhood. What distinguishes the upbringing of boys from that of girls, with the result that the latter become more susceptible to depression? We have to consider both the prescribed ideals and the training the children receive, and the opportunities they are given for achieving the ideals.

Little girls are taught above all to be good, to be biddable, and to put the family first. To have a career, to become 'something' is not the primary goal. A mother wants to teach her daughter to be a good wife and mother, to be important in the family. The aim of a boy's upbringing, on the other hand, is to make him important in the community. But what has this to do with depression? One result of these often unexpressed goals is that girls have fewer opportunities than boys for testing their own power, for trying themselves out in a variety of spheres. Boys are given greater freedom away from the control of their parents. Boys are allowed to play more violent games; they do not have to be at home as much as the girls; they are not encouraged to do odd jobs around the house as often as girls are expected to, and so on. Boys are given a chance to develop qualities such as daring and courage; they have opportunities to build up their physical strength and security. The result is likely to be a vicious circle, as Viestad *et al.* have pointed out: the boys become stronger and more curious; the girls idealize strength in boys and undervalue it in themselves (Viestad *et al.*, 1977).

These principles of upbringing must leave girls with a narrower range of action opportunities and, therefore, fewer chances of acquiring self-esteem. To develop faith in ourselves we need to try out a variety of activities to see whether we can master them. Furthermore, the traditional upbringing described above perpetuates the sexual roles from one generation to the next. The adult woman will almost certainly regard home and the family as her main sphere of operations. To this subject we will return later.

6.2.4 Tasks at home and at work

What kind of tasks do women spend most of their time doing? Are they such as to give prestige, opportunities for influencing others, and scope for self-realization—in other words, things that help to counteract depression? The reader will know my view already, namely that this is not the case. Perhaps the situation of many men is little better, and there is some empirical evidence that it is among men in similar restricted situations that male depressives are more likely to be found. At present, however, I want to consider the kind of working lives that are typically male or typically female. The typical female job is underpaid, carries low prestige, and provides little opportunity for influencing the work process. These are limitations that serve in different ways to reduce the scope for action, thus cutting down opportunities for acquiring self-esteem. Women are in less demand than men in the working world; nor does society facilitate their entry into that world by arranging for the care of young children.

In seeking to explain the higher incidence of mental disorders among women Gove and Tudor (1973) refer to the work women do in the home. They claim, on a basis of a wide range of empirical evidence, that women tend to regard their work in the home—bringing up children and looking after the house—as frustrating; such tasks carry little prestige and are rarely even noticed by others; it is easy for the housewife to become passive. A change seems to be on the way here. Many people are beginning to recognize the value of work in the home, partly because younger men are more willing to take part in it today. If this trend continues it will be to the benefit of both women and men. The greater understanding, and perhaps also respect, that they will have for each other's work cannot fail to add to their mental wellbeing.

The usual outcome at the present time, however, is that the woman finds herself doing two jobs. She is under even greater pressure, partly because she works longer hours than her husband every day (Gove and Tudor, 1973) and partly because she is often compelled to undertake typically female tasks both at work and at home. Gove and Tudor also make the interesting point that women's jobs are rarely commensurate with their occupant's educational background. There is probably a great discrepancy between what women feel they are capable of and what they actually do. As Linsky (1969) showed (see p. 13), the incidence of depressive disorders is higher in societies where opportunities for occupational success are inadequate in relation to the educational level.

6.2.5 Role losses

An explanation that is often suggested for the high incidence of depressions among women is that, particularly in middle age, women suffer the loss of several of their roles. For instance, they lose the mother role: children acquire ideals and habits of their own, sometimes in open conflict with their parents. And it is the mother who feels this loss most keenly; she has been closest to the children, it is her self-esteem which is most closely bound up in them. Another role she may lose is the female role; she is treated less as a woman and more as an object; her husband perhaps turns his attention away from her to younger women. Yet another role to disappear may be the daughter role; with the loss of her parents the woman also loses contact with that early-life manifestation of what she has learnt to regard as supremely important, namely the family.

Pauline Bart (1974) has made a penetrating study of depression, in particular during the female menopause. In traditional psychiatry these involutional depressions are linked chiefly with hormonal changes. Bart studied the case histories of 533 women and interviewed 20 of them. The women were between the ages of 40 and 59. Bart's general conclusion was that their depression had its roots in role loss. She also made intercultural comparisons, and found that in four cultures where meaningful roles were available to women in their fifties, middle age was not regarded as a particularly difficult period.

Since one's conception of self is learned by the selective identification of certain roles which appear to be the most congruent, self-esteem stems from a sense of adequacy in the most salient roles. Because the most important roles of women in our society are those of wife and mother, one might predict that the loss of either of these roles could result in a loss of self-esteem—resulting in a feeling of worthlessness and uselessness that characterizes most depressions. (p. 145)

Bart emphasizes that for the women in her study the loss of the maternal role was particularly critical. The loss of the wife role was also important, but it was not a loss that was particularly marked in middle age. The women included in my own earlier investigation were generally younger, and we could not have expected the loss of the maternal role to be as important in their lives. But we did find that their problems were frequently connected in some way with the home situation. The men's problems were much more often connected with the situation at work.

It is not only that women are more frequently afflicted by role losses; more significant is the fact that the relative importance of their roles is very great, since their total role repertoire is much smaller.

> . . . a man has two major sources of gratification, his family and his work, while a woman has only one, her family. If a male finds one of his roles unsatisfactory, he can frequently focus his interest and concern on the other role. In contrast, if a woman finds her family role unsatisfactory, she typically has no major alternative source of gratification. (Gove and Tudor, 1973, p. 814)

If all the meaning in a person's life comes from one source and this source is destroyed, that person will be particularly vulnerable to depression.

6.2.6 The female role in general

We have already touched on certain features of the female role that provide at any rate partial explanations of the problems we have been discussing. There are, however, some aspects of the female role as a whole which together can perhaps give us a more cohesive picture.

According to one interpretation of the problem, which stems from psycho-dynamic theory, women seldom develop strong and socially accepted ego-ideals. Few women are encouraged to worry about the meaning of life, in the sense of thinking what they want to do with their *own* lives. As a result they exist, as Vinde (1977) has put it, in a constant state of mourning for what they have never had. The same author points out that the depressed woman is nevertheless *less* verbally questioning and aggressive than the normal non-depressed woman, and suggests that the depression serves in itself as a way of maintaining loyalty to the feminine role. According to this view, a show of aggression would be a manifestation of disloyalty to the woman's 'sexual' identity. For a man the show of aggression is part of the masculine role.

To show aggression openly also represents a questioning of the *status quo*; but women have been brought up to live for others and not for themselves; it is not for them to question. Many women tend to be martyrs, the very opposite of the aggressive type. They define themselves in terms of what they do; they all too easily assume colossal burdens.

To use Becker's terms again, we could say that the pattern of sexual roles in Western societies forces women in general to restrict their own range of possible actions. Women allow their lives to become bound up with the home and the family, since this is what they have learnt will give them the greatest self-esteem. And the pattern of actions often becomes permanent, since the actions themselves are continuous and repetitive. In other words, the all too often rigid nature of female action patterns comes from the woman's tendency to put her trust in her children rather than in herself and in circumstances extrinsic to the family's life. If this limited sector is then exposed to some severe event, the woman has no alternative repertoire of responses which can repair the loss to her self-esteem, and the risk of depression is great. Moreover, it is actually more likely that something serious will happen to threaten self-esteem within the family, just because the family is a limited—almost a unique—phenomenon. It is almost always easier to find a new livelihood than to repair a family or build a new one. A blow to a man's self-esteem in one sphere of action is unlikely to have such serious consequences, since he can more easily compensate in other areas (for example, problems at home may be partly offset by his enjoyment of a stimulating job).

The results of our study suggested that the roots of female depression are often bound up with family life. We can now exemplify this by the case of O, one of our interview subjects.

O is a middle-aged woman, now living alone in a rented apartment. Following a divorce a few years ago, she has started to isolate herself and has become increasingly passive. The people she knew before the divorce were mostly her husband's friends, and at the time of the divorce she decided to move from the town where they had been living together. She had three grown-up children. The eldest daughter lives in the same neighbourhood, but she and her mother rarely manage to meet more than twice a week. Her fear of contact is so great that she has had her telephone number listed.

The marriage had been a torment to both partners. The husband was very dominating, and the couple found it impossible to communicate with one another. In the process of getting divorced their conflicts became more marked. There had also been trouble with the two youngest children, who had both been involved with the police and were on probation. The husband wanted to take a stern line with the children, while O supported them and paid their fines for them. O has now bound herself up in the children; she says that they mean everything to her. The only contact she has apart from this is with a couple of members of the religious congregation to which she belongs. But she hasn't yet dared to invite these people to her home. Another of O's problems is her sister, with whom she cannot get on at all. Her main reason for moving was that she couldn't cope with her sister. The sister has also on occasion sought psychiatric treatment for hysteria. The sister often calls O on the telephone and asks a lot of awkward questions about the children.

O's father was an artisan in central Sweden. He died when O was at primary school. It came out in the course of the interview that the father was often violent, and beat O's mother (who died about 10 years ago). Before her divorce O was working at an old people's home, which she remembers as a very positive experience. It was rewarding, helping the old people. She now works in the daytime, looking after children for a family in the neighbourhood. It is mostly a question of seeing to the children and the house, while the parents are away. She would probably rather get another job in an old people's home, where she would have adults to talk to. But she seems to be paralysed by her earlier problems and bound up in the children; she finds it difficult to take the first steps towards changing her own life.

There was not much more to be learned from an interview with O's eldest daughter, the one with whom O has the closest and most frequent contact; all we really found out was that the daughter didn't seem to know much about her mother's life. The daughter first mentioned the problems of the sister and the youngest daughter. According to her, O did nothing but worry about the youngest daughter. She also believes that O regrets the divorce, finding it harder to be alone than to put up with all the quarrelling.

Here we have a woman who has spent most of her life concentrating almost exclusively on her family; it is hardly surprising that she suffers from depression when she no longer has a husband and her children now have lives of their own (partly in conflict with their mother). She no longer has access to those actions which used to give her at least a relatively secure self-esteem, and she has not been able, or been helped, to compensate for this by acquiring any new repertoire of actions. The repression she suffered under her husband, and to some extent under her father, has made her afraid. This fear has become internalized as part of her own personality, and it renders her incapable of daring to change, of daring to make contact, of daring to get close to people.

An aspect of O's situation and women's situation in general that links up with the problems discussed under subsections 6.2.1 to 6.2.5 above, is the development of fixed ways of behaving, of rigid action patterns. The young girl is assigned a predetermined place in the world; her security is bound up to a great extent with other people (her mother, her husband, her children). Both as a girl and an adult she learns to repress her desire to *question*. The anger which must sometimes be called forth tends to be transformed into guilt feelings and turned in upon herself. She cannot find a permitted solution in drinking, since this encourages that *open expression of feelings and aggressiveness* which is unacceptable as part of the female behaviour pattern. Family life becomes rigid and the woman is caught up in many routines. At the same time, the family is probably the societal institution most firmly attached to the maintenance of tradition, the institution which only changes when other constituents of society have already changed (Viestad *et al.*, 1977). The jobs that women can find to do outside the home are also restricted in range and demand little of them in the way of independent action.

On a basis of a fairly extensive empirical investigation Kaplan (1977) suggests that the roots of women's depression lie in the limited range of action available to them.

In the case of males Kaplan found that high depressive affect was significantly associated with, among other things, reports of receiving less attention from parents than siblings during childhood, of having done better or not as well in life as siblings, and of having had a higher or a lower standard of living than most of the other families in the neighbourhood while growing up. In the case of females, high depressive affect appeared to be associated among other things with having been raised on a farm, having been in the lowest social class during childhood, having had four or more siblings, having been part of a family whose members were not as close as the members of most of the other families around, and with reports of not doing so well in life as siblings.

This difference was explained in terms of differential sex-role socialization that inhibits the use of response patterns by females which would reflect their attribution of blame (in blameworthy circumstances) away from self. The fact that sex differences in depressive affect were observed only under conditions where greater requirement for inhibition of such responses might be expected provided support for this interpretation. (Kaplan, 1977, p. 108)

Thus, in situations which give little scope for initiative women are expected to show *restraint*: they are forced into what can with full justification be called rigid action patterns.

And in what setting are women most exposed to the kind of expectations we have been describing? Certainly in the family where she has to fulfil the various roles of wife, mother, and daughter. 'The most convincing evidence that social role plays an important role in the vulnerability of women to depression is the data that suggests that marriage has a protective effect for males but a detrimental effect for women' (Weissman and Klerman, 1977, p. 109).

In a study of depressed, young, unmarried college students in the USA, Hammen and Padesky (1977) found no sexual differences in the severity of depression. They were, of course, studying a group of the population in which the expectations imposed on men and women are likely to be more similar than in other groups. Nevertheless, Johansson (1970) found sex-based differences even in this age group. But it is important to note that Hammen and Padesky's study was concerned with the severity of depression. There are no grounds for believing that simply because women are depressed more often, their depression must necessarily be more severe. It seems, in fact, that once a man becomes depressed at all, the trouble is likely to be more serious. There is another parallel with alcoholism here: female alcoholism, when it occurs, is generally more serious than male. When it is no longer possible to hold out, although the rules of the prevailing culture say that one should, the fall seems to be all the greater. But to return to the example of the American students, the point is surely that the difference between the sexes is firmly related to the social context, to factors there which can threaten self-esteem. The reader may have been wondering why more women do not actually become depressed, in view of all the factors that seem to be ranged against them. The point I have tried to make is that women are generally more exposed to the loss of roles and the loss of self-esteem, since their sexual role is more strongly bound up with fixed action patterns (to be a martyr, to occupy a predetermined position, not to show aggression, to show restraint, etc.). This sexual role is imposed in its purest form on women with families, married women, and it is in this particular context that role loss or loss of important and accepted meanings are most likely to occur. The married woman risks losing those things that mean most to her, those things on which she has staked her all. There is thus a large group of women who are less exposed to the risk of losing self-esteem, namely younger women who have not yet built a family, and older women. Another reason why more women are not depressed despite the obvious risks is that women are also more likely to seek psychiatric help for depression (Weissman and Klerman, 1977; Hammen and Padesky, 1977) as well as more prepared to ask for help from relatives and friends (see p. 106). There is less pressure on women to hide their feelings, in particular their gloomy feelings, and they feel less fear than men of admitting their dependence on others (pride does not stop them seeking help). In this way women often manage to stop a disappointment or crisis from going so far as to provoke a depression. And this may also help to explain why a man's depression, once it has become a fact, may well be more serious than a woman's. His help-seeking actions come into play much later in the day.

The reader should remember that we have been discussing sex-based differences on a very general plane. There are also some men who have had little chance either during childhood or later to take independent action, to become aware of their own value; there are men who are not allowed to show aggression, whose range of possible actions is circumscribed. And many men do therefore develop depressions. Conversely, there are women who are given the chance to break out of the traditionally confined female role. Nevertheless, in general, our society rewards and reinforces certain traits in men and in women. The reasons have their roots in tradition ('It's always been like this'), in economics (the division of labour, which has become increasingly pronounced in our economy, works more smoothly if women look after the home), and in the historical distribution of power (women have had little influence on economics, politics, culture, and science). It is perhaps not too much to say that economic efficiency and the extrinsic instrumental goals that hold high priority in Western society, hit women hardest. It has become increasingly important to achieve a great deal in competition, at the cost of *meaning* something to each other. It is not surprising that this results in emotional conflicts expressing themselves as depression. Depression is connected at a deep level with a sense of worthlessness, and in a society geared to *doing* this sense is likely to be most profound in those who have directed their lives towards *being*.

6.3 THE PARTNER RELATIONSHIP

We have seen that the relationship with the husband is a very important factor affecting a woman's mental health. It also emerged from my earlier investigation, however, that certain features of the partner relationship are extremely critical to both women and men when it comes to susceptibility to depression. Two factors in particular seemed to make people more vulnerable to the pressures caused by severe events in the relationship itself or outside it, namely heavy demands emanating from the other partner and lack of depth in the contact between the two partners. I will discuss these two factors in more detail below, but would first like to mention that by 'partner relationship' we referred in our study to relationships between two people who were either married, living together, or otherwise involved in a stable and serious relationship with one another; further, the questions about the partner relationship referred to the period preceding the negative or depressive patch.

6.3.1 Demands in the partner relationship

Perceived demands may refer to anything from small day-to-day details to the overall acceptance of the partner's own self-image. When we asked our subjects 'Do you feel that your partner makes demands which are difficult to bear?' we were trying in the first place to discover their feelings on this last point, and the formulation of our question meant that we were asking about negative rather than positive demands. It is difficult to say whether or not we managed to uncover what we wanted, but the interviews we held with close relatives of our respondents suggested that the question was understood in much the same way by everyone concerned.

The overall nature of the relationship with the partner seems to have a clear impact on the predisposition to depression. On the specific question of heavy demands, there were big differences between our three groups (patients, depressed controls, and non-depressed controls).

Thus almost half the depressed perceived their partner relationship as being full of demands during the period prior to the onset of depression. Furthermore, the difference between the patient group and the depressed controls was considerable. The figures varied in the patient group from 43 per cent (out-patients) to 88 per cent (neurotic patients) who claimed that there were heavy demands in the partner relationship. The demand variable appeared to be 'independent', i.e. there was no very marked connection between it and any other variables. The only connection to be noted was that *only* in the case of the non-depressed was there a relatively high statistical correlation between demands in the partner relationship, dominance in the partner relationship, and number of functions at work.

A possible explanation of the results may be that people judged their relationships as more demanding in retrospect than they had actually found them to be at the time, since the crisis had followed the period under discussion and had perhaps coloured the memory of it: people tried to find an explanation for the problems that had arisen. However, the idea that the results suggest this kind

Table 5   Demands in partner relationship

	Non-depressed (%)	Depressed controls (%)	Patients (%)
No heavy demands	86	65	44
Heavy demands from partner	14	35	56
	100	100	100
	$n = 109$	$n = 43$	$n = 48$

of rationalization is not supported by the interviews with close relatives. In fact, the close relatives were more inclined than the patients themselves to describe the relevant relationship as very demanding. We should not ignore the possibility that the relatives may have received this impression from the patients' subsequent description of events; but there is no support for such a supposition, while there was much in the patients' own accounts to indicate the real existence of heavy demands in the situation before the depression broke out.

What can be regarded as even more certain is that these people *perceived* heavy demands being made upon them by their partners, and this fact alone is important. Thus we can interpret demands in two ways: as actual and as perceived demands. And what are the consequences of a relationship characterized by heavy demands? It seems to me that a demanding relationship can promote a depressive development in many ways. If one partner has definite ideas about how the other should live, this imposes a restriction on the second partner's scope for action. The situation is even more difficult if the demands are not openly expressed; this generates fear that spreads to much of what the second partner undertakes. Unexpressed demands are also the most difficult kind to counteract; there is nothing to come to grips with, nothing to discuss. There are also demands that are not only openly expressed but expressed with great emphasis; the recipient is left with no possible opportunity for alternative action. In both cases one partner's range of action opportunities is being restricted by the other. Such a restriction will probably be felt most acutely by a partner whose main sphere of activities is the home. She (since it is almost always a woman) has no other less demanding sphere into which she can escape; and even if she could find such a sphere, she is probably still dependent on her husband as the most important source of self-esteem.

But this restriction on the scope for action is not the only consequence of a demanding relationship; probably the most important result is the creation of rigid action patterns. People who are being subjected to heavy demands easily become totally bound up in the person who imposes the demands, particularly if it is someone who means a great deal to them and with whom they spend a lot of time. In a demanding relationship of this kind a definite type of behaviour is clearly expected; there is very little opportunity for the subordinate partner to do anything to alter the repertoire of available actions. He or she becomes trapped in a fixed and determined world. A certain way of being is also the *only* way of being.

It may be difficult to distinguish between the concept of 'limited range of action' and the concept of 'rigid action patterns'. The difference is essentially that a 'limited range of action' implies the existence of alternatives but these are inaccessible or forbidden. 'Rigid action patterns' means that everything is blocked; no other actions are possible (see also pp. 156–157).

It was fairly certain, as I have mentioned, that respondents who admitted to a demanding relationship really did *perceive* heavy demands emanating from their partners. Such a perception can be seen as evidence of limitations and blockage in that person's experience, but it can also probably be regarded as reflecting external circumstances: the very feeling that demands are being made on us means that we regard certain actions as the only possible alternative and the actual demands of the other person would hardly affect us so strongly if we thought that alternative solutions were available. In other words, we would not perceive the demands as heavy if we actually had access to a variety of possible solutions.

It is a question of a complex interplay between external and internal reality. The concept of 'demands' can only be understood in terms of the situation intrinsic and extrinsic to the individual. The imposition of demands induces a social–psychological state that renders the individual more susceptible to depression. But the reverse can also be true, namely that a person with low self-esteem and a limited range of action is more likely to find himself in situations where he is exposed to heavy demands; he lacks the resources necessary for controlling his environment, which in this case means an inability to manage the relationship with the partner. Either he has not learnt the art of manipulation, or for some other reason the pair relationship is inequitable. Perhaps one partner has much greater skill in verbal expression, for instance, so that he finds it easy to exercise power and increase his demands on the other partner.

6.3.2 Depth in the partner relationship

Depth in the partner relationship was one of the variables that differentiated most clearly between the depressed and the non-depressed (see Table 6). The question with which we intended to measure the depth of the relationship was: 'Can you talk to ... about almost anything?' This question, too, can be understood in several ways. There are presumably certain things which are impossible to talk about; also, two people may be so close that they understand one another without exchanging words. The question allowed for this last possibility, since we asked whether people *could* talk to one another, not whether they did so.

Forty per cent of the depressed as against 7 per cent of the non-depressed said that they were unable to talk to their partner about almost anything. It might have been expected that the underlying situation reflected here would be much the same as that uncovered by our previous question about heavy demands in the relationship. But in fact there was only a very slight statistical correlation

Table 6   Depth in partner relationship

	Non-depressed (%)	Depressed controls (%)	Patients (%)
Lack of depth in partner relationship	7	33	46
Depth in partner relationship	93	67	54
	100	100	100
	$n = 109$	$n = 43$	$n = 48$

between the two variables. Another variable, however, did show a strong correlation with depth in the partner relationship, namely involvement in tasks at work calling for independent action. In other words, many people who had no such involvement also lacked depth in the relationship with their partners. The statistical correlation was particularly marked in the patient group (0.55), but was non-existent in the non-depressed group. This last was not particularly surprising, since few people in this group described their partner relationship as lacking in depth. Is it possible that a lack of opportunity or flexibility in working life affects a person's flexibility in private life, or even vice versa? Generally speaking, it seems likely that difficulty in acquiring 'meanings' in one sphere will make it more difficult to acquire them in others. Or the results might simply be evidence of a certain 'life style'; some people never commit themselves very deeply to anything, either at home or at work. However, this last explanation is contradicted by the fact that the patients actually had *closer* contact with their children and colleagues than the normal population. The impression I received personally from the interviews, and which seems to be confirmed by this last point, was that the depressed are capable of achieving depth in a personal relationship. Where such depth is lacking it often seems to be a question of high expectations that fail to be realized; two people start living together and one finds the other to be something less than the hero or heroine they had previously seemed to be. Disappointment is not a good basis for an open relationship, and some compensation can perhaps be found in discussing problems with colleagues instead. My own and other studies have shown that the antecedents of depression are often connected with disappointment in the partner relationship, and this will naturally affect answers to a question such as the one we were asking, although our question actually referred to the period prior to the onset of symptoms.

Returning briefly to the question of male and female roles, I should also mention here a very interesting tendency in my study. It cannot be statistically confirmed, since there were so few depressed men in our material, but within this limited material we found no marked difference between depressed men and depressed women on the question of demands in the partner relationship. On the other hand, only two of ten depressed men admitted to a lack of depth in their relationship with their wives. On this last point I imagine that the difference can be explained by the probably lower expectations nursed by men in this respect; it is probably also more difficult for men to acknowledge to themselves that there is anything missing, since talking about feelings and problems is not generally regarded as very legitimate behaviour among men.

That the severely depressed woman finds it difficult to communicate with her spouse has been confirmed by Weissman and Paykel (1974) among others. Compared with matched normal controls, the depressed women admitted to considerably more problems in the intimate relationship of marriage. But such manifestations of serious disturbances in a relationship during the depressive phase must, I think, have their roots in the earlier state of the relationship. Brown and Harris (1978) show that 'high intimacy' protects many people from becoming depressed in the presence of a provoking agent. They even found that high intimacy could neutralize other vulnerability factors for depression—early loss of mother, three or more children under 14 years of age, and lack of employment. What is perhaps even more interesting is that high intimacy appeared to be connected with social class. Generally speaking, the working-class women in Brown and Harris's study rated low on confiding relationships with husbands and boy-friends. This result agrees with my own finding that people who lacked depth in their partner relationship often had jobs requiring little of them in the way of independent action. To be able to open your mind to someone else, to enjoy the intimate exchange of confidences with others, is perhaps more highly valued and more easily attainable in the middle strata of society.

Brown and Harris propound a theory to account for the poor partner contact of the woman who is predisposed to depression. 'Women low in self-esteem might well choose to marry men with whom it is difficult to have a confiding relationship just because they feel they will never find anyone more suitable who is willing to stay with them' (p. 266).

Although this explanation certainly fits some cases, in most others I believe it to be unfounded. My view is the opposite: these women have instead had high but unfulfilled expectations of achieving a confiding partner relationship. And my empirical findings regarding the intimate contacts enjoyed by the depressed with their children and colleagues, in other words in relationships which do not depend in the same way on finding the one right person, appear to support my proposition. Nor did I find any connection in my study between demands and depth in the partner relationship. Involvement in a demanding relationship may be evidence of a predisposition to accept and resign oneself in the way Brown and Harris describe, and if a correlation had existed between these two variables (depth and demands), there might have been confirmation for their conclusion. But there was no such correlation.

In what way does an absence of depth contact in the partner relationship affect a person's ability to cope with serious personal problems? To be able to talk to another person implies the existence of opportunities for action, in this case the opportunity to discuss possible ways of resolving the crisis, the opportunity to get support and help in discovering how the crisis may have arisen. In such confiding contacts both parties learn about the other's world; action opportunities are generated. If, on the other hand, there is little confidence in the relationship, the two partners will not be able to reveal alternative actions or meanings to one another. And from the lack of verbal contact may spring a general linguistic impoverishment which in itself constitutes a further narrowing of the possibilities available.

Thus we have seen that lack of depth in the partner relationship can first of all limit the scope for action and make people more susceptible to depression. Secondly, it may result in a loss of action opportunities which will have immediate consequences. If two partners find it difficult to talk openly to one another, they are probably also lacking in understanding of each other's idiosyncrasies. When one partner gives expression to complex and unexpected feelings, or behaves in a way that he has never behaved in before, the second partner will find it difficult to recognize the forces at work and will thus miss the internal action opportunities. Thirdly, lack of depth in the relationship may reinforce a depressive development which was not originally connected with the partner. To a person in the grip of approaching depression, the feeling of being lonely in the company of another must be very hard to bear. Fourthly, the lack of a confiding relationship between the two partners makes it difficult for the second partner to understand the interlinking forces at work. Without this understanding he cannot help to break down the paralysis that prevents the depressed individual from acting on his own.

In conclusion I will describe one of our cases in which it seemed to me that a close and confiding relationship between the respondent and her husband, and between the respondent and other people, helped to prevent the development of a depression.

A is a woman of around 40. For the last ten years or so she had been working for the same firm as a stockroom assistant. She enjoyed her work and got on well with her colleagues. With two of the women at the office she felt she could talk about almost anything. She appeared to have an excellent relationship with her husband. She lived with him in a typical working-class district. Her parents-in-law lived in a flat on the floor below. I was able to interview both husband and wife on the same occasion. They seemed very open in their answers, and I received a generally sympathetic impression of them both. A couple of years ago A's father was found to have lung cancer (her mother had died 15 years previously). She had been made particularly miserable by her father's rapid deterioration after the doctors had at first given her some hope of his recovery. A spent many nights at her father's bedside, which of course made her work seem more of a strain than usual. Otherwise, however, A coped with the difficult situation surprisingly well. Her husband was supportive and helped to look after the dying man. He even says now that he and his wife came closer to one another during this period. They don't have a wide circle of friends; they spend most of their leisure time with the husband's parents. They both look upon his parents as hers too. Apart from her parents-in-law, an old friend (who was also a colleague and a relative of A's) did a great deal to help her to cope with the crisis without becoming depressed. The friend was in the same situation as A with a father who also had cancer. The two women used to meet several times a week, and they supported one another in their trouble. A also explained that her job and her trips to the country with her husband had made it easier for her to cope.

A's husband confirmed A's picture of this period, and said that he had been at least as sad as his wife about his father-in-law's illness. 'We both felt exactly the same about it.' Just when they heard the news about the cancer, A's husband was ill with pneumonia. He explained that A and her father had always had an excellent relationship (A and her husband had known one another since A was nine) and she and her father were very close.

A's feelings and thoughts were shared with and confirmed by her husband. They had an equal relationship; they supported each other on equal terms. Neither of them had to play the martyr; neither of them had to sacrifice himself to the other. The tragic event brought them closer together. The deep community of feeling they enjoyed thus meant that her father's serious illness actually extended their range of action opportunities. They were involved in a positive cycle, unlike those who cannot talk to one another in everyday life, who then find it even more difficult to do so in a crisis, and who are subsequently left even more out of touch with one another than before. The case of A shows that it is possible to emerge from a crisis with greater strength, having been able to show one's feelings and to work constructively on them.

CHAPTER 7

Friends, work, and social class

Up to now we have been discussing the implications of past life events and present or past family bonds for the development of depression. In this chapter we will leave the family and look at the role that work and leisure time may play in this context. Are certain jobs more likely to pave the way for a depressive reaction in an adverse situation? And is any social class more disposed to depression than others? This question embraces several factors connected with the repercussions that a culture—the organization and distribution of power in a society—may have in the shape of depressions suffered by its individual members. My main focus of interest in this chapter will be the possible links between social class and depression. Before embarking on the more sociological aspects of the subject, I would like to mention another sphere of activity that is often outside the home and apart from the family, namely leisure-time pursuits and contacts with friends.

7.1 PLEASANT ACTIVITIES AND FRIENDS

It seems likely that those who are particularly susceptible to depression will probably lead rather a restricted life outside the everyday routines of their homes and their jobs. But how can we discover the content of a person's leisure time from personal interviews? In my investigation I asked about regular leisure-time activities, those that occurred more often than once a fortnight. I also asked about any regular non-kin leisure-time companions.

As regards the number of leisure-time activities, the average was the same for the depressed and the non-depressed. This meant that *before* a depressive or negative period both groups had an average of at least three leisure-time activities in which they regularly indulged. I expected that at least when I asked specifically about leisure-time activities involving *social* contacts, I would find some difference between the depressed and the non-depressed, but even here the number of activities undertaken varied very little.

My hypotheses on these questions were based mainly on behavioural theory (see p. 5). It has been suggested, for instance, that the depressed have received less positive reinforcement for their behaviour than other people. Indulgence in pleasant activities can be said to generate positive reinforcement. Lewinsohn and MacPhillamy (1974) based their argument on a Pleasant Event Schedule containing 320 events which could be regarded as 'pleasant'. Older people proved to have participated in such pleasant activities less than younger people, and the depressed less than the non-depressed. The older people's subjective enjoyment of the events did not vary with the number of events participated in, while among the depressed a lower pleasant activity level also meant that the participant was finding the activities less satisfying. And it is, of course, just this combination—lower satisfaction and fewer activities—that is symptomatic of depression. Thus, as Blaney (1977) points out, these results are really tautologous. If they are to be used to support the behavioural assumption, it will be necessary to establish a decline in the number of activities even *before* the onset of the depression.

One of the criticisms that could be levelled at my own study is that the people interviewed were not asked to say whether the activities in which they participated were satisfying and pleasant. I was trying to establish whether their leisure-time activities were important to them, which is probably—although not necessarily—often the same as their being satisfactory. The most serious objection, however, and one which applies to other similar studies as well, is that the same importance is ascribed to the most varied activities. Even if certain activities are singled out—as I single out club activities, for instance—these may still mean very different things to different people. It may be a case of activities that form part of an individual's repertoire of actions, requiring little extra commitment and no stepping out of the normal, regular pattern. In other words leisure-time activities may not always broaden an individual's range of action opportunities or provide him with a source of increased self-esteem. A study of the subjective import of the activities, similar to my study of the content of personal relationships, might have been useful.

Nevertheless, I conclude from my own results—and I have found nothing to contradict my view in any of the studies I have examined—that the impact of leisure-time activities on self-esteem is very slight compared with the significance of the partner bond and the relationship with parents. And when it came to the number of leisure-time activities at the time of the interview (i.e. after the depression), the depressed group—and the patient group in particular—actually engaged in more leisure-time occupations than the non-depressed. Perhaps they were compensating for the failure they perceived in their family life, by engaging in something which they felt they could master?

One way of establishing whether there is anything in this last assumption is to look at the kinds of leisure-time activities that were most common in the different groups. Dancing and club activities were more common in the patient group compared with the others, while sport and culture predominated among the depressed members of the control group. Sporting activities were also relatively common among the non-depressed. It was interesting to note that these last were more often involved in sporting activities requiring the participation of other actors, while the depressed members of the control group spent more time walking, cycling, and so on. The difference in activity pattern between the groups was fairly small, but it nevertheless indicates a tendency; the depressed group, particularly the depressed patients, devoted themselves to the kind of activities in which people *seek* contact with others; the non-depressed, and to some extent the depressed in the control group, devoted themselves to activities that *depend on contact* (or where there *already is contact*) with other people. I suggest that these results may support my hypothesis that in their various leisure-time activities depressed people seek compensation for the frustrations of family life.

We may also be able to learn something from this unexpected result if we look at certain other variables that seem to be connected with participation in many leisure-time activities. Those people in the non-depressed group who were involved in a variety of activities in their leisure hours, also proved to have many meaningful work contacts, many deep social contacts, and many different functions at work. This is the pattern that could be expected of the flexible individual; but the interesting point is that *none* of these variables correlates with leisure-time activities in the two groups of the depressed. This appears to confirm my assumption that leisure-time activities in themselves have very little to do with the low self-esteem of the depressed personality, which depends predominantly on conditions in the family and to some extent on conditions at work. On the other hand, we can assume that in the case of the non-depressed personality, access to many varied leisure-time activities may contribute something towards the feeling of general satisfaction.

It should always be remembered, however, that individual differences can easily be missed in comparisons between large groups. Although the lack of social activities may mean a lot to a few people, the statistical average reduces this significance to a minimum. Case G provides an example of a depression which was probably partly caused by a lack of social activities.

G is a 25-year-old woman who grew up in a working-class family in northern Sweden. Four years ago she sought psychiatric help for a depression which she thought had developed when she stopped taking the contraceptive pill. The interviewer felt that the interview helped G to gain insight into her situation. G was surprised to discover during the talks that her depression was probably connected with her life situation; there had been several adverse factors in the period prior to the onset of the depression.

G had stopped taking the pill and had subsequently gained a lot of weight. She had recently moved to Uppsala and was badly missing her best friend. She avoided social contacts. Her life seemed so dull that she ate too much, sometimes so much that she was sick. Her only leisure interests at this time were reading, sewing, and sometimes going for a walk in the country or going to the cinema. Whatever she did, she was almost always alone. Just before the onset of the depression she had been involved in a relationship—though not a very close one—with a man who had been both dominating and demanding; neither of them could really get through to the other. When G moved to Uppsala, her mother—who was still living in the north of Sweden—missed her daughter very much. G also felt that they were too far away from one another, and this made her feel guilty about moving. She had moved to Uppsala to take a job as a laboratory assistant. To begin with things were also difficult at work; there were two 'camps' and G did't feel she belonged to either of them.

Thus there were several negative factors which could have contributed to this depression; none was immediately obvious or particularly conspicuous, but together they went a long way towards explaining the depression. It is not so much a question of sometimes being alone, of not having many interests that involve other people; it is more a question of being left entirely on one's own (and without voluntarily having sought isolation). If you are frustrated at every turn, trapped in a situation with no apparent way out, the last straw will be the *total* lack of anyone to trust and to share interesting activities with. And it is in the light of this that the role of friends in connection with depression should be considered. Friends can play a positive role in adversity if there is no backing and no possibility of support or change from close relatives.

A research team in Australia has examined the possible association between social bonds and neurotic symptoms. The depressive symptoms appear to dominate in their rating scale. In a study of a group of patients (1978a) and another of a group of people in the community (1978b), Henderson *et al.* found a strong inverse relationship between social bonds and the presence of neurotic symptoms. The authors define three types of social relationship: persons with whom a close attachment is maintained; friends or non-kin with whom a voluntary, desired, and affectively comfortable relationship exists; and acquaintances encountered in the transactions of day-to-day living (1978b, p. 464). The research team also tried to establish whether there was an express desire for better social relationships and whether any of the social interactions were unpleasant (rows, etc.). In a sample of the normal population it was found that the level of neurotic symptoms depended to a great extent on available attachments, adequate attachments, and unpleasant social interaction. These results tie up with my own findings regarding the lack of confiding communication between the depressed and their partners and parents, and the demanding nature of these important relationships. I am assuming here that the 'attachment' referred to concerns the close kin, although unfortunately it is not clear whether this is actually so. But it is interesting to see that friends and acquaintances have little effect on the level of depressive symptoms. A similar study was made of 50 patients (37 depressed) and 50 matched controls. In this case, too, it was found that the patients claimed only half as many good friends and half as many attachment figures as the non-neurotic. Further, the patients were more inclined to perceive contacts with the 'primary group' (kin, friends, work associated, and neighbours) as affectively unpleasant. But it is difficult to draw any definite conclusions from this material since the questions were asked during a period, and referred to a period, when the respondents were depressed. The authors were aware of this problem, mentioning, for example, that the symptoms may have made it less pleasant for the patient to seek social encounters, which in turn made him less sought-after.

Henderson *et al.* (1980) have now designed a longitudinal study, in which they will interview a large population at four-monthly intervals; they will also interview close relatives or friends of the respondents. The first interviews have now been reported; an attempt has been made to see whether a deficiency in social bonds holds in its own right, or whether the individual concerned has experienced life-stress. The neurotic symptoms increase with the lack of social bonds. Zung's scale of depression has also been applied, but these results have not been reported. However, even if Zung's scale suggests the same trend, it does not seem to me that Brown and Harris's hypotheses have been upset (see below), since these—like my own—are primarily concerned not with an explanation of different levels of neurotic or depressive symptoms, but with what actually makes a person become depressed.

Brown and Harris (1978) showed that a person with a confiding relationship (in the first place with a partner and secondly with parents or other close connections) ran much less risk of becoming depressed when faced with an adverse life experience. Only 2 of 62 women who lacked a close and deep partner bond became depressed in the absence of such an experience. Brown and Harris also studied the frequency of the interaction with relatives and friends, but this has no effect on the possible occurrence of a depression, provided the need for intimacy was satisfied within the family.

In my study I found that patients, the depressed controls, and the non-depressed had on an average about three 'contact units' whom they met regularly (more than once a fortnight). The term *contact unit* referred to groups of people who are met in the same context at roughly regular intervals and who are all more or less equally important to the subject. If we disregard these units we find some slight difference between the groups. The non-depressed meet about 10 people, the depressed controls about 9 people, and the patients about 7.5 (the average rating includes people encountered regularly but less often than once a fortnight). The difference between contact units and the number of single leisure-time companions seems to suggest an important explanation of the results reported in Henderson *et al.* (1978a). These authors found that the depressed individual is eager to meet people, and he spends as much time with others as do the non-depressed. But the depressed person is also anxious to dominate the discussions, to be at the centre of interest, and not to risk making *faux pas*. The larger the setting of the encounters and the more people there are involved, the greater is the risk of being lost in the crowd. In such a situation the depressed has no control over developments and the anxiety he is so eagerly trying to avoid revives. Much the same mechanisms apply in making contact outside the primary group; he is afraid of the unpredictable and therefore avoids such contact. He prefers to meet people he already knows well, preferably on his own.

I thus assume that certain characteristics of the depressed personality, in particular the fear of anxiety, make him unwilling to establish contact with a great many different kinds of people. While this probably plays little part in *generating* a depression, the restriction it involves may hasten the development of a depressive personality; there is little opportunity for learning how to handle many situations and many types of people; action becomes set in rigid forms.

It is hardly surprising that the withdrawal from any but a few friends is most marked at the time of the actual depression. All depressive traits will naturally be accentuated at this time: the depressed individual is very much afraid of fear; he sees things in terms of black and white; he has no confidence in himself while also desperately wanting to receive all the attention available. These characteristics of the depressive personality, in particular the fear of anxiety, are most clearly apparent in the neurotically depressed.

Once again, however, I would claim that in certain situations involving severe personal problems a large circle of acquaintances can have a markedly positive effect. Let us look at a case in which it seems possible that depression was avoided partly because a man had many friends and a job that offered him plenty of variety.

K is a man of about 30. He was divorced a year ago, but did not suffer any resulting depression. There was nothing especially remarkable about his childhood, except that his mother was depressed and was admitted for hospital treatment when K was 10. He also mentions that he felt some strain in connection with arranging his father's funeral a few years ago.

K has a responsible and varied job. He is part-owner of a firm. His job involves driving round Uppsala and the surrounding area delivering and collecting goods. He also does a lot of other things in the company. Just before the divorce he was also studying at evening school.

This meant that he was often out in the evenings, and his wife met another man. It was the wife who asked for the divorce. K says that there was a deep bond between him and his wife, but that she was demanding and dominating. The divorce did not worry him very much. He admits to feeling some guilt at first and he wanted the marriage to go on, but in the end he accepted that his wife wanted the divorce. His mother was worried that he might not be able to cope, but was surprised to see how well things turned out. K says that he sees no point in thinking too much about his problems; it's better to start doing something, which he did as soon as he moved out of the marital home. He now regularly makes up a foursome with good friends. They have even started a club for divorced men, which meets once a month. He also has three female friends whom he sees regularly.

There is nothing in K's background, apart from his mother's depression, to predispose him to the development of depressive responses. It is, of course, difficult to gather from K's own remarks what his wife really meant to him and to his life. Perhaps he is suppressing his disappointment. But the case does surely suggest that for the non-depressive personality the possession of a large number of good friends may contribute to the avoidance of depression or the ability to cope with a depression reasonably well. My more general conclusion, however, is still that the nature and extent of the friendship group is far less important in this context than the partner bond or the relationship with parents. The implications of the work situation will be examined in more detail below.

7.2 THE WORK SITUATION

Are people in certain jobs more susceptible to depression? In my study I used a new Swedish socio-economic job classification based on the predominant trade union or professional affiliation (workers' organization, white-collar workers' organization, and entrepreneurial organization) and on the training require-ments. It seemed to me that this classification provided a more useful and telling picture than the traditional classification by social group. A comparison based on social group (social class) will be presented in the following section.

In a comparison between the depressed and the non-depressed in our study no single occupational category was found to predominate, but there was a difference between the depressed in the control group and the treated patients. For example, we found that a high proportion of the former belonged to the specialist category (engineers, teachers, journalists, supervisors, and so on). I shall return to these results in a later chapter where I discuss the characteristics of those who seek psychiatric treatment (pp. 103–104)

We also examined the nature of the contacts maintained with work colleagues. As regards the content of the relationships (depth, demands, dominance) no very noticeable differences could be distinguished between the groups. Three possi-ble explanations occur to me. First, the nature of the relationship with work colleagues seldom has any decisive effect on the possible development of a depression. Secondly, many people seek escape at work from their problems at home. At least there are people to talk to at work; and their companionship is probably particularly desirable because of the circumstances at home, even if the domestic problems are not actually brought out into the open with workmates. The third explanation is closely related to the second, namely: any problems that do confront the individual at work are relatively insignificant compared with the family troubles, and people are therefore less likely to complain that colleagues are making what an objective observer might regard as unreasonable demands. The ambition to succeed in family life usually means so much more than any aspirations to do well at work.

However, the reaction pattern of the depressive personality revealed itself more clearly in other ways. The depressed person had significantly fewer people at work with whom he talked (i.e. in the period prior to the depression). After the depressive period the difference between the groups was roughly the same: all three acknowledged more present-day contacts, which suggests that the memory factor played the same role regardless of group affiliation.

The fact that the depressed talk regularly to fewer people at work probably helps to explain why they report surprisingly few difficult relationships there: many of them presumably avoid any contacts which they feel might prove difficult. At this point my proposition about the number of leisure-time contacts is again relevant: I assume that in his eagerness to control what is happening around him and to avoid anxiety, the depressed person eschews any contacts about which he is in any way uncertain. Sometimes, however, this is not possible; he may be more or less compelled to accept certain contacts or the job may call for a large team of collaborators. The interesting point, which appears to support my hypothesis, is that only the depressed are unable to cope with a large range of contacts at work; and those of the depressed who do form part of a wide occupational contact network are also those who mention a comparatively large number of negative contacts in their jobs. There appears to be a statistical correlation between the number of occupational contacts and the proportion of *demanding* occupational contacts, and between the number of occupational contacts and the proportion of such contacts characterized by dominance on the part of the other person ($r = 0.40$ and 0.47 respectively). Neither of these relations appeared in the non-depressed group. It thus seems that the depressed personality is uneasy in the presence of large numbers of people, since he cannot then control the situation.

The question in this section of our study which revealed the greatest differences between the groups concerned the respondent's perceived job responsibility. This question was put only to those in paid employment (the proportion of wage-earners was somewhat greater in the control group than in the patient group). (See Table 7.)

Seventy per cent in the non-depressed group see their jobs as responsible, compared with 53 per cent in the depressed group (significant difference). Not very surprisingly, it is mainly the unskilled and the semi-skilled workers who feel that their work calls for no independent action on their part. It is interesting that the general difference between the depressed and the non-depressed is equally marked in these two categories (e.g. 29 per cent of the unskilled in the depressed group claim to have responsible jobs compared with 47 per cent in the non-depressed group).

In a broad study of mental health and job content Gardell (1980) has shown how the degree of autonomy in a job affects self-esteem. The studied population consisted of 414 people employed in the pulp and paper industry and 640 people employed in the engineering industry, all operating outside any major metropolitan area, in communities with similar consumption patterns and similar recruitment bases. In both these industries Gardell found that those whose jobs had a high degree of complexity also enjoyed greater self-esteem. Job complexity was defined in terms of, for instance, vocational training required, responsibility, and variation of task. An interesting point was the absence of any clear connection between job complexity and psychosomatic disorders, anxiety, or general satisfaction. But one wonders whether the tendency to depression would not have varied between workers with high and low levels of responsibility, particularly in view of the central role that self-esteem plays in depression. As Table 7 shows, my study provides some support for such an assumption.

Table 7   Perceived job responsibility

	Non-depressed (%)	Depressed controls (%)	Patients (%)
Independent tasks	70	56	50
Some independent tasks	11	15	15
No independent tasks	19	29	35
	100	100	100
	$n = 104$	$n = 41$	$n = 52$

Another of my results also points in the same direction: I found that on an average the jobs of the depressed embraced fewer functions than the jobs of the non-depressed (24 per cent of the former and 30 per cent of the latter had jobs embracing two or more functions). But the difference was not significant. By functions I meant activities that were part of the job but which had very little to do with one another. The concept corresponds more or less to Gardell's 'variation of task'.

The apparent link between depression and non-responsible work can depend on several factors. One might suppose that people with depressive personalities would *perceive* their work as less responsible than it really is. But the idea that the depressive personality thus 'infects' his work situation with perceived but unrealistic uniformity is not supported by my earlier proposition—for which my investigation gave empirical support—that the depressed seek compensation at work for problems in the family. Nor did the close relatives' assessments of the respondents' work situations provide any support for such an assumption. Instead it seems more likely (a) that people with depressive personalities actually seek non-responsible jobs because of their fear of putting a foot wrong and of being unable to command any part of such a varied and fragmented world (see, for example, case N, p. 35), *and* (b) that non-responsible jobs reinforce a depressive development.

Regardless of whether or not a person has chosen a non-responsible job because he already has a depressive personality, the job in itself will also affect the way he develops as a person. A dull job lacking in responsibility provides little opportunity for demonstrating his own unique nature. It is more likely to reduce him to a puppet, giving him no chance to confirm his identity; his worth consists of little more than the value of the product he works to produce. The lack of personal responsibility implies a large degree of dependence on others; the worker's own range of actions is severely curtailed, which in turn affects his confidence in himself and in his own capabilities not only at work but in life as a whole. Another effect of doing a dull and undemanding job is probably a tendency to fall into rigid action patterns. So much of what you do follows a regular routine; you are expected to emit certain set responses in certain set situations. Perhaps you perform the same action repeatedly, always with the same result. Or you have to answer the same questions over and over again ('What time is the next train to Waterloo?'). You have no chance to practice flexibility of response; no chance to act on your own terms and in answer to your own needs. You are locked in your settled patterns.

7.3 SOCIAL CLASS

The question of social class and depression has been widely studied but the findings are rather contradictory. Some studies have shown a higher proportion of depressed at the lower social levels; others have shown the opposite. Generally, however, no particular connection between social class and depression has been established (Fredén, 1978; Nijhof, 1978; Munro, 1966a; Schwab *et al.*, 1967; Hare, 1955). There are fairly clear indications, on the other hand, that other socio-psychiatric disorders, such as schizophrenia, psychopathy, alcoholism, and drug addiction are more common among the lower social classes. And these disorders—perhaps for this reason—have received more attention from social-scientific researchers, while the social aspects of depression have been somewhat neglected.

What is there in the nature of depression which makes it relatively independent of social class? In trying to answer this question I shall describe and examine the methodology of several studies which have analysed the connection between social class and depression, and in particular I shall interpret the results of these studies in terms of Becker's theory. What aspects of society are likely to nourish the possibility of threats to self-esteem, what aspects are likely to reinforce rigid action patterns or restrict the range of opportunities? Is there any social class that is particularly vulnerable in any of these respects?

I have examined and compared several studies which are concerned with the relation between social class and depression, hoping to discover what has led to the widely differing results reported. Most of the studies refer to the Scandinavian countries, Great Britain, Holland, or the USA, i.e. countries which are fairly similar in terms of culture.

Where differences have been noted, the tendency is fairly clear: the depressive psychoses involving an element of the manic (manic-depressive psychosis) are more in evidence in the higher social classes (Bagley, 1973; Woodruff *et al.*, (1971). Two Norweigian psychiatrists (Grünfeld and Salvesen, 1968) excluded manic-depressive patients from their study and found that patients with reactive depressive psychosis had less favourable socio-economic backgrounds than had been expected. No decline in class affiliation was found in the case of depressive patients after the first hospital visit (the drift hypothesis). Thus it seems that the higher social classes exhibit more depressions of a somewhat inexplicable and, it can be assumed, internally generated nature, while the lower social classes incline towards depressions of a more obvious social stamp.

Most of the studies are concerned with inpatients. Where depression has been examined in a normal population, a negative relation between social class and depression has generally been found (Brown and Harris, 1978; Johnsson, 1970; Warheit *et al.*, 1973). Nor did I find in my own study that any particular social category predominated in the patient group. On the other hand, there was a preponderance of people from the lower social strata among the depressed in the control group (35 per cent as against 27 per cent). One probable explanation of this predominance among the non-patients is that depression manifests itself in different ways in different social classes. Schwab *et al.* (1967) have shown that members of the lower social classes sometimes tend to express their hopelessness and despair in physical symptoms (headache, backache, and so on). A person with a headache is unlikely to go to a psychiatrist, and even if he does, the psychiatrist may find it difficult to identify the underlying depressive situation. My own investigation provided indirect confirmation of this. The more severe depressions appeared to a greater extent than expected in the lower social groups, among both the depressed and the controls. Could this be because their defences in the shape of somatic symptoms were inadequate at that stage and the depressive problems became overwhelming?

Although it has been established that depressions are two or even three times more common among women than among men, only one of the studies in my survey included a comparison of sex, class affiliation, and depression. Johansson (1970) found that depressions were much more common among men of working age (30–54 years) in the lower social classes than among women in the same age group (even among the women, however, there was a certain preponderance in the lower social classes). This result thus suggests that male depression is something of a class phenomenon. In all the studies social class was established according to occupation and the educational requirements of the job. In several of the studies the woman's social class was based on the man's occupation. It is not, therefore, very surprising that the woman's social class appeared to be of minor importance, in view of our findings in the previous chapter. I have suggested that male depression is more closely linked to the work situation and that female depression is more likely to have its roots in the home. Naturally the man's work situation will also affect the woman's situation in the home (e.g. crowding, lack of common leisure, and so on), and this is probably what Brown and Harris's study of a London suburb reveals when—contradicting my thesis—it shows a preponderance of depressions among working-class women.

This brings us to another aspect of many investigations of this type. Almost all the studies in my survey refer to fairly large towns and their surroundings, obviously because that is where university research departments are to be found. Brown and Harris (1978) compared their study of a London suburb with a smaller investigation which they conducted in the Outer Hebrides. There they found *no* social class differences in connection with depressions. Birtchnell's (1971) study of depressed men (inpatients and outpatients) was also conducted in Scotland (north-eastern Scotland), and this suggests a preponderance of depressions in the lower social classes. The difference between Brown and Harris's study and Birtchnell's may depend on the fact that Birtchnell restricted himself to male patients. The cultural–geographical implications may thus be counterbalanced by the sexual, and by the fact that the studied population consisted entirely of patients.

It is interesting to note that clinical assessments also identify more depressed people in the higher social strata, compared with diagnoses based on the subject's (or patient's) own answers to set questions (rating questions). What is the difference in these two ways of 'measuring' depression? And why are they different, when the rating scales are actually based on clinical diagnoses? Zung's rating scale (1973), which I used in my study, considers the following factors: (a) mood disturbance, (b) psychological disturbances, (c) physiological symptoms, and (d) psychomotoric disturbances. Naturally the way these factors are combined is of key importance. In Zung's rating scale the somatic and psychomotoric disturbances are given relatively great weight (accounting for 7 of the 20 questions). In clinical assessment, on the other hand, emotional and psychological factors probably carry much more weight. This assumption is supported by Schwab *et al.* (1967). It is important to remember that the clinical diagnosis also allows for causal factors (personality development, precipitating factors, etc.) and takes into account reactions to antidepressant therapy. A psychiatrist can probably 'discover' a depression more easily if underlying factors can explain the symptoms to him, and he is more likely to see such explanations if the social distance between himself and the patient is not too great (i.e. they belong to the same social class).

Schwab *et al.* (1967) have compared rating scales (Beck's and Hamilton's) and clinical assessments, and examined the diagnoses reached by the two methods for the same patients. The examinations concerned 143 patients in a *medical* hospital department. According to the rating scales, depression was most common in the lower social classes. The medical practitioners, on the other hand, diagnosed 32 per cent of the upper-class patients and 8 per cent of the lower-class as depressed. Of course, the material was selective, and we should not perhaps draw conclusions as though it were of a purely psychiatric nature. However, it is usually the general practitioner or medical student who makes the first selection, and it is at that stage that a preliminary diagnosis of depression is arrived at. Schwab's team concludes that physicians regard depression as an 'upper-class disorder'. This may be because they belong to the upper class themselves and therefore find it more difficult to recognize symptoms in the lower classes where depression, according to Schwab, is more likely to assume somatic forms. Schwab's hypothesis agrees with my own assumption that physicians may find it difficult to understand the background to a depression in the case of their lower-class patients.

In Schwab *et al.* (1968) and Chwast (1966) it is also suggested that criminal activity in the lower social classes may be an expression of depression. Aggression is directed outwards towards society, instead of inwards with a resulting depression. Chwast investigated present depression among a group of juvenile delinquents convicted of minor offences. He used psychological tests and found that almost half of the young people were clearly depressed. Chwast postulates a link between depression and violence, including in violence the extreme forms of suicide and murder. The background these young offenders had in common was their strong feeling of hopelessness, the feeling that they were society's losers. But should we not expect—at least if we stick to the classical psychodynamic theory—that criminals will have a lower level of depression, since their aggressions are directed outwards? It seems to me, as it does to Chwast, that in fact they do exhibit the characteristic signs of depression (feeling of hopelessness, low self-esteem, uncritical view of themselves and society, limited range of action), but that the *external* manifestation of these symptoms often assumes the force of destructive or aggressive actions. This is something of a self-contradictory phenomenon since it contains both outward-directed and inward-directed anger.

Agitating depression appears to be more common in industrialized and commercialized cultures. Lesse (1968) cites some studies from India and Japan.

This type of depression has been found predominantly among the children of highly educated and professionally working mothers in large metropolitan cities such as Tokyo and Bombay. In light of Chwast's findings, we could conclude that these depressions might have found even more violent expression if the subjects had not been controlled by middle-class norms (e.g. respect for society) and the knowledge that they still had a chance to make something of their lives in the society in which they lived. Altogether it seems to me that the studies discussed show how closely the depressive symptomatology is linked to societal conditions. However, the whole discussion presupposes that there is a definite, independent, psychological or medical state which can be called depression. Farbrega (1974) calls for a definition of depression in terms that are independent of culture. He assumes that certain features of depression are common to all cultures, but that its manifestations differ from one cultural context to the next. Farbrega also assumes that the biochemistry of depression (interrelated neurochemical and neurophysiological changes) is a constant factor. Unlike Farbrega, Ernest Becker does not assume a medical or biological common denominator in depression: he postulates that depression is entirely an expression of social phenomena (even the psychological phenomenon, the ego, is a social construct). But Becker also assumes that all depression is subject to a common social–psychological dynamic.

How, then, can the social–psychological concepts of self-esteem, range of action opportunities, and rigid action patterns help us to understand the links between society, social class, and depression?

What factors can precipitate a depression by constituting a threat to self-esteem? In Chapter 3 we saw that *losses*, and particularly the loss of a partner, often trigger off depression. In our present context we therefore need to consider the *meaning* that losses may have in different social classes. The romantic love idea—'the only one for me'—is probably more widespread in the middle classes. It is also in the middle and upper classes that partner loss represents a great threat to a woman's self-esteem, since she often stays at home. My study showed, for example, that a severe difficulty sometimes fails to develop into a depression if the subject has an important role outside the family and supportive colleagues available to help. Partner loss in thus likely to appear much more severe to a woman at home; the activities which are important to her and which provide her self-esteem have suddenly been drastically reduced.

Brown and Harris (1978) showed that depressions were much more common among working-class women than among middle-class women (23 per cent as compared with 5 per cent). Further, class differences were found only in the case of severe events affecting the home, i.e. events concerning the economy of the household, the home itself, the husband, or the children (apart from difficulties connected with health or the socio-sexual situation). Working-class women ran three times as great a risk as middle-class women of experiencing a severe event connected with the home.

Brown and Harris also classified different kinds of difficulties: it is not a question of clearly defined events but rather of substantial problems that have lasted for more than two years. The results are similar to those reported above, but it also appears that health problems are different in the different classes. In the case of severe events and difficulties connected with the home and health, however, big differences between the social classes appear only when there are children still living at home. Brown and Harris's study invites the conclusion that working-class women with children at home are exposed to the greatest pressure, and that this can lead to depression.

I conclude from this that severe events and acute problems impose a greater burden on working-class women with small children. For these women the physical space (crowded living conditions) as well as the economic opportunities must be strictly circumscribed. The children are constantly under their feet, it may be difficult to get anyone to help with them (no close relatives available), the woman may be doing two jobs (one at home and one 'at work'), and the children put a great strain on the family finances. The same authors' comparative study in the Outer Hebrides confirms this interpretation; no class differences with regard to the presence of depression could be found there. The people of the islands were firmly rooted in a known social context; they had not been exposed to that depletion of their range of action which often results when people are forced to move, particularly to anonymous suburbs.

Phillips (1968) refers to the famous Midtown study in the USA, in which a strong link was found between low social class and poor mental health. But it was *not* possible to blame the much higher incidence of mental disturbances in the lower social strata on any preponderance of stress factors in these classes; people appeared to develop mental disturbances regardless of the *number* of stress factors. On the other hand, the overall stress picture—perhaps involving physical illness, job worries, socio-economic anxiety—had a greater impact on 'positive feeling' in the lower levels of society. In the upper social classes the expression of positive feeling did not differ much between those who had been exposed to many stress factors and those who had only been exposed to a few. Positive feeling is very similar in this context to the concept of self-esteem.

Phillips, like Brown and Harris, shows that the context in which the severe difficulty arises is the determining factor. The different social classes generally suffer *as often* from severe difficulties, but the generally problematic life situation of the lower classes means that the critical event acquires greater negative impact. People at this level in society do not have as much to fall back on in the way of acquired self-esteem and available action alternatives. We have seen, for example, that household problems in general and health in particular are more likely to result in depression in the lower social classes. This could be because the severe difficulties have more effect on such things as strained finances (making it necessary to work both inside and outside the home) and crowded conditions, perhaps in a small flat, and people in these social groups are probably less likely to seek help outside their own social circle. Thus the social and economic conditions in which the lower social classes live can mean that difficulties are perceived as more severe.

In the upper social classes other problems seem to some extent to assume an importance that makes them threaten or even diminish self-esteem. Marital difficulties and problems connected with the partner are a common cause of depression. This can certainly be explained in part by the prevailing happiness ethic and the love ideal continually projected by the mass culture. Thus in these classes it is ideological and cultural factors that are more likely to accentuate certain problems. And marriage is naturally also a factor of some considerable importance to a woman who is not compelled to go out to earn her living.

It seems to me that the concept of the rigid action pattern is particularly important in any study of depression and social class. Researchers of the psychoanalytic school emphasize that manic-depressive patients often have a history of exposure as children to high moral demands on the part of their parents (Cohen *et al.*, 1954), that as adults they set great store by social approval (Gibson, 1958), and that they are performance-oriented, conventional, and authoritarian in their attitudes (J. Becker, 1960). These are all factors which seem to me to suggest rigid action patterns, an insistence on certain ideas and types of behaviour. The only diagnostic group which shows a preponderance in the upper social classes is, not surprisingly, the manic-depressives.

In a comparative study of different cultures Murphy *et al.* (1967) found that in all the countries studied the middle classes showed throughout the most typical symptoms of depression (e.g. undervaluation of self, thoughts of suicide), while the depressions of the lower classes were more outward-directed (e.g. excitement, theatrical mourning). The authors explained their findings in part by citing the probably stronger superego (conscience) of the middle classes and their greater social solidarity (in the broad sense of striving for common goals, etc.). Their general conclusion is that depression does not seem to be contingent on a specific culture, a particular religion or any social class; it is connected rather with the degree of social solidarity in the relevant society, i.e. on the extent to which the individual feels constrained to live up to the dominating social expectations of a particular society. My own comment here is that the upper classes presumably adopt such dominating aspirations or ideologies all the more wholeheartedly for having had a large part in their creation.

A Finnish psychiatrist has written a very interesting article in which he lists typical mechanisms in our society that reinforce depressions in the individual (Siirala, 1974). It is more fruitful, he suggests, given the way that our Western society functions, to ask why some people do *not* suffer from depressions. He discusses various characteristics of our society that appear to have strongly depressive overtones. Among other things he mentions the medical profession's view of depression, which to a great extent coincides with the clinical picture revealed by the depressed person. There is also the poverty of the medical language which encourages us to establish quick, superficial, and unreflecting social contacts, reacting to people as stereotypes rather than varied individual personalities. This sort of behaviour resembles what I have called rigid action patterns. A similar social-behaviour parallel with depression can be discerned in the buying and consuming of goods. In the capitalist economy we are expected to become dependent on goods; at the same we are not to remain content with those we have, but are supposed to seek ever greater satisfaction from new products. Fromm-Reichmann has described the cause of the manic-depressive psychosis as an unconscious registration of failure to establish dependence on a partner, when the latter satisfies all needs. Neither in consumer behaviour nor in adaptation to the partner is it our own needs that we consider, and in both cases we strive continuously to advance without achieving satisfaction.

Another clear parallel between depressive symptoms and certain features of our society is what Siirala calls the merit-doctrine. In the family where the depressive persons grow up, people are accepted only when they have fulfilled certain specific functions (e.g. coped with school); love is conditional. In our society we are regarded as full members only when we have proved ourselves as consumers and workers; approval is conditional.

What is lacking in Siirala's analysis is any attempt to define the role of compulsion and the various power relationships. Who gains from the merit-doctrine, who exploits it, who controls the consumer society? We have already asked who has most wholeheartedly adopted these principles of human behaviour in our society, and the answer we gave was: the upper social classes. The answer is presumably the same here. And I assume that these classes are thus to a greater extent the victim of their own 'depressive culture', to use Siirala's term.

In conclusion, let us look at the third of the crucial concepts derived from Becker's theory, namely limited range of action. How does this tie up with social class and depression? The success ideal described above has been adopted in the main by all classes, although presumably most eagerly by the upper strata. Which class, then, will find it easiest to live up to the ideal? By definition the upper classes must be regarded as having succeeded best. And if we examine the action opportunities available to different social strata, it is fairly obvious that the lower classes have the fewest openings: the biggest group of unemployed consists of young people of the working class; the working class suffers most severely from closures; the lower social classes have altogether less chance of finding the work they want. It has also been shown (e.g. by Johansson, 1970) that the lower social classes have fewer leisure-time opportunities, less opportunity for enjoying non-mass-produced culture, worse health, and so on. In other words, they are caught up in all sorts of circumstances which limit their range of action.

Language is also a major action resource. The language of the lower strata in society is both less comprehensive and less varied than the upper-class equivalent, partly as a result of less adequate schooling. But far more important than this is the fact that these strata have less command of the language of power, i.e. the language of the upper groups in society. Deficiency in language will lead, as Becker would put it, to deficiency in action opportunities.

The lower social classes have been compelled in various ways to conform to a way of life that limits their range of action. This restricted range of action probably also depends on a different way of evaluating the world (a different norm system): their life experience gives them less means for learning about, and accepting, what present-day society can offer, i.e. what is regarded as 'the good life' by the upper social strata.

To summarize: the upper social classes are subject to high expectations (their own and other people's) regarding their success in achieving certain cultural goals. The lower social classes have less chance of achieving these goals, since social realities put more obstacles in their way. I thus suggest that these two circumstances, corresponding to the concepts of rigid action patterns and limited range of action, cancel each other out, with the result that no social class is more subject to depression than any other. The lower social classes generally command fewer action opportunities than the upper classes, while the latter tend to develop rigid behaviour patterns. Frumkin (1955) analyses psychological disturbances in general in rather similar terms:

. . . one might say that the etiology of lower socio-economic-status-group mental illness (and crime) is generally sociogenic in nature, whereas in the upper strata of society, mental illness is generally more psychogenic. Thus, the etiology of middle-class mental disorders, being somewhere in between, i.e. more or less equally sociogenic and psychogenic, or simply social-psychogenic, in origin, reflects characteristics of both the extreme strata of society. (p. 155)

Thus depressions in the lower social strata stem mainly from difficult social and economic conditions, whereas upper-class depression is contingent to a greater extent on psychological and cultural conditions. This agrees with my earlier hypothesis regarding the factors that typically precipitate depression at the different levels in society (see pp. 91–92 above).

What Brown and Harris (1978) have shown is that the total societal structure (and not only the class structure) should be taken into account. The women of the lower social strata in the Outer Hebrides did not suffer from depression to the same extent as the working-class women in the big metropolitan areas.

A crofting housewife has more opportunity than an urban housewife to perform a range of tasks, which, barring meteorological disasters, are limited and successful. Being brought up upon the island will have given the woman from her earliest years a wider range of contacts and thus interpersonal role identities. (p. 252)

In Becker's terms these women have access to many actions in many spheres. We can assume that the lack of action opportunities in the lower strata of society is most conspicuous, and that the risk of depression is therefore greatest, in highly urbanized societies with a high level of technology and an inadequate sense of solidarity in the local community. And obviously all these factors tie up both with each other and with class conditions.

That the impact of class-related factors will also depend on the particular social setting is clearly shown in another recent study (Brown, in press). In the Hebrides it was found that depression was comparatively common following the death or imminent death of someone close, and that as a provoking factor it was much more common than it was in Camberwell. Social bonds are much stronger in the Hebrides; people live for the family, which embraces a fairly extensive group. The frequency of contact with relatives, for example, is higher than it is in Camberwell. I would conclude from this that in the Hebrides rigid action patterns probably characterize behaviour in both the middle and the working classes. On the other hand, those social conditions that reduce the scope for action so markedly among the working-class women in London are far less important in the Scottish islands, and class differences do not therefore have much effect on the overall pattern of depressive disorders.

Let us return to the question we asked at the beginning of this section: what is there in the nature of depression which makes it less dependent on social class differences than other mental disorders? Using Siirala's terms we could say that the upper classes are the victims of their own depressive culture just as much as the lower classes are of theirs. We have here a culture, a dominating social ideology, characterized by the kind of rigid action patterns that distinguish depression from most other mental disorders.

CHAPTER 8

Why some people seek treatment

What sort of people seek psychiatric help when suffering from depression? Almost all the documented assumptions and theories about the nature and causes of depression are based on material relating to treated patients. But there are hardly any grounds for assuming that these people are particularly representative of 'the depressed'. Perhaps those suffering from certain kinds of depression are more likely than others to turn to physicians for treatment. We are thus faced with the problem that the definition of 'depression' is based almost exclusively on the help-seeking sector of the depressed population. But even in studies with this fundamentally clinical orientation, it has been found that many people are depressed without ever contacting phychiatric institutions.

As a general practitioner Watts (1966) made an investigation of depression in England and Wales. He likens the incidence of depression to an iceberg: he estimates that the visible part of the iceberg, the part which comes to the attention of the physicians, represents about 10 per cent of all depressions. At the tip of the iceberg he puts suicide which accounts for 0.01 per cent of depressions in one year, followed by committed patients 0.01 per cent, voluntary patients 0.07 per cent, psychiatric outpatients 0.2 per cent, general practitioner outpatients 1.2–1.5 per cent (of which half are diagnosed as endogenous depressions), and finally those who never report their depressive problems to any physician, whom he estimates at 15 per cent of the population. The last of these figures is taken from an interview study in a London suburb, in which 17 per cent of those over 16 years of age claimed to have depressive symptoms. In a nationwide Swedish investigation (Johansson, 1970), 3.6 per cent (15–75 years) answered that during the last twelve months they had been 'depressed or very low'. In 1957 Inghe and Åmark (1958) carried out an investigation in Stockholm on a random sample of the population (488 people). At the time of the interview 18 per cent of the women and 13 per cent of the men said they were depressed (as many as 40 per cent claimed that they had felt depressed on some previous occasion). As in the Swedish study mentioned above, the interviews were conducted by interviewers untrained in psychiatry and were coded by the psychiatrists Inghe and Åmark. In analysing the material Inghe estimated that 6 per cent of the cases could be classified as depression; Åmark's figure was 11 per cent. Thus we can see that different studies lead to very different results, due mainly to variations in the populations (age, region, and so on), to the representativeness of the different populations, and to varying definitions of depression. But these and other studies to which I shall refer below do nevertheless suggest a high incidence of depression in our society.

In the study which seems to me to be the most reliable, namely Brown and Harris (1978), it was found that of 458 women interviewed in Camberwell in London, about 15 per cent had experienced depression in the year concerned. There were more or less equal proportions of onset cases and chronic cases. In addition to this a further 15 per cent had suffered depressive symptoms during the same period, but these were not sufficiently serious to be classified as cases. The investigators classified depression on a basis of a standardized clinical-type interview (Present State Examination or PSE). In our study we also started from a traditional clinical definition of depression (see p. 17). We found that 29 per cent of our control group had felt depressed at some point during the last five years. Since 80 per cent of our control group were women (and depression is two to three times as common among women), and since the period covered was relatively long, this result was hardly unexpected. My own general conclusion is that in a normal population between 5 and 10 per cent will become depressed during one year and of these about 1 per cent will seek psychiatric treatment.

What then, distinguishes the help-seekers from those who try to solve their depressive problems in some other way? Three main differences emerge: (a) different nature of the depression as such: particularly among in-patients it is more serious; (b) social support from friends and others for those who do not seek institutionalized psychiatric help: (c) different attitudes to depression or psychiatric problems. I shall be discussing these three points below.

8.1 THE NATURE OF THE DEPRESSION

Perhaps the most natural reason for seeking psychiatric help is that in the circumstances—the sufferer feels so ill or so desperate—it seems the only thing left to do; the help-seeker is quite simply *more* depressed than the non-help-seeker. Brown and Harris found a significant difference between patients and community cases as regards the overall severity of the depression (11 per cent of the community cases were severely disturbed, compared with 44 per cent of the outpatients). We did not find such a marked difference in our study in which outpatients scored an average of 55 points on Zung's rating scale and the depressed controls 52 points (the definition of moderate depression was set at 48 and of severe depression at 55). But the differences were more marked in both investigations when inpatients were included. There is thus considerable support for the proposition that depressed patients are generally suffering from more severe depression than the depressed who do not seek psychiatric help.

How can a severely depressed person take hold of himself sufficiently to seek psychiatric help? The initiative does not usually come from the sufferer himself; contact is made or arranged by somebody else. In half of the patient cases in our study, the initiative had been taken by some other person; in the case of the in-patients, i.e. those with severe depression, the proportion was even higher. In most cases it was the patient's general practitioner—a doctor whom the sufferer dared to approach since they had previously been in touch with one another—who decided that contact with a psychiatrist had become necessary. Close relatives who had become unable to cope with the situation also often felt compelled to initiate contact with the psychiatric system. A third point of entry into the psychiatric system was from some other department of the hospital, e.g. perhaps the gynaecological department where the patient may have been treated during a difficult pregnancy.

Generally speaking, I would suggest that the patients' problems were more acute than those of the depressed controls; the nature and extent of their difficulties probably caused them to perceive their own situation as so acute that they (or some other person) considered it necessary to make contact with a psychiatrist. The severity of the problems underlying the depression is, ultimately, a question of subjective judgement, but it may be possible to try to rate the *extent* of the problem 'objectively'. Brown and Harris (1978) show that during the 38 weeks before the onset of depression 23 per cent of the patients and 12 per cent of the onset cases had experienced three or more severe events. Similarly the double burden of severe events and major difficulties was more common among the patients. This gives us one explanation of the greater severity of the patients' depressions, which is indirectly supported by Surtees and Ingham (1980). Ingham and Surtees approach the problem from the other end, studying the sequels to contacts made with the psychiatric system on account of depression. In follow-up interviews seven months later it turned out that those who were still depressed had experienced substantially more life-stresses during this period than the patients who were now judged to be healthy.

It is not difficult to understand why the accumulation of severe events and problems leads to depressions of greater severity. If self-esteem is attacked or threatened from several quarters at once, there is not much for a person to cling to. The situation is most critical when more than one opportunity for satisfying activities are withdrawn, i.e. if things are very difficult, for example, at home as well as at work. In our study, too, inpatients proved to have been exposed to multiple threats to their self-esteem to a greater extent than either the outpatients or the depressed controls (see pp. 37–38).

As we have seen in earlier chapters, depression can manifest itself in many ways. Are particular symptoms more common among the psychiatric help-seekers? Wing *et al.* (1977) compared the symptoms of depressive cases in the normal population on the one hand and the symptoms of depressed inpatients and depressed outpatients on the other. Symptoms that were common among the inpatients were hallucinations and delusions, pathological guilt, slowness, and underactivity, while these symptoms were not usual among either the outpatients or the general population cases. These differences tallied with the degree of severity of the depressions in the three groups. On rating scales these symptoms are generally regarded as signs of depressive psychosis; at the same time, seeing things that are invisible to others, feeling guilt for the misfortunes of the whole world, extreme passiveness—these are all regarded as sharply deviant symptoms in our culture. It is when confronted with symptoms of this sort that most people will identify a mental *disorder* and it is generally accepted that the mentally ill should have psychiatric care.

Weissman *et al.* (1975) have identified another characteristic of the help-seekers, namely greater anxiety (feelings of tensión, fearfulness, and phobias) and above all more somatic anxiety (trembling, dizziness, and headaches). Patients also manifest more of the somatic symptoms of depression, such as anorexia and weight loss. It is worth noting that the patients had 'ordinary' depressive feelings on top of their somatic difficulties. Schwab *et al.* (1967) claims that many patients in the lower social strata show their depression *only* in somatic terms (headaches, stomach pains, and so on) and therefore often escape classification as depressed. Weissman's study makes it clear that anxiety is what finally makes these people react: 'I must do something to get rid of this oppressive anxiety.' If the depression and anxiety are combined with headaches, trembling, loss of appetite, and so on, it is rather natural to turn to a physician, i.e. to seek somatic treatment. The doctor probably finds no organic problem, but he suspects some type of psychological difficulty and refers the patient to a psychiatrist.

There are thus three aspects of the nature of depression that affect help-seeking behaviour: the severity of the depression, the culturally deviant nature of the symptoms, and the presence of several somatic symptoms as part of the depressive picture. The person who feels low but who can just about cope with everyday matters, who suffers no hallucinations or delusions and who has no particular physical problems, is typical of the depressed who do not seek psychiatric help. The interesting point here, however, is why this person does not fall into a severe depression and thus become compelled to make contact with the psychiatric system when a stressful event occurs in his life. This question will be discussed in more detail in the following section.

8.2 SOCIAL SUPPORT

In our study the greatest difference between the depressed controls and the depressed patients is to be found in the way the depression is resolved. If we look at the social circumstances *before* the depression, the difference between the two groups is not so marked. What is most noticeable is that the patients had been subject to *a greater number of* negative factors than the depressed controls. They did not seem to have been able to find support or help anywhere, and there was nothing to stop the negative cycle: their self-esteem was impaired, they could not bring themselves to act, they received no reinforcement of their own worth, their self-esteem was reduced even further. The partner bond, in particular, seems to have been a source of stress to the depressed patients, who complained of heavy demands and a lack of close contact with their partners. If two people have difficulty in understanding one another at the best of times, it must be even harder when one of them is depressed. It must be very difficult for the relatives of a depressed person to cope with, and to understand, the special language of depression. How can two partners talk about emptiness, guilt, the lack of meaning in life, and so on, when they cannot even discuss openly such simple subjects as who is to wash the dishes? The result is (a) that the sense of isolation increases and the depression becomes more severe; (b) both parties perceive the problem as being beyond their powers to solve, and as requiring the help of experts; (c) the depressed person feels a need to escape from the home. There is some support for this last point in the answers we received to another question. The depressed controls confessed to a stronger feeling of subjection in relationships with parents and friends than the patients, while the patients were more dominated by their partners and professional colleagues. Thus the patients felt more dominated in relationships which they could not avoid; their need to escape must therefore have been greater. The interesting point here is that a negative perception of the partner bond was general among the inpatients but not among the outpatients. The outpatients did not feel subjected to heavy demands from either children or partners, and this was presumably one reason why they did not want or need to go into hospital.

We have now examined in some detail the nature of the situation prior to the onset of depression, and the way in which this may affect help-seeking behaviour. What other alternatives for help are available once a person has become depressed? We asked the respondents in our study whether they had looked to their friends for help with their problems. We can see from Table 8 that, as was to be expected, a larger proportion of the depressed controls turned to their friends for help (67 per cent of the depressed controls as against 44 per cent of the patients—a significant difference).

As can be seen, the greatest difference between the two groups appears in 'partner contact' and—most of all—in 'contact with other friends' (i.e. non-kin, leisure-time companions). There is hardly any doubt—and the more un-structured oral accounts only served to emphasize this—that those who become depressed in the control group turned more frequently and more extensively to close friends to try to talk about their problems. That this did not always achieve the desired result is irrelevant in the present context. What matters is that the depressed controls sought alternative solutions to their problems; there were

Table 8   Looking to friends for help with problems

	Depressed controls (%)	Patients (%)
No contact with friend	33	56
Looking to partner for help	11	4
Looking to parents for help	7	3
Looking to brothers and sisters for help	7	3
Looking to children for help	—	—
Looking to other relatives for help	2	4
Looking to professional friends for help	7	9
Looking to other friends for help	33	21
	100	100
	$n = 45$	$n = 67$

presumably supportive people or groups to whom they could turn. The depressed controls presumably had a more confiding relationship with their friends than the patients enjoyed, and they were therefore prepared to seek help from these same friends when life became difficult. The importance of supportive friends can be illustrated by the case of R, a woman in the control group who had suffered a fairly mild depression.

R was a friendly woman of about 40 with an open manner. She regarded herself as having been depressed, but she did not rate particularly high on the scale (mild depression). She had been feeling rather low for about two years, but the crisis had been at its worst in the summer of 1972. At that time she had felt very depressed almost continuously.

R and her husband ran their own shop together. In the spring of 1972 there had been a lot to do, and as usual they had hoped to get everything dealt with by the summer. A misunderstanding with the accountant meant that R had to sit down and re-do the whole of their complicated income tax return. The worst blow was that they unexpectedly had to pay VAT on a car, owing to a mistake made by R. If they had bought the car ten days earlier, they would have avoided this payment. At two weeks' notice R and her husband had to pay almost 5000 kronor in VAT for the car.

R wanted to get in touch with someone to help her with her depression, but she didn't know who to turn to. She had a medical check-up, but this contact with the doctors obviously didn't help much. One person who was really supportive was a friend with whom R was always able to talk about her problems. The two women enjoyed an open and mutually satisfactory relationship, in which the friend, too, was able to air her worries. R said that her family (husband and three children) also stood by her and supported her, but, of course, her husband had a lot to do. There is little to suggest any particular problems in R's intimate relationships. At their summer cottage by the sea, the family kept open house and seemed to lead a pleasant and relaxed social life. R admitted that they lacked any really close friends to do things with at the weekends, but she herself had a number of leisure interests. Among other things she belonged to a sewing circle together with her best friend.

R's best friend was also interviewed. She seemed to be rather like R, and she drew much the same picture of the situation as R had done. There had been a lot of problems all at once, it had just been too much. As well as the mistakes in the tax return, her friend mentioned that R was worried about her eldest daughter, who was having a baby although she had not yet finished her training. Furthermore, a colleague of R's had died in a motor accident and R's father-in-law was not at all well. But the friend was not quite sure whether all this actually happened during the spring and summer of 1972.

The friend pointed out that R was expected to cope with everything, particularly in the shop where so much seemed to depend on her. The friend didn't think that R and her husband talked about their personal problems very much. They had a lot to do; they got up early and went early to bed. R could confide in her mother. Naturally the relationship between R and her friend was also discussed. The friend told me that every Monday after the sewing circle they would go back to R's house and have a good talk. The two husbands would go to the friend's house. R's friend felt that the sewing circle provided a means of acquiring self-confidence; the women all helped one another, and made one another feel good.

The depressed controls, R among them, seem to have had a more positive partner relationship and comparatively little trouble in opening up about their problems. These two factors certainly act upon one another: if a person has a relatively uncomplicated relationship with her partner, it will naturally be easier for her to discuss her personal or their common problems; nor is she so likely to feel guilty about turning to other friends for help; if the partner bond is spontaneous and easy, neither party will feel he or she is going behind the other's back in also seeking support elsewhere.

When people turn to others with their problems, they are generally looking for two things. First, they need confirmation of their own despair, of the fact that they are depressed and need support; only then can the other relieve their pain. Secondly, they need some of the 'rights' of the ill; somebody to take care of them, to let them occupy the centre of attention. If the other person can provide understanding and perhaps even suggest possible solutions, there may not be any need for professional help.

Work was another social support factor which we found to be more common among the depressed controls than among the patients. Quite a large proportion of the depressed controls said that work had helped them to overcome their depression (21 per cent as against 7 per cent in the patient group). That the difference was not greater was due to the fact that for many of the controls work represented the 'dominating problem' (see Table 2).

Somewhat paradoxically, most of the patients who claimed that work was a positive factor in their lives belonged to specialized professions. Among the depressed controls, on the other hand, there were comparatively many manual workers who mentioned work as a positive element. This result can be explained, however, by the fact that for the 'specialists' among the depressed controls work was the dominating problem. Our findings seem to suggest that people in specialized professions are at greater risk of becoming depressed as a result of their work situation, but that they are better equipped to cope with a depression which is *not* connected with work. The positive effect of work, with this one reservation, seems to be confirmed by another of our results. When we asked about the underlying causes of a *positive* period in their lives, 30 per cent of the control group mentioned work as against 14 per cent of the patient group. Two conclusions can perhaps be drawn from this: that the work situation of the depressed controls made it easier for them to cope with their problems, and that the depressed patients were more inclined to orientate their lives towards their families and were thus particularly vulnerable when a crisis occurred. The first of these arguments is supported by an American study (Mostow and Newberry, 1975), in which depressed housewives were compared with a matched group of depressed working women. The working women were more severely depressed at the first psychiatric contact, but tended to recover faster than the housewives. The overall improvement was more marked in the working women than in the housewives. The authors conclude that work provided the depressed women with both protection and distraction.

However, work is not the only activity which can help to relieve depression. Involvement in leisure-time activities can also help to contain a depression within manageable limits. In our investigation one-third of the respondents claimed that various leisure-time activities had helped them to cope with their situation. There was no difference in this respect between the patients and the depressed controls, and this accords with their stated involvement in leisure-time activities which was also generally the same. Our questions about work and leisure seemed to underline the importance of *activity* to those who are poised on the brink of depression, and in particular of activity which can be perceived as worthwhile. Doings of this kind help to concentrate the mind on something other than the problem, perhaps even bringing a new perspective to bear on it so that some solution suggests itself. 'Life *can* be worth living, even for me.'

Is any particular social class more inclined to seek psychiatric treatment for depression? Does the social situation as a whole affect the severity of the depression and determine help-seeking behaviour? In our study we found a certain preponderance of help-seekers in the lower social groups (35 per cent sought help as against 27 per cent who did not, which is not a significant difference). The difference might have been greater if the patients had been in a traditional mental hospital rather than in a teaching hospital. However, there is not much difference in social class affiliation between different types of institution in Sweden as there is, for instance, in the USA. Klerman and Paykel (1970) found that in the general hospital in their study about half the depressed patients came from the lower social strata, while the state mental hospital took as many as 96 per cent of their patients from this level of society.

To complement the grouping into social classes, which is always rather approximate, I classified the subjects in my study according to certain socio-economic criteria. I chose two main dimensions: position on a scale, manual workers–white-collar worker–entrepreneurs, and the educational requirements of the job. This classification gives more substance to the various professional designations than a categorization by social group. In our study we found among other things that as many as 41 per cent of the depressed controls as against 18 per cent of the patients belonged to the category 'engineers and specialists' (e.g. teachers, supervisors, journalists). Quite a large group among the patients were students (20 per cent as against 12 per cent).

How can we explain the preponderance of specialized professions among the depressed controls? We have seen that non-work-related depression is relatively common in this group, but only among those who did not seek psychiatric treatment. The difference between the help-seekers and the others may mean that problems at work do not often generate so severe a depression as to compel the sufferer to seek psychiatric help and/or that problems connected with work are easier to resolve. I further suggest that people in specialized professions are more likely to set their self-esteem at risk, but that by means of their work they have generally been able to build up greater self-esteem than other people. At work they can control and influence events. They have to learn self-reliance. They have a value; they cannot be easily replaced. And work of this kind is generally endowed with high prestige. All these factors will contribute to self-esteem. At the same time, such work involves 'daring' and experimenting with new ideas. There is probably nobody to share the responsibility with, and the risk of threat to self-esteem is therefore great. Perhaps, too, the cultural convention that emphasizes the importance of personal strength in high-powered, high-status jobs discourages any idea of seeking professional help. 'I will (should) manage to cope with this depression myself; I don't need to bother a psychiatrist.' There is probably also a practical problem: the specialist is pressed for time, his job calls for personal continuity; it is difficult to be away for sickness or for undergoing psychiatric treatment. Furthermore, the specialist occupies a particular cultural role in our society; he has 'a career'. It is hardly likely to help him in the promotion stakes if he becomes known as a man with mental troubles. Or at any rate, this is what he may believe: he must put a good face on things and go on fighting.

At the beginning of this chapter I suggested that people who seek help from the psychiatric system are generally suffering from a more severe depression than those who do not seek such help. The severity of the depression and the support which the sufferer receives from his surroundings can, of course, be regarded as two disparate factors that affect help-seeking behaviour. Nevertheless, the two phenomena are in fact often connected. The depression may actually become aggravated *because* the sufferer lacks a confiding relationship with the partner and has had difficulty in getting support from relatives and friends and, in particular, from work. The greater severity of the depression is in itself a sign that the sufferer cannot see any solution to his problems, that he is being pushed further and further into passivity and self-pity. The opposite process is, of course, also possible, but as a parallel development: as the depression becomes more severe, other people—partner, close friends, and colleagues—find it more difficult to cope and ultimately withdraw their support.

8.3 ATTITUDES TO PSYCHIATRIC TREATMENT AND TO PSYCHOLOGICAL DEVIATIONS

Is depression a disease to be cured by taking medicine? Is that what most psychiatric treatment consists of? If this is what the depressed person and his family or friends believe to be right there is not much doubt that psychiatric help will be sought when the need arises. If, however, the depressed person has a vague idea that psychiatric treatment will involve him in responsibility for his own improvement, in analysis and searching discussion of his problems, while he himself believes more in the 'illness needs medicine' approach, he may refrain from seeking expert help. Or perhaps, in some cases, the patient may be longing for a thorough discussion of his problems, but finds the psychiatrists looking at it all from a medical point of view. We did not investigate such attitudes systematically in our study, and what follows is therefore based on my own more general and subjective impressions and on my interpretation of the predominant trends in present-day traditional psychiatry.

I suggest that people who seek psychiatric treatment tend to have a comparatively deterministic and medical view of depression. They want to hand the problem over to the expert: they cannot see any possibility of influencing the situation themselves. They also see their depression as something which cannot immediately be explained, and which must therefore have somatic causes. What, then, is more natural than to turn to a doctor-cum-psychiatrist, an expert and 'medical' doctor in one?

There is also a tendency to individualize the problem, both in traditional psychiatry and on the part of the person seeking psychiatric help. The same tendency is to be found among friends and acquaintances who regard the sufferer as 'disturbed' and 'sick', and who encourage him to seek psychiatric treatment. Harrow et al. (1969a) asked a great many questions in their study about the patient's view of himself, the partner's view of himself, and their pictures of one another; this was then compared with their view of the 'average person'. The assessment of the patient—both the partner's and his own—was more negative than the assessment of the partner and the average person. After eight weeks during which the patient was in hospital, this negative attitude, though less marked, still persisted. It is particularly interesting to note that all these patients attended family therapy sessions, and yet one partner was still regarded as 'the patient', the one who was 'sick'. These findings tallied with what Harrow et al. (1969b) had reported about the views of the families of hospitalized adolescents. The parents of the depressed adolescents regarded their offspring in rather a negative light. And the adolescents themselves had a lower self-image than other non-depressed patients. Even more interesting was that after eight weeks in hospital the young people themselves perceived a greater improvement in their condition than their parents did. Harrow concludes that parents and the staff of the psychiatric hospital stamp an inpatient as sick: 'It must be quite a severe depression since they felt compelled to hospitalize him.' This stress on illness further impairs the patient's self-image. To hospitalize someone represents a last resort; for the patient's point of view this must have negative implications.

Coyne (1976) follows an interactionist approach, somewhat along these lines. He points out that the way a depressed person related to other people is such as to lose him their support. He often complains about his family, reacts negatively towards them, thus arousing in them guilt feelings and aggression towards himself. In their disappointment or sorrow or anger over him, they will tend to avoid him, which increases his isolation and reinforces his depression. I suggest further that the negative reaction to his surroundings will be even stronger in the hospitalized patient; he feels abandoned and isolated in his depression. 'Those people at home don't understand me at all; they want to get me out of the way because I bother them.' If he projects this attitude on to the family, their reaction is unlikely to be positive. And even if they reaffirm their love and his value in their eyes, he sees this as just one more proof of their falsity. 'They are only saying it because I am depressed, but what they really mean is. . . .'

Watts (1966) suggests three main factors which probably discourage people from seeking psychiatric treatment when they become depressed. 'They [those who do not make contact with a psychiatrist] find their symptoms hard to describe, they feel that they should be able to "snap out of it" themselves, and even mild depressives carry with them a sense of shame that they have let themselves slip' (p. 116).

The second of these factors ties up with my proposition that the non-help-seekers are those who, perhaps because of their positions, feel that they ought to be able to solve their personal problems by their own efforts. The first and third factors are more related to general attitudes to psychiatric problems (depression) and to ideas about psychiatric treatment.

The sense of shame, of being inadequate, of not being sufficiently strong, must be more difficult for a man than for a woman to accept. And, indeed, we found in our study that there was a greater preponderance of women among the hospitalized patients than among the outpatients or the depressed controls. The patient, the psychiatrist, and the patient's relatives and friends all find it easier to admit that a woman is depressed, and this in turn makes it easier for all parties to accept that she may have to be hospitalized. Nor should it be forgotten that a woman's social situation, also, generally makes hospitalization easier to accept. Because her work is generally in the home or in a low-status job the acknowledgement of a depression severe enough to warrant hospital treatment is not as likely to have a negative effect on her career.

CHAPTER 9

Depression as a medical problem

The traditional, clinical view of depression differs markedly from the approach to be found in Ernest Becker's work. I have already discussed the medical approach in Chapter 1, and would now like to examine in a little more detail the research results on which the medical model is based. What justification is there for regarding depression as predominantly a medical problem, and for thus referring depressed people to medical treatment? Is there a social and psychological explanation for the attachment of a medical diagnosis to the depressed? Is there any alternative explanation for those apparently inexplicable depression which recur regularly without any observable external event to trigger them off? In discussing these questions I will start from the dichotomy in traditional psychiatry between those who divide depression into the endogenous and the exogenous and those who see all depressions as springing from a continuum of external and internal causes.

An endogenous depression is defined as one whose cause lies mainly within the individual. There may be an inherited disposition to react to stress with a depressive response. What actually touches off the depression may be spontaneous hormonal changes, amino changes, carbohydrate changes, or electrochemical changes in the brain's biochemical structure; or the cause may be some other environmental factor. Or there may be a fundamental lack of some biochemical substance in the brain, which predisposes to depressive reactions. The important point is that the experience of depression is assumed to *depend on* some biochemical deficiency or defect in the brain; the manic-depressive psychosis is one of the types of depression assigned to this group. Exogenous depressions, on the other hand, are said to depend mainly on external, psychological circumstances, and they can be subdivided into reactive and neurotic depressions. It should be noted that the classification varies somewhat from country to country; in the USA and England, for example, neurotic depression often includes what in Scandinavia are known as reactive *and* neurotic depressions. This subdivision is based mainly on the proximity in time of the basic cause of the depression, and on its apparent degree of complexity. A diagonsis of neurotic depression means that the patient's depression is thought to spring from personal conflicts in childhood and adolescence and to be connected with his personality and with severe external events. In the case of reactive depression a specific external event is assumed to have preceded the depression and is regarded as a sufficient explanation of its occurrence. This strictly dichotomous view of depression as endogenous or

107

exogenous predominates among clinical psychiatrists. The opposition claim instead that *all* depressions are *in varying degrees* determined by both external and internal causes. The first section of this chapter is concerned with these two schools and with a criticism in particular of the dichotomous view. In section 9.2 below I discuss another question that embraces both schools: why do we make a medical diagnosis of depression? For those who, like myself, feel dubious about the medical approach, what other explanations of the 'endogenous' depressions are available? In a final section I shall try to provide a social–psychological explanation for these depressions which otherwise appear so inexplicable.

9.1 PRESENTATION AND CRITICISM OF CLINICAL RESEARCH

Most clinical psychiatrists support the classification of depressions into the endogenous and the exogenous. One of the main justifications for the classification is that people with a diagnosis of endogenous depression react positively to drug therapy and electroconvulsive therapy and the dichotomy therefore appears to have a practical base. Slater and Roth (1969), two prominent members of the Newcastle school, have claimed in their monumental psychiatric textbook that there is strong evidence of a qualitative distinction between the two types of depression. They cite as typical of endogenous depression (a) genetic factors, (b) positive reaction to electroconvulsive therapy and antidepressant psychodrugs, and (c) the fact that apparently insignificant everyday events are sufficient to provoke a depression. Typical of the reactive (or exogenous) depression, on the other hand, is that it has occurred in response to the stress of circumstance, and that a purely endogenous mood change is unknown to the patient.

The main genetic studies on which these writers base their arguments are Angst (1966) and Perris (1966). It appears that 12–15 per cent of the studied manic-depressive psychotics (bipolars) had close relatives suffering from the same disorder, while only 1 per cent had relatives suffering from depressive psychosis (unipolars). The converse was true of the unipolars, i.e. 10–12 per cent of their close relatives had also suffered from depressive psychosis, while about 1 per cent of their relatives were bipolars. Kringlen (1972) describes some other genetic studies, in which identical twins have been compared with non-identicals. Various studies have found that anything from 33 per cent to 98 per cent of the identical twins of manic-psychotics also suffer in the same way. The corresponding figures for non-identical twins lie between 0 per cent and 39 per cent.

Factor analysis is often used to illustrate the disparate nature of endogenous and exogenous depression. To put it simply, symptoms that occur together are combined in the factor analysis into one factor or dimension. Carney *et al.* (1965) performed a factor analysis of 36 symptoms (items) and found that those which were positively correlated with endogenous depression were also positively correlated with a positive reaction to electroconvulsive therapy. Several other factors (e.g. 'absence of adequate psychogenetic factors in relation to illness') also correlated positively with symptoms typical of endogenous depression (see

p. 2). They thus constituted a main factor or dimension. Kiloh and Garside (1963) obtained similar results, as did also Rosenthal and Klerman (1966), i.e. that there were two distinct depressive syndromes.

Thus, different reactions to medical treatment, and in particular to electroconvulsive therapy, are often cited in support of a dichotomous classification of depression. The Swedish psychiatrist Jacobowski (1961) can illustrate this view: 'Another reason [apart from the symptoms] for the assumption of a biological mechanism in the above-mentioned diseases [the endogenous] is the fact that these depression only respond to physical treatment . . .' (p. 100).

Forrest et al. (1965) can represent those who propound the third argument in favour of this classification, namely that environmental factors can go only a very little way towards explaining endogenous depression. These authors found that among the 11 manic-depressive patients in their study (note the low number) none had lost a close relative during childhood, whereas 56 of 197 reactive depressive patients had done so. Five of the manic-depressives had been exposed to 'environmental factors' within the last three years (social isolation, role loss, somatic disease), while 135 of the 197 reactive depressive patients had been so exposed.

Already in the 1930s several members of the London school, i.e. those who were critical of the division of depressions into the endogenous and the exogenous, were making their voices heard. Mayer and Lewis were two British psychiatrists among others who supported the continuum hypothesis (Kringlen, 1972). Lewis found that the deeper one delved into the background of a depressive patient, the more likely one was to find a traumatic event which had triggered off the depression; conversely, the roots of an exogenous depression could be found to go back long before the time of the identified traumatic event.

Even such a genetically oriented scientist as Angst (1966) admits that no state can be classified as purely endogenous or purely exogenous. Constitutional factors (i.e. inherited factors) and environmental factors interact with one another. In reactive depression the constitutional element is less specific and, conversely, in endogenous depression the effects of environmental factors are less specific.

Costello et al. (1974) have shown that patients who acquired more points on a scale measuring endogenous depression also came high on the scale of reactive depression ($r = 0.86$). Most of the patients were to be found in a continuum 'from high overall depression (high scores on both dimensions) to low overall depression (low scores on both dimensions)'. This study suggests that it is hardly meaningful to distinguish between depressions that are more, or less, endogenous.

It is often claimed as a major justification for distinguishing between endogenous and exogenous depression that patients suffering from the former improve as a result of electroconvulsive therapy. In a broadly based study (1080 patients) Kendell (1969) shows that there are greater differences in outcomes following ECT within the psychotic group than between the psychotic group as a whole and the neurotic groups as a whole. Kendell finds it more meaningful therapeutically to obtain a 'diagnosis score' for every patient on a basis of the number of typical endogenous symptoms (see p. 2) compared with the number of typical reactive symptoms. It was in cases where there were many typical endogenous symptoms, and few reactive symptoms, that there was a positive reaction to ECT treatment. Kendell belongs to the London school and he presented this study as an argument in favour of the continuum model of depression. There was further support for this hypothesis in that patients with a diagnosis of psychosis also often had symptoms judged to be neurotic, while the neurotic patients often gave evidence of psychotic symptoms. The bimodal distribution proclaimed by Carney *et al.* could not be established; in other words it was impossible to identify one group revealing typical endogenous symptoms and another revealing typical neurotic symptoms. In Kendell's study a great majority of the patients were clustered round the middle of the psychotic–neurotic symptom scale, i.e. the distribution was unimodal.

This presentation of the continuum hypothesis constitutes an implicit criticism of the dichotomy school. But there are also grounds for a more explicit criticism, in particular a criticism of methodology. It is difficult to refute the factor analysis studies on empirical grounds, although Kendell succeeds in doing so up to a point. It seems to be claimed that by finding two relatively uniform factors, the dichotomous nature of depression has been proved. Let us assume that we repeat such a study and that we also obtain two relatively distinct factors or dimensions, but that the syndromes are somewhat different. It is still possible to claim that there are two types of depression. The aim of the factor analysis is just this, i.e. to pick out different factors or dimensions, but if the analysis is to have any point these factors must be linked to an independent external criterion. Nor is it possible in a factor analysis to establish causal relationships; we can only say that in many cases certain symptoms do appear in the same individual.

Beck (1967) has another criticism of this kind of investigation. In the factor analysis studies there is no control of age, sex, or other demographic variables. We know that there is a high correlation between endogenous and exogenous depression and age. Brown *et al.* (1979) found 45 years to be the average age in the psychotic group in their study, compared with 29.5 years in the neurotic group (see also pp. 118–119).

Kendell (1968) suggests that the dichotomy demonstrated by representatives of the Newcastle school is a result of the halo effect; in other words, if one type of behaviour is observed in an individual, it is assumed that other types of behaviour are also present, although no proof of this is evident. What is involved is a one-sided and stereotyped way of looking at people. We may recall that Siirala described traditional psychiatry as a stereotype. Kendell reminds us that the evaluations in the Newcastle studies were made by psychiatrists who were convinced that there were two distinct types of depression, namely the neurotic and the endogenous. The evaluations were made at the end of the interview with the patient, when the psychiatrist could not have helped imposing his own 'global concepts of stereotypes' on the subject concerned. Kendell assumes that these global concepts affected the individual assessments, so that endogenous symptoms were overemphasized in cases where an endogenous depression was suspected. This danger must have been particularly great, since it was known that the purpose of the study was to demonstrate the importance of the distinction. Kendell supports his hypothesis regarding the halo effect with the evidence of an experiment of his own. Psychiatrists who assessed a group of patients were asked about their own attitude to the nature of depression, i.e. whether they considered it meaningful to distinguish between endogenous and neurotic depression. Their assessments of the patients were then compared with Kendell's own. There was a clear relation between the attitude of the psychiatrists and the way they assessed the patients with respect to endogenous symptoms. Psychiatrists who upheld the dichotomous model of depression, saw the patients as very much more 'endogenous' than Kendell; those who were ambivalent in their attitude assessed the patients as somewhat more 'endogenous' than Kendell; and those who adopted the continuum model of depressive illness assessed the patients in much the same way as Kendell.

Leff et al. (1970) carried out an intensive longitudinal study of the environmental factors that preceded severe depression in 13 patients with endogenous symptoms and 27 with non-endogenous symptoms. Their most important result was that the endogenous and the exogenous groups had experienced stressful events equally often in the period preceding the onset of depression. Furthermore, the types of stressful events were much the same in the two groups, with the threat to sexual identity being the most common (in 30 of the 40 cases). It is particularly interesting to note that information about these events emerged first after several intensive discussions with the patient himself and with his 'significant other'. A social worker talked to this 'other' (usually the partner or a parent) once a week, while the patient had individual therapy at least twice a week with a psychiatrist; there was no ECT treatment. It was first when the precipitating events came into central focus in these discussions that their role in the life story of the individual patient was understood. The method used by Leff et al. also seems to me to imply a criticism of the research methods of traditional psychiatry, in which the material is based on a few discussions exclusively with the patient, and in which there is no particular focus on environmental factors (rather the opposite) or on the personality of the individual patient, and where patients with an endogenous diagnosis have often been given ECT treatment which presumably results in temporary deficiencies in memory. It is therefore hardly surprising that in many cases of severe depression it has proved difficult to identify any underlying environmental factors.

In our study we obtained certain results which support Leff et al., although in this respect our findings are not as well-founded as Leff's. Our comparison was based on 13 patients with a diagnosis of endogenous depression and 19 with a diagnosis of exogenous depression. The material was also based on a single discussion, but this was geared to stressful events and environmental factors. I found that the endogenous patients claimed to have experienced more stressful events since the age of 18 than the reactive patients (2.9 as against 2.5). Age cannot explain this difference; the endogenous patients were, in fact, somewhat younger than the reactive patients, which is not generally the case. It is interesting to note that the endogenous patients mentioned 'events which had spoiled important plants' more often than the other patients. A relatively common event mentioned by the reactive patients was 'a serious accident or severe illness'. Events which are less easy to pin down appeared to be more common among the endogenous patients. Nor was there any noticeable difference between the two diagnoses when it came to the 'dominating problems'. The few patients who were unable to mention any particular underlying problems were divided equally between the endogenous and the reactive diagnostic group (about one in five in each group). But, as I have already mentioned, we must be very cautious about drawing any conclusions from these results, since they were based on such a small sample.

But Brown and Harris (1978), working with a larger sample, were equally unable to find any differences in the underlying environmental factors between psychotic and neurotic patients. They found that 71 per cent of the psychotic patients had suffered either a stressful event or a major difficulty before the onset of depression, compared with 80 per cent of the neurotics. The psychoses correspond to endogenous depressions and the neuroses to exogenous depressions.

But are there not, nevertheless, good grounds for supposing that manic-depressive psychoses have a biological basis? It is often pointed out that these depressions recur regularly, alternating between manic and depressive phases. Beck (1967), who bases his findings on comprehensive clinical research, refutes the notion of the definite manic-depressive 'cycle'. What is more common, he points out, is 'a wide variation in the interval between recurrences' (p. 98).

There are also objections from the psychodynamic school to the traditional view that manic-depressive psychosis is a clearly defined endogenous disorder. Cohen et al. (1954), in a study to which I have referred several times before, describe the intensive psychotherapy given to a group of manic-depressive patients. The writers conclude that the manic attack is a defence against depression; it can either precede the depression, in which case the patient is unable in the long run to withstand the underlying depression, or it may represent an escape from a depressive state with which the patient cannot cope 'into something more tolerable'. As one of their patients put it, 'I am crying underneath the laughter . . .' (p. 122). The point I am trying to make here is that manic-depressive psychoses rarely recur at regular intervals, and that the manic attack does not differ qualitatively from depression—two points that are usually cited as proof of the endogenous character of the manic-depressive psychosis. I will return in the last section below (pp. 120–121) to a psychosocial explanation of this disorder.

Biochemical research (Akiskal and McKinney, 1975) has not been able to provide unambiguous support for either of the models (the dichotomous classification or the continuum model). The catecholamine hypothesis, which I have mentioned before (pp. 2–3), has proved difficult to confirm. However, Ashcroft and Glen (1974) have found that patients with depressive psychosis without manic elements have a reduced level of transmitter substances both during the depressive phases and following improvement. This seems to indicate that there is a biochemical 'defect' in the personality, but that this may have either a biological or a psychological cause. None of the biochemical investigations that I have examined includes any extensive longitudinal studies of patients, particularly *prior* to the depression. Is the biological defect a result or a cause of psychosocial changes? On a basis of these studies we cannot decide which comes first, the hen or the egg; the deciding factor is the model to which we subscribe.

This last brings me to a general criticism of both sides in the psychiatric debate; it applies particularly to the advocates of the dichotomous classification, but also to some extent to the London school. It can be summarized under the following headings:

(1) Inadequate control of social factors
(2) Lack of any form of societal or cultural analysis
(3) No link-up between the various levels (biochemical, individual, social)
(4) Vagueness as to whether precipitating events represent a sufficient, a necessary, or a contributory factor in the development of depressions
(5) Little allowance for the subjective character of precipitating factors.

As regards the first point: attempts to control *social factors* are limited to those that are easy to quantify; but there is no study of any complex social relationships, such as can be found, for example, in schizophrenia research (see Lidz, Bateson, *et al.*). Another weakness is that the social factors are seldom controlled by matching against a random sample from a normal population. Such control groups as are used are generally drawn from other psychiatric groups or from the somatic wards of the hospital concerned.

Questions that arise in connection with the second critical comment are: What is the researcher's or psychiatrist's own societal role? How do the psychiatrist's values and beliefs affect the interview situation and the interpretations of the patient's own statements? (See Kendell, 1968.) What role do *cultural expectations* play in the development of depressions?

As regards the *level* of the analysis, I would like to see more discussion of how far behaviour and experiences can be explained in biochemical terms and, conversely, how far biochemical factors can explain the individual's behaviour and experiences.

A *precipitating factor* is sometimes taken to mean an external factor which can contribute to the development of an endogenous depression. But the term is also used to refer to an external factor that is necessary to the classification of the depression as exogenous. Furthermore, it is seldom stated explicitly in the case of either endogenous or exogenous depression whether 'precipitating factor' refers to a sufficient, a necessary, or a contributory factor.

Under the fifth heading I refer to the *subjective character* of the depressive experience, which is rarely considered in psychiatric research. When a diagnosis is made it is the psychiatrist who ultimately decides whether or not a depression can be linked to some specific event or cause. Events which the patient, with his particular life history, has perhaps found overwhelming, may be ignored by the psychiatrist as trivial.

Some of these criticisms could also be levelled at my own study. I have not gone far enough in placing the problem of depression in a societal perspective, and the social factors I have discussed are rather 'simple'. But I have tried to remedy this drawback by referring to other studies and by providing my own investigation with a broad theoretical framework.

9.2 WHY THE MEDICAL DIAGNOSIS?

'Physicians think they do a lot for a patient when they give his disease a name,' said Immanuel Kant (quoted in Costello *et al.*, 1974).

What is the point of distinguishing between *different* depressive states by making a medical diagnosis? It is very doubtful, as the above survey has shown, whether depressions can really be divided into those that depend on external and those that depend on internal causes. Furthermore, many psychiatrists appear dubious of the therapeutic value of the distinction between endogenous and exogenous depressions (Kendell, 1968), and they anyway often disagree about which label to attach to individual patients. The validity of specific diagnoses of depression is thus low. Kreitman (1961) quotes diagnostic agreement ranging from 12 per cent to 47 per cent (the studies on which he bases his figures do not refer exclusively to depressions).

Individual diagnoses will naturally depend to a great extent on what the psychiatrist sees in the patient when they meet. Hinchliffe *et al.* (1975) carried out a series of observations of depressed patients and a control group and found that the patients interacted verbally and non-verbally in one way with a stranger and in another way with their spouses. Videotape recordings were made of free discussions between the depressed patient and the spouse, first during the inpatient phase and later after discharge. The same method was used in observing interaction with a stranger and in observing interaction between members of the control group and their spouses. The non-verbal language observed included hand movements and posture. Interaction with the spouse was very different in the two groups. The depressed patients showed a high degree of tension, negative expression, and self-preoccupation, and in non-verbal communication they showed diminished non-verbal patterns of communication and body congruence. What is particularly interesting to our purpose here is that the depressed revealed a somewhat different interaction pattern with the strangers; among other things there was less negative expression and their speech was more rapid. The authors conclude

that it is the social system that both produces and maintains the state which we call depression, i.e. psychological symptoms are 'carried by' the interaction . . . . It suggests that it would be inappropriate for a psychiatrist to extrapolate from his own interaction with a patient to the patient's life with his spouse. (p. 171)

All this is highly relevant to the diagnosis of endogenous depression, which emerges from just such an interaction between a stranger (the psychiatrist) and the depressed subject. If 'the stranger' assumes from the start that the depressive symptoms are lodged in the individual, and that he himself is the expert who is going to find out what they are, it will often be difficult for him to understand a depression that is perhaps the result of a tangled interaction between a husband and wife, consisting of complex emotional and linguistic blockages. If he cannot *understand* human behaviour but is determined to *explain* it, he will be only too ready to fall back on a diagnosis that reduces the individual to a biological entity whose symptoms lend themselves to a concrete and accessible explanation.

The reason for a psychiatrist's failure to get close to a patient may simply be that the depressed individual cannot or will not discuss with anyone, possibly not even with himself, what has caused him such great inner distress. Rowe (1978) suggests that this may explain why patients with a diagnosis of endogenous depression react so positively to ECT and psychodrug treatment; they feel themselves supported and cared for, relieved of their pain, in a way which they find acceptable. What actually caused the pain can remain hidden; it does not have to be explained. The sense of shame is probably very important here. This kind of patient is generally ashamed of his depression, in particular of its cause which is just what he is trying to bury deep within himself. The medical treatment helps to free him from the shame that weighs on him so heavily; he hasn't done anything wrong, he is simply 'ill' — he must be, because the doctor says so, and the treatment is making him 'better'. Feelings of shame and guilt are closely related to the assumption of personal responsibility: 'I have done something I could have avoided.' By treating the patient with psychodrugs and ECT the psychiatrist frees him from some of this burdensome personal responsibility, and it is hardly surprising that at least for a time the result is a sense of relief and liberation.

A team of Danish women has written a book on women and psychiatry (Vinde, 1977), which is very critical of the concept of endogenous depression. It was found that women hospitalized for the first time with a diagnosis of manic-depressive psychosis are generally between the ages of 50 and 54 years, and the authors express some scepticism over the 'sudden' appearance of the condition after so many years. At the same time they recall the major social changes that women undergo at just this age (see pp. 65–66). The authors point out that reactive psychoses also predominate in the 40–50 age group, which seems to support their argument in favour of a social explanation. The 'diagnostic culture', as they see it, relieves the psychiatrist of the necessity for any real commitment to the patient or her situation: he need pay no serious attention to her experiences or to her possible criticism of himself. And, of course, the psychiatrist who makes a medical diagnosis is not called upon to view the psychological symptoms in a social or societal context.

There seem to be several reasons why a medical diagnosis comes readily to hand in cases of depression. It provides the psychiatrist with a convenient posture that exempts him from involvement in the patient's family and other social relationships. It is also and above all a convenient solution since the psychiatrist is trained in the medical rather than the psychological or social disciplines. And if he belongs to a scientific tradition in which explanations according to 'cause' and 'effect' are paramount, the dichotomous view of depression is going to fall very nicely into place in his conceptual world. The more he distances himself from the purely biological being and approaches the social and existential, the more difficult will it be to find a simple explanation of human behaviour. And since the depressed individual is unlikely at first to do or say anything to suggest the presence of a psychosocial or existential problem, is it not natural that the psychiatrist should seize upon an explanation and a treatment that the patient apparently both accepts and desires?

9.3 A SOCIAL EXPLANATION OF 'ENDOGENOUS DEPRESSION'

My own view of the type of depression that is generally regarded as 'caused from within' (the endogenous) is a combination of a continuum model and a social–psychological model deriving from Becker's theory. I suggest that genetic factors are more important in certain types of depression than they are in others, while also arguing that people who suffer from the so-called endogenous depressions are more likely to reveal characteristics of the kind I have ascribed to the *depressive personality*. I shall elaborate this second assumption in the present section.

There seem to me to be at least two possible reasons why people are unable to identify a specific cause for their depression, thus laying themselves open to classification as endogenous depressives. The first is that their personality is so markedly depressive and their *self-insight so deficient*, that they find it difficult to interpret their own reactions; because they are trapped in such a limited mental range, they have difficulty in looking at themselves from different perspectives. Over the years the depressive subject has increasingly narrowed his view of existence to embrace only the certain and the predictable—in other words, very little beyond his own self. In the face of the unexpected, of something which disturbs his restricted conceptual world, he is at a loss to explain the events to himself let alone to other people. Looking for explanations means assuming different perspectives; for the individual who restricts himself to a single view which for some reason is no longer available or valid, no alternative exists; he has no other mental standpoint from which to look at himself. The situation must be particularly paralysing if the underlying problem is a complex one, perhaps going back to childhood.

Brown *et al.*(1979) found an interesting difference between psychotic and neurotic patients which, it seems to me, can be explained in terms of the model outlined above.

During childhood or in the two-year period preceding the onset of depression a high proportion of the psychotic patients had experienced the death of a close relative (60 per cent compared with 16 per cent of the neurotic patients). More of the neurotic patients, on the other hand, had experienced loss in the form of separation (22 per cent as against 6 per cent). In both cases the loss during childhood referred to parents or brothers or sisters, and in adulthood to spouse or child. The differences persisted under age controls. The interpretation of these results which I suggest below appears to be supported by the figures for the severely psychotic patients, of whom 74 per cent had experienced the death of a close relative.

The death of a close relation is almost always a very distressing event which people try to reject in all kinds of ways. They deny that it has really happened; they fall back on many other defensive mechanisms so as not to have to feel and think about it. The walls which people build around themselves and their experiences make it difficult for them to see and understand what is going on outside in the real world. It thus also becomes difficult to make the connection between external circumstances and personal experience, and there is little fertile ground in which self-insight can grow. That the death of someone on whom we are dependent for our self-esteem is more difficult to handle constructively than loss through separation probably depends on three circumstances: (a) loss through death is a genuinely more painful experience, (b) death often occurs unexpectedly, allowing no time or opportunity for a successive adaptation to the new situation such as is often possible in the case of a separation, and (c) death represents a traumatic event over which we have no control. Together these factors drive the individual to erect strong defences, to shut himself more firmly than ever into his narrow conceptual world for fear that the same disaster should happen again, and this reduces even further his opportunities for gaining self-insight. In this situation the slightest upset may be enough to precipitate a depression if in some way it recalls the earlier traumatic event. The walls that the sufferer has erected collapse, reality threatens to submerge him completely, he loses his foothold in reality and falls into a psychosis.

Let us now examine the second of the possible social–psychological explanations of so-called endogenous depression that seem to me to be particularly relevant. The central concept here is that of the *self-fulfilling prophecy*. In general terms this means that if people believe something will happen, it will happen, and specifically in our present context that a strong conviction that depression may ensue can contribute to its actual development. First, just this strong belief in their own predisposition to depression is common among those with an endogenous diagnosis. No particular event need have occurred before the onset of the depression, apart perhaps from a slight feeling of being low or tired after a bout of influenza or something similar. The feeling of uneasiness may then have been recognized ('one of my bad patches') and blown up to full depression status ('I always get depressed in the spring', or 'The doctor says my depression is an illness and there's not much I can do about it'). Thus the process may assume an identifiable form: 'If I get this queer feeling, I know a depression is coming on.' That a conscious train of thought like this can have consequences in the shape of a severe depression may seem surprising. Part of the explanation may lie in the lack of self-insight that I have already discussed; people cannot understand *that* they cannot understand. Also, the advantages that illness (i.e. in this case the depression) bring are probably another factor. Rowe (1978) reports a conversation in which both a husband and his depressed wife benefited in some way from the woman's depression:

'When I'm not depressed he's moody and miserable and when I'm depressed he changes.' 'In what way?' 'Becomes more friendly, . . .' Q. 'More the sort of person you'd like him to be?' A. 'Yes.' (p. 51).

The husband may not have wanted his wife to be active and independent, so that when she assumed a role in which *he* had to be strong he was immediately more considerate towards her. If there is something to be gained from depressive behaviour it will certainly not be long before the depressive experience occurs. We can recall here the observations reported in Hinchcliffe *et al.* (1975) in which typically depressive behaviour was most marked in interaction with the partner. Perhaps the patients benefited (were shown more consideration) from thus demonstrating weakness, but they were probably also using the opportunity to transfer their own guilt feelings on to their partners.

Thus both the explanations I have suggested presuppose that among those suffering from the type of depression known as endogenous there will be a preponderance of depressive personalities with a marked proclivity towards rigid action patterns. In cases of inadequate self-insight and subjection to self-fulfilling prophecies, the common denominator is just these rigid action patterns. The distinctive characteristics of the manic-depressive individuals as described by Cohen *et al.* (1954), Gibson (1958), and J. Becker (1960) can all be subsumed under this same heading (see pp. 46–48). One of the results of my own investigation which seems to confirm the high incidence of rigid action patterns among patients with a diagnosis of endogenous depression was that these people had a large number of non-kin, leisure-time companions with whom, however, they generally enjoyed a rather superficial relationship. On the other hand, their interaction with their colleagues at work was slight. It is possible to choose our own friends, and possible, therefore, to choose the kind who do not demand any very deep commitment and who do not threaten our conceptual world. At work it is not so easy to remain in control, and this kind of contact is therefore avoided. Further empirical confirmation of this argument comes from the fact that 'endogenous depression' is most frequent among older people. Brown *et al.* (1979) found that the average age in their psychotic group was 45 years, while in the neurotic group it was only 29.5. The authors suggest that the losses afflicting women in middle-age are much harder to bear than losses in earlier years. It is at that stage in life that earlier loss of a close family member hits the psychotic harder than the neurotic, and the kind of strong defence system and lack of self-insight that I have discussed above may, of course, follow. And the older we become, the more likely we are to be forced to leave the shelter of our old established walls. It seems to me to be equally or even more important, however, that as we become older we also generally become more firmly enmeshed in a fixed conceptual world: not only has our conceptual world itself become more limited, but our own actions have also become more settled in routines and more difficult to alter. This psychological and social aspect of reality is expressed in the theoretical concept of the rigid action patterns which, I suggest, are more characteristic of the older generation.

Let us return to my two assumptions regarding inadequate self-insight and subjection to self-fulfilling prophecies. In the following case there was apparently 'nothing special' to explain the patient's depression, but it seems to me possible to identify certain elements suggesting that both these explanations may be relevant here.

M is a 40-year-old woman with a diagnosis of endogenous depression. For quite a long time she has been taking lithium which makes her feel like a vegetable; she experiences no swings in mood at all. She is eager to label her problems as an 'illness', and this has probably increased the consideration she gets from her family and their acceptance of her state. Previously they used to minimize her problems, told her to pull herself together and asked her, 'What on earth's the matter with you?' Now they say, 'Oh dear, you've got one of your turns', and treat the whole thing as a matter of course. She admits that she doesn't really want to talk to the family about it much, and that she's fairly happy with things as they are. After the interview M says she thinks her memory must be poor; she has had so many depressions that she can't remember them all separately. But the interviewer does not think her memory is bad; with a little thought M seems able to remember and give honest answers.

M says that she has been depressed every autumn and spring since she was 18. The depressive periods generally last about two months. She was also depressed after the birth of each of her children (three of them). At the beginning of 1972 she sought psychiatric help for the first time, and was admitted to the psychiatric ward for about a week. She was given a lot of psychodrugs and became hyperactive. She can't identify any special underlying cause of her depression. She looks back now on the way she felt as unreasonable, proof that she was ill. She thought people were all stupid and life was awful. She felt as though she stood outside herself.

M grew up in a typical upper-class home. Her father was a highly qualified professional man, and her mother was a 'kind of super upper-class housekeeper'. In high school M became pregnant and had to leave. After the child's birth she was extremely depressed (this was her first real depression). Subsequently she has been depressed and suffered from migraines after the birth of her other children.

In the period before she first sought psychiatric help, M was a housewife. She had a large circle of acquaintances, including several close friends. She was very active in various clubs, and had numerous other leisure-time interests. During this period M's father died after a long illness. M's relationship with her father had always been good, although they restricted their discussions to generalities and didn't talk about anything personal. M has never had much contact with her mother on any level. She feels that her mother has imposed heavy demands on her, has always dominated her. M's husband, like her father, has a highly qualified job, in which he is very happy. In 1971 her relationship with her husband was rather worse than it is now, mostly because of her personal problems. Even so, she felt they could talk to each other about most things.

As I see it, the depressive process began with M's expulsion from high school, which must have been a hard blow for a girl of her upper-class background. One factor that supports this interpretation is the depression that followed the birth of all her children. This recalled the one event in her life which she had always avoided talking about, and which probably weighed most heavily upon her, namely her first pregnancy and her expulsion from school. Although this is certainly not the whole explanation of her depression, she ascribes *no* explanatory value to it at all, which suggests poor self-insight on her part. An element of the self-fulfilling prophecy appears at the very beginning of the case description: the doctors, M's husband, the rest of her family, and M herself all regard the depression as an illness which recurs without M being able to do anything about it. Moreover, M has won certain benefits for herself as a result of her 'illness', which have probably helped to reinforce it.

In conclusion, I will return briefly to the manic-depressive psychosis. Cohen *et al.* (1954) and others deny, as we have seen, that there is any qualitative difference between the depressive and the manic phases. The manic phase, in fact, constitutes a defence against depression. Siirala (1974) describes the similarities between mania and depression rather differently, arguing that there is a concealed hubris in the depression that manifests itself in the manic state. He likens the manic-depressive state to an iceberg: the sufferer is either trapped under the iceberg (depression) or skating over its surface (mania). With this metaphor Siirala wants to emphasize the element of hardness and coldness in mania.

Cohen *et al.* (1954) describe the vicious circle in which the manic-depressive may become trapped: when the manic defence no longer yields the gratification he craves the patient starts using depressive techniques; he complains and whines to elicit the affection he requires, but generally succeeds only in arousing greater aversion in those around him. '. . . the patient redoubles his efforts and receives still less. Finally, he loses hope and enters into the psychotic state where the pattern of emptiness and need is repeated over and over again in the absence of any specific object' (p. 122). This description of the manic-depressive state comes close to that propounded by Ernest Becker (1964, pp. 135–136). The similarities between mania and depression that Becker mentions are the lack of self-criticism, the loose grip on self-esteem, and the attachment to a narrow range of social rules. Outside the family the manic-depressive is involved in a continual hunt for enhancements to self-esteem, but he never manages to reach a point where he feels safe. When the world beyond the family becomes too threatening he is compelled to concentrate his life within the home. There he achieves some self-esteem—not much, perhaps, in the light of the limited scope for action that the family permits, but that little seems fairly firmly based. The manic state has been exchanged for the depressive.

A common element in the pictures of the manic-depressive painted by Cohen, Siirala, and Becker is the high but unrealistic level of aspiration. It is in the vain attempt to satisfy their own high aspirations that such people enter the manic state; ultimately, however, when they realize they cannot become the heroes or heroines they would like to be, mania gives way to depression.

CHAPTER 10

Ernest Becker's theory of depression

10.1 INTRODUCTION

Ernest Becker (1924–1974) was a professor of politics, sociology, and anthropology. He was active mainly at Simon Fraser University in Canada, and at Syracuse University and the University of California at Berkeley in the USA. That his theories have received surprisingly little attention in the psychiatric debate can probably be explained in two ways: his arguments as presented in his books are far from easy to follow, and he is extremely critical of the traditional view of depression. Few behavioural researchers have in any case paid much attention to the riddle of depression, so there has been no body of scientists available to unravel and pass on Becker's multidisciplinary theory.

I had intended at first to refer to Becker's theory of depression as one theory among several others (see p. x), but I became increasingly attracted by the breadth, and even more by the depth, that I discovered in Becker's work. At each new reading I had new 'aha experiences'.

Becker's theory is often very difficult to untangle, partly because it is multidimensional and its concepts are derived from various theories and traditions. It is frequently unclear, for example, which level of existence he is referring to at any one point in the argument: man's general conditions or the particular circumstances of the individual. A third important level can also be distinguished in the theory, the level comprising what we could call man's cultural conditions, i.e. determinants of behaviour stemming from the particular culture concerned. There is also some difficulty in separating his references to man's external and inner lives. In restructuring the theory here I have tried to distinguish between the exterior and the inner life, whereas Becker often concerns himself with both levels at the same time. Thus in the following theoretical analysis it is *my* choice of various aspects of human life that provides the basis of the argument.

I have taken the following levels as my point of departure:

(1) Man's ontological (existential) position
(2) Conditions contingent on culture
(3) Life outside the self (external life)
(4) The inner life.

This frame of reference can be summarized in a simple model (see Figure 1). We could naturally insert more boxes and arrows into this model, but my aim is

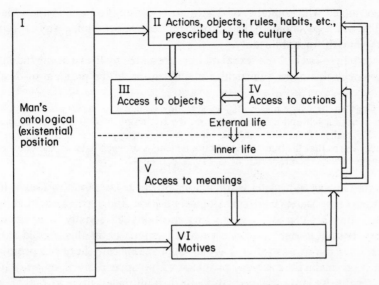

Figure 1 Becker's theory—a model

to keep the argument as simple as possible. It should also be mentioned that the arrows do not represent any direct causal relationships; for the time being we can let them indicate the factors which are most closely associated with one another. According to Becker, what we call *causality* is at least partly a question of the point at which we enter and exert influence in a system. This interpretation is extremely relevant to traditional medical psychiatry: as Becker sees it, the psychiatrist seeks for causes *within* the patient, since it would be much more difficult to tackle the whole family and altogether daunting to think of tackling society as a whole.

It can be seen from the model that Becker gives great weight to man's ontological position. He posits that all life's manifestations are in some way connected with our fear of death. But he then adds that we are also afraid of life, a fear that is a result of our terror in the face of death. 'How can we make anything meaningful of our lives, when we are anyway going to die?' But the fear of life is a fear connected particularly with the idea of self: because of our self-awareness we can accumulate conscious experiences, and with these comes the knowledge that we can change. Our experiences can call forth fear; and we dread what the future may hold in store for us. Above all it is the fear of the repercussions on our future life of the mistakes and choices of today that constitutes the greatest problem of life.

The general human problems that Becker discusses are not the result of biological drives; they derive entirely from our existence as human beings with an ego or 'self'. This is what makes us aware of our mortality. The fear of death is reflected in all aspects of our lives, even if we often manage to mask the fear fairly successfully. Becker claims that even the great Freud succeeded in repressing the idea that man's fundamental dread is his terror of death. And yet Freud was often occupied with thoughts of death, never ceasing to ponder upon his own end. The whole psychoanalytical movement became, for him, a way of trying to qualify himself for immortality.

According to Becker, the sexual matters presented by Freud as the fundamental human problem are a particular manifestation of the problem of death.

This brings up the whole matter of why sexuality is such a universal problem. . . . The person is both a self and a body, and from the beginning there is the confusion about where 'he' really 'is'—in the symbolic inner self or in the physical body. . . . The child gradually learns that his freedom as a unique being is dragged back by the body and its appendages which dictate 'what' he is. (1973, pp. 41–42).

It is particularly in his later work, among others in *The Denial of Death* (1973), that Becker emphasizes man's ontological position, and in particular that man is the only animal to be aware of his own mortality. Personally, I am uncertain whether Becker is right to place so much emphasis on this. Could not the realization of our own mortality have the opposite effect to the one he postulates? Might it not make the everyday problems of life appear trivial, may not life be easier because we know that everything we do is ultimately unimportant? Becker, as we have seen, suggests the opposite, namely that since our lives will come to their irrevocable ends, it is actually more difficult to find any meaning in them. Although this argument is central to Becker's thought, I do not feel that the different emphasis I give to it need affect the *social–psychological* theory presented below.

Another point which should be mentioned at the outset concerns Becker's definition of the depressed person: it is not always clear whether he means by this the potentially depressed or the patient suffering from acute depression. In fact, he often seems to be referring at one and the same time to what I have called the depressed personality and to people who are actually suffering from depression. In *The Denial of Death* depression is described in the first place as one long process untouched by any real qualitative change.

In the other two of Becker's works on which I base my analysis—*The Birth and Death of Meaning* (1971) and *The Revolution in Psychiatry* (1964)—some critical event in a person's life is generally regarded as the cause of depression. People with particular personality characteristics which have been forming throughout their lives run the greatest risk of becoming depressed as a result of a critical event, and the precipitating cause is usually a severe threat to self-esteem. But in these books, too, Becker appears to be referring only to the individual who *has become* depressed. Altogether three elements seem to be involved in the determination of what Becker calls the depressed patient or the depressed person:

(1) Characteristics that predispose to depression
(2) The actual process of becoming depressed
(3) The state of being depressed.

It is not possible to distinguish between these three phases, since they are so intimately interwoven. Where I feel that Becker is emphasizing any one of them, I shall say so. In referring to the potential depressive I speak of the *depressed personality*; where Becker seems to be including all three phases I speak of the *depressed person*, and where I feel that he is chiefly concerned with those who are, or have become, depressed, I use expressions such as *the depressed* or *the person who has become depressed*. One reason why the reader of Becker's works can easily become confused about his concepts, is that he uses traditional psychiatric terminology but gives the words quite different connotations.

It is well to be clear at the very beginning that these words [among others *depression*] are used only as pointers; in the present stage of knowledge and history it would be impossible to communicate without them. As they are used here they mean quite different things than they do in medical psychiatry; they permit us to conceptualize ways of being in the world, ways of reacting to experience, to which no medical valuation is attached. (1964, p. 6)

In this context it is appropriate to point out that Becker makes no distinction between endogenous and exogenous depressions, or between other kinds, simply because he regards all depressions as springing from external and interpersonal sources. Between the different types of depression he sees only a difference in degree. Psychosis represents the most serious type (in which, as Becker sees it, the depressed person's problems have become most aggravated). I believe, however, that psychogenetic factors are not unimportant (I associate myself in principle with the continuum hypothesis, see pp. 108–111). At the same time I feel that among those suffering from so-called endogenous depressions, there is a preponderance of people with the personality traits characteristic of the depressive personality.

10.2 MAN'S CULTURAL CONDITIONS

Becker's culture concept is rather vague, and he uses the terms 'culture' and 'society' without distinguishing very clearly between them. Culture or society in Becker's theory is associated with various general ideas and conceptions rather than with any superordinate rules of economic life. He seems to put emphasis on the ideological rather than the economic structure of society.

The particular culture in which he lives has both a positive and a negative impact on the life of the individual. The positive impact derives from the culture-related rules, customs, and ideas that make it possible for people to acquire self-esteem. To Becker, a major function of a culture is to provide a framework of continuity for our self-esteem. Although theoretically we have an infinite choice of paths to self-esteem, if we want to be sure of the lasting nature of that self-esteem we must choose a path sanctioned by our culture. As we shall see later, unwavering self-esteem is of vital importance in the avoidance of depression.

As well as providing security for our self-esteem, a second positive function of a culture is to provide us with security in our lives. Self-esteem and anxiety are closely related. In Becker's view, a fundamental element in human life is our striving for self-esteem and our avoidance of anxiety (see p. 145). Thus our culture should supply us with certain predictable procedural norms which make it easier for us to avoid anxiety. What can a culture supply in the way of a predictable framework? One secure peg for self-esteem is provided by the status associated with certain jobs, which gives us an *ipso facto* value and means that we do not have to be judged and graded. Another peg consists of prescribed social roles in our culture: there are certain actions we are expected to perform, and which we therefore do perform, as woman, nurse, mother, car-driver, 20 year-old, and so on.

This last also brings us to the negative impact of the culture on the life of the individual. The culture restricts the possible range of actions, i.e. the dominating social system *limits* the possibilities which *could* be available.

Thus the culture prescribes, within the broader framework of man's existential conditions (which are also reflected in the culture), the limits of the possible. The first external or existential framework consists in the fact that we have to die. The second interior or cultural framework consists in the fact that we live together with other people and are thus bound by common rules.

Since we are so eager to acquire self-esteem without suffering anxiety, we are readily disposed to adopt whole cultural systems without discrimination. Our culture—acceptance may come about indirectly through our upbringing or directly in confrontation with external reality. It seems to me that Becker makes much the same link between culture and the individual as Erik H. Erikson, namely that the culture supports and underpins the kind of upbringing and education that produces good, strong children in the terms of that very culture (Erikson, 1963, pp. 149–150). Thus we conform early to the prevailing cultural system. In any particular society certain roles, rules, customs, and so on will therefore come to dominate to the exclusion of others. But not all are able to accommodate themselves to the ordained rules or to accept the rules as applying to themselves; at the same time it is impossible for them to step outside the cultural system. As a result they are regarded as deviants. They are then all too likely to lose the main advantage that accompanies acceptance of the cultural system, namely a *secure* sense of self-esteem.

If the acquisition of self-esteem is our paramount goal, we will probably focus on the whole range of possibilities offered by our culture; but we then run a great risk of being overwhelmed and missing everything, of ending up outside society in a state of anxiety and low self-esteem. If, on the other hand, a secure existence seems to us to be the most important goal, then we are likely to accept without argument the dominating values that prevail in our culture, with the result that we will find it difficult to realize all the myriad opportunities of life or to assume a heroic role (see p. 149). Thus, it is a question here of what the individual makes of the culture he lives in—what life does he prefer? But at the same time it is a question of what the culture or society can offer him, and of whether he really can choose! To Becker this last is a crucial element in all 'mental' disorders. 'If we want to "stamp out mental illness", it will mean putting the control of means–ends sequences back into the hands of people who need to make choices, or who want to make them. It will mean making rational means–end matching explicit for as many as possible' (1964, p. 211).

It seems to me that Becker is clarifying here the relation between culture and the individual. What is important is that we should be able to *control* the means–ends sequences ourselves. That many people today cannot do this depends in Becker's view on society. Society presents us with all the means–ends sequences that are possible, but within that framework we *can* choose what we believe will give us the greatest self-esteem. Those who fail in this choice are described as 'mentally ill'. Our parents recommend and pass on to us certain limited means–ends sequences, but we live in a rapidly changing culture and by the time we grow up many of these sequences have become irrelevant. It is thus more difficult in our Western culture to find a tenable range of actions or meanings, since old and new experiences are frequently in conflict. Access to a wide range of possible actions is important to the avoidance of depression. This may be one reason why depression appears to be becoming increasingly common in our society.

Becker suggests a further explanation of this phenomenon.

But consider the situation in traditional society. There the extended family is the rule, and not the small, tight, nuclear one that is familiar to us. The consequence of this is that the life-chances and life-meaning of the individual do not depend on a few objects. Meaning is generalized to a whole range of kin. The extended family provides a continuing source of esteem and affirmation for the individual actor, *even though significant figures drop out.* (1964, p. 127)

A society that is open to the dissemination of alternative ways of achieving certain goals provides a better opportunity for coping with stressful life situations. But the most important point about this quotation is not that there are many significant others to whom the individual in traditional cultures can turn in a crisis; it is that the individual is not dependent on a few significant others and he can therefore build up a *secure* sense of self-esteem. Access to a large audience almost certainly reduces the risk of becoming dependent on a few others.

In *The Denial of Death* Becker refers to another aspect of the problem of man's ontological position: ' . . . that neurosis is also historical to a large extent, because all the traditional ideologies that disguised and absorbed it have fallen away and modern ideologies are just too thin to contain it' (1973, p. 177). I shall not attempt to distinguish here between depression and neurosis, but it seems to me that Becker is saying that the problems arising from man's existential conditions never had cause to rise to the surface in traditional societies. Religion was able to explain the human situation.

10.3 LIFE OUTSIDE THE SELF (EXTERNAL LIFE)

By our external life is meant here the life of our everyday doings. It is this which makes a decisive impact on our conscious mind; it determines what we can predict, what we would like to do, what we feel and how we look upon the world–all the things which together I have called our inner life. In the external life Becker emphasizes the importance of access to actions, not least in connection with conditions predisposing to depression. And in this last context it is actions connected with other people that are of paramount importance. I shall distinguish below between significant relationships or *objects* (10.3.1), accustomed doings or *external actions* (10.3.2), and the restricted and rigid nature of the actions, or *strict control of actions* (10.3.3).

10.3.1 Access to objects

Following Becker's terminology, I refer to significant relationships as *objects*. Becker in turn borrowed this designation from psychodynamic theory. A problem arises here in that Becker sometimes includes things as well as people in the term, although when he discusses depression he presumably refers only to other people. It is also possible to discern yet another connotation of 'object' in Becker's work, which is closer perhaps to the concept of action (to be discussed in the next section). One person can represent several sub-objects to other people; and sometimes one person may interact only with a very limited part of another (i.e. with a few sub-objects only). However, in the following argument *object* will be used exclusively to refer to *significant relationships* or what we could call *significant others*. In other words, it is a question of people who are important to our self-esteem. What objects become important to us in this sense? Volkart, to whom Becker refers in this section, suggests that they are the people whom we 'love, honour and obey' (Becker, 1964, p. 127).

Becker claims that 'the whole life-meaning is invested in objects' (1964, p. 153). We cannot create life significance and provide ourselves with a meaningful existence without objects. To put it simply, we could say that the greater our access to objects, the richer will be our life; and this in turn means that we will be less vulnerable in situations of personal crisis such as divorce or bereavement. Access to objects is intimately related to the significance of action. Thus it is not the object in itself that gives life its meaning, but the interaction with that object. It is essentially this loss which can easily lead to depression in a person who loses a significant relationship through divorce or death. 'To lose an object, then, is to lose someone to whom one has made appeal for self-validation. To lose a game is to lose a performance part in which identity is fabricated and sustained . . . . Unless the individual feels worthwhile, unless his action is considered worthwhile, life grinds to a halt' (1964, pp. 112–113). The objects in themselves are the basis of our self-esteem, but self-esteem is created and maintained in action, in interaction with objects. If we lose an object, we also lose meanings (see p. 138); our self-value is impaired, with the result that life becomes less worth living. Object-loss is harder to bear for those who have bound up their lives with few objects, since the resulting reduction in the range of possible actions will have a greater relative impact.

Lonelines (i.e. the absence of objects) does not only mean that our range of possible actions is limited. If we have few people to whom we can relate, we will also receive a limited picture of ourselves. As Becker puts it, loneliness is a 'moratorium on self-acquaintance'. We just do not have enough opportunity to test our own power, as we must do if we are to understand our limitations and possibilities. Difficulty in recognizing his own possibilities, at least outside his accustomed sphere (usually the family), is just what characterizes the depressive personality.

As well as giving us no chance of testing our own resources, the absence of objects denies us the opportunity to present parts of ourselves for evaluation by others. This can quickly lead to a vicious circle: few people to provide us with a self-image → limited self-image → fear of trying out possibilities, and so on. It is this process that underlies Becker's description of the depressed person as being *too uncritical* in the few relationships to which he does have access. (This question will be discussed in somewhat greater detail on p. 144 below, in connection with the inner life.) In this respect the depressed person can be distinguished from the schizophrenic, who is *too* critical in reacting to the experience of his relationships. The depressed person is firmly convinced that he understands the nature of reality: what others are like, what one ought to be like, what one can expect of others, and so on. In order to obtain confirmation of his world view, he often seeks what he believes to be the perfect object.

When we look for the 'perfect' human object we are looking for someone who allows us to express our will completely, without any frustration or false notes. We want an object that reflects a truly ideal image of ourselves. But no human object can do this; humans have wills and counter-wills of their own, in a thousand ways they can move against us, their very appetites offend us. (1973, p. 166)

Tragically, the depressed person often believes he has found the perfect object in his partner or child. An uncritical attitude of this kind in relation to objects means that he is considering selected aspects (action patterns) of the other person, i.e. interacting with a few sub-objects only. The depressed person seeks security in his relationships in order to avoid anxiety, but there is a great risk of the whole situation backfiring: if anything should deviate from the apparently stable action pattern in the object, the subject's self-image—which is generated by and through the object—will be gravely impaired. 'I can't trust anything any more.' In such a situation it is all too easy to fall into the self-pity and passivity of a depression.

10.3.2 Actions

By *actions* are meant the things that we generally do. But the term includes not only actions in which we are directly involved but also those whose consequences we feel able in some way to predict. How much variation is there in the actions we generally perform? Or, as Becker would put it: how great is our access to possible actions? And can we control these actions?

Access to actions

The reader is certainly aware by now that *action* is one of the key concepts in Becker's theory. Drawing on the psychology and philosophy of John Dewey,

Becker says that 'by definition "mental illness" refers to action that bogs down, or that is constricted within an extremely narrow range' (1964, p. 3). Both these conditions can be said to apply in depression, where the range of possible actions of a person, whose access to action is anyway limited, is further reduced.

In the previous section I described the intimate connection between access to objects and access to actions. 'By definition, to constitute an object is to create a behaviour pattern. To lose an object is to *lose the possibility of undertaking a range of satisfying action*' (Becker, 1964, p. 125). Naturally the amount of satisfying action that disappears in connection with object-loss will vary. Becker does not mention that object-loss could in certain circumstances mean an *increase* in opportunities for satisfying action, but this alternative is hardly likely in the case of the depressed. Depression is generally precipitated by an object-loss which involves a reduction in opportunities for satisfying actions, i.e. actions which generate self-value; the severity of the consequences can be explained by the insecure self-esteem of a person whose range of possible actions is already restricted.

[depression] develops in people who are afraid of life, who have given up any semblance of independent development and have been totally immersed in the acts and the aid of others. They have lived lives of 'systematic self-restriction,' and the result is that the less you do the less you can do, the more helpless and dependent you become. (1973, p. 210)

It is through action that self-esteem is acquired. Since people who lack self-esteem find it difficult to undertake actions generated by and depending upon themselves, they are helpless in social life, and have less opportunity to develop independent actions of their own. And so we have another vicious circle. The negative process may have started in early childhood, thus restricting the growing child in his attempts to explore the world.

10.3.3 Strict control of actions

We also need to be able to control our accustomed actions. It is difficult to interpret Becker's concept of *control*, since it includes several components which are not easy to keep separate. Two important attributes of control as he sees it are the actor's ability to *steer* action in a desired direction and the *durability* of the actions themselves.

The steering of action is particularly important in the development of identity (self-development). But if we are to have opportunities for testing our power, we must come up against some sort of obstacle. Becker claims that before evolving a social identity we have already tried out our possibilities on an organic level. It is *after* some need-satisfying action has been blocked that an identity can be evolved. We need confrontation with obstacles in order to test our strength; at the same time, however, our actions must yield results. There is thus conflict between two kinds of need: the more obstacles we meet, the less likely we are to remain in control of our actions; but if we are *never* frustrated at all, we will never learn to control our actions. In other words a well-balanced degree of frustration is best.

In this context Becker stresses that a child can 'be undermined by considerable maternal attention and love' (1964, p. 46). Too much attention and love leaves a child no chance to develop its 'own' resources; it becomes completely dependent on its parents. As a result, this child will tend to rely on others in adult life. He cannot, and dare not, exploit his own resources and this, as we shall see below, is something that characterizes the depressive personality. Becker does not postulate any direct link between different methods of upbringing and the depressive personality, but it is possible to conclude from his argument that the child who receives too much love (in the form of all-absorbing attention) and the child who is not allowed to do things on his own both run the risk of developing a depressive personality.

Becker discusses a similar problem of balance in a context of adult life.

We might say that there were roughly four levels of power and meaning that an individual could 'choose' to live by:
1) . . . the Personal one. It is the level of what one is oneself . . .
2) . . . the Social: . . . one's spouse, his friends, . . .
3) . . . the Secular . . . the corporation, the party, the nation . . .
4) . . . the Sacred . . . it is the invisible and unknown level . . . . (1971, p. 186)

If we direct our lives exclusively towards any one of these levels it will become difficult for us to comprehend the human situation in all its aspects. Consideration of all four levels is necessary to mental health. The depressed person focuses his life too narrowly on the social level at the cost of the individual level. It is a question of where he places his trust. The depressed thus puts more trust in others (social level) than in himself (individual level).

If we create and learn to control action patterns within one limited area—for example, the family and the home—the actions tend to become narrow and to persist over time. It is this second element in his concept of control (namely the durability of actions) on which Becker lays particular stress. He points out in several contexts that the depressed person controls his actions all to well, and his behaviour therefore falls into certain determined patterns. A person who chooses to rely entirely on someone else rather than on himself, is at great risk of letting his actions become over-controlled (rigid).

There is a certain contradiction between access to actions and control of actions which can be summarized in the following postulates:

(1) If we have access to many actions (in many areas), we have less chance of controlling these actions
(2) If we have access to few actions (in few areas), we may learn to control these actions all too well.

The converse also applies. The depressed subject has access to few actions of *his own*; he has stopped investigating the world and feels able to predict the way the people around him will act (he has reduced his world to encompass only the predictable). There is thus a negative interaction between excessive control of actions and access to actions.

Why is depression more likely to afflict those who keep tight control over their actions? Sooner or later there must be some change in their lives, since society—particularly nowadays—is itself constantly changing. There may be a divorce, a child may reject its parent's view of the world, a new position may impose unfamiliar routines, and so on. For the person who has restricted his life to certain fixed actions, a negative change will assume huge proportions, since controllable actions are important to his self-esteem. It will become more difficult for him to handle his depression (which therefore becomes more severe), since the restricted and predictable world he has chosen has given him little opportunity even to consider learning new (alternative) actions which could help to shore up his self-esteem.

10.4 THE INNER LIFE

10.4.1 Unprocessed actions

Becker criticizes the way in which the term 'unconscious' has been applied in traditional psychodynamic theory. He sees no justification for speaking of 'unconscious drives'. At the same time he emphasizes the importance of what the child learns about himself and others before he has a developed language at his disposal. In fact, however, this preverbal, learned knowledge has essentially the same implications for the adult's life as 'the unconscious': it affects our lives but is difficult to control.

He [the child] is unaware, of course, of his conditioning, and is not able to frame alternatives in words at this early time—nor even to suspect that alternatives exist. . . . But, still contrary to the Freudian thesis, these subverbal and preverbal motives (perceptions) *are not presocial*. They are learned in *social interaction*, and are not born into the world with the child. (1964, p. 63)

It is thus because the child cannot formulate alternatives that the first socially learned action patterns have such a strong impact on his later life. The child does not perceive the existence of alternatives, and in a new situation cannot therefore obtain help from other solutions. Added to which, as an adult, he will find it difficult later to handle social motives of whose origins he is unaware.

Preverbal motives may also come into conflict with motives learned at a later stage, as the child's control of its own experiences increases with the development of its ego (see next section). Problems will thus arise in the future when the preverbally learned behaviour patterns and motives—in which knowledge of reality, ego-conception, and motives were all largely determined by some person or persons outside the self—come into conflict with behaviour patterns and motives learned later. Becker throws his spotlight on a further aspect of this problem, pointing out that our ability to choose freely among different action alternatives is crippled from the start. I interpret this as meaning that we learn preverbally that *we cannot choose*, and that we never entirely recover from this abandonment of our free will.

The behaviour repertoire

It is not always easy to understand the distinction in Becker's theory between *action scheme* and *meaning*. Becker applies the term *meaning* sometimes to processed and sometimes to unprocessed actions, and in some passages the latter are also designated *action scheme* or *behaviour repertoire*. It seems to me that it may sometimes be important to be able to distinguish between actions which have been processed by the ego and those which have not been so processed. What I call the *behaviour repertoire* here thus refers to the original layer of our behaviour; it is something which we do not understand and which we have not processed with the help of language. All our fellow animals rely on a fund of experience which has never been subjected to advanced linguistic processing, and we can therefore say that their behaviour is governed solely by behaviour repertoires. Human action, on the other hand, is mainly determined in the first place by 'meanings' (i.e. processed actions, experiences, etc.).

Before turning to the discussion of meanings, we should first look a little more closely at the human behaviour repertoires. Becker seems to suggest three types of experience that constitute these repertoires. One is the preverbally learned behaviour that we have already discussed, the second is behaviour which could be described as reflex actions, and the third consists of certain immediate impressions such as can be found in artistic creation.

However, it is a simplification to say that there are three types of behaviour repertoires and one area of 'meanings'. It would be more appropriate to speak of a continuum starting from reflex actions at one extreme and meanings on a very high level of abstraction at the other. Where exactly we then draw the line between behaviour repertoires and meanings will depend on when we consider that the conscious experience and language play a dominating part in behaviour.

An important point in Becker's theory is lost if we disregard the concept of behaviour repertoires. We cannot develop meanings of real substance except on a basis of actions (1964, p. 97). People do sometimes create 'meaning-games' which have no roots in action, but they are useless as a basis of predictable behaviour. The creation of 'meaning-games' is characteristic, for instance, of the schizophrenic patient.

We could extend our continuum now to include the concept of *meaning-games* which would give us the following: behaviour repertoire – meaning – meaning-game. The meaning-game is thus the manifestation of our conscious processes that lies furthest away from the behaviour patterns derived from actions outside the self. But this, too, is a simplification, since we have to allow for the degree of abstraction in meaning. A meaning that combines many possible actions in accordance with some principle (e.g. 'If we have a capitalistic organization of production . . . *then* we get alienated people', or 'If there are few meanings . . . *then* we get depressed people') must also be said to lie far from behaviour

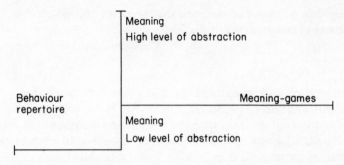

Figure 2 A continuum from behaviour repertoires to meaning-games

repertoires on this continuum. If we try to visualize the conceptual distances only, we could get something on the lines of Figure 2.

It is interesting to examine in this context why people who enjoy social-role success sometimes break down. Becker suggests two possible explanations for the depression of some great figures such as Nietzsche, Weber, and others (1964, pp. 73f). Meanings on a very high level of abstraction often lack any direct link with behaviour repertoires, i.e. the individual has rarely been involved in all the actions on which the chain of meanings is based. His inner security requires that meanings should have some link with organismic actions in the real world. The depressed geniuses were 'unanchored', living too much in the world of ideas and too little in any social reality. Becker's second possible explanation is that from childhood these people suffered from self-value deficiencies for which they tried to compensate as adults by means of symbolic successes. In other words, they lacked any basic trust (see p. 146). Perris and Espvall (1973) have studied depression in a group of Swedish patients all of whom had enjoyed social-role successes. Their results seem to support Becker's argument: (a) they were shy and reserved, which may reflect a lack of roots in organismic action (they were 'unanchored'), and (b) they had severe inferiority complexes (cf. lack of basic trust).

There is another aspect of depression among 'geniuses' which seems to fall in with Becker's first explanation. If a person becomes deeply absorbed in some theoretical problem, the problem may in the end become almost real to him (materialized); in the extreme case he may start to live his life according to the theoretical constructs. Since the real world is generally far more complex than this, and since the 'genius' has anyway very limited experience of interaction with the world on a practical level, there is a risk of his becoming disappointed with himself and falling victim to depression.

10.4.2 Ego

It seems appropriate to discuss the ego here in a section between the behaviour repertoire and meanings. It is the ego that makes possible the development of meanings from what I have called the original layer of behaviour. To Becker it is our possession of an ego that differentiates us from other animals. The ego can be defined in general terms as the unique control we have over our own behaviour. 'When we talk about the ego we are referring, simply, to the unique process of central controlling behaviour in a large-brained animal' (1971, p. 15). What is unique is that as human beings we can *consciously choose* between different action alternatives (1971, p. 7).

The four chief attributes of the ego are:

(1) The ability to abstract
(2) The ability to divide reality into time sequences
(3) The ability to wait and delay a response
(4) The ability to see oneself (self-awareness).

The ability to think in abstract terms depends on the possession of a language. Without symbols of some kind it is not possible to abstract, i.e. to subsume several topics or objects under a single whole, according to some principle. (The role of language will be examined in greater detail in the next section.) The ability to abstract can be regarded as superordinate to the other three attributes of the ego.

Posssessing an ego, we are able to perceive time. 'Without an ego the animal exists in timelessness, unable to face itself with precision in a world of sensations' (1971, p. 16). With the help of the unique control over our behaviour with which the ego endows us, we can not only divide life into time sequences but also place ourselves in a time stream. This means that we can even 'see' ourselves in time past (we can live on our memories), and we can envisage the way the future will unfold. The ability to divide life into time sequences presupposes an ability to abstract; the ability to place ourselves in a time stream is made possible by our self-awareness.

This complicated interdependence of our ego-attributes embraces even the third attribute, namely the ability to wait and delay a response. Because we can place ourselves in a time stream, we do not have to react immediately to a particular stimulus.

The fourth ego-attribute, the ability to perceive ourselves apart from other objects, is—like the other attributes—exclusive to human beings. The ability to 'see' oneself constitutes an abstraction in which the self is the object.

Before we are able, with the help of language, to evolve self-awareness, consciousness of the body has already been established. 'If the child has been allowed to gain an "organismic identity" by relatively free actions and self-controlled manipulation of his world, he has more strength and resilience toward the vagaries of social systems' (1971, p. 26). Becker does not seem to claim that body-awareness is *necessary* to the emergence of self-awareness, but possession of a firmly established body-awareness (organismic identity) will provide better conditions for the development of a substantial ego. Piaget goes one step further in his development theory, claiming that body awareness is a necessary condition of ego-awareness.

According to Becker, the ego has its origins in social life. On these grounds, he claims that depression must be a social phenomenon.

Since the ego is rooted in social reality, since self-esteem is composed of *social* symbols and *social* motives, depression becomes a direct function of a cognitively apprehended symbolic world. Nothing less than a full sweep of cultural activity is brought into consideration in the single case of depression. (1964, p. 111).

The ego evolves inasmuch as we learn to control *social* reality. The nature of the control will naturally depend on the kind of reality that the ego is called upon to face. Becker appears to mean that, if depression is indeed connected with self-esteem and if the ego is a social construct, then depression must be conditioned by social reality. Essential to this argument is that self-esteem is either a part of the ego or a direct consequence of the ego.

What constitutes the depressive personality, in terms of the ego-function? Becker provides no explicit answer to this question. He demonstrates that the depressive person has very strong control over *certain* aspects of behaviour, and that he can locate actions and objects both spatially and in a time stream. At the same time he is unable to exploit the ego-attributes in many other areas (see, for example p. 131). Moreover, the depressed personality has limited self-knowledge (see p. 144) and low self-esteem, factors which are probably connected with inadequate self-awareness. In fact, we can probably say of the depressive person that he has a *relatively weak ego*.

It is perhaps more interesting and fruitful to consider the implications of the ego in connection with traumas. The development of the ego calls for the presence of obstacles to be overcome. But time must be available for the handling and manipulation of the obstacles, for placing them in their context. What is crucial with regard to traumas is that they are events which completely overwhelm us and deny us the necessary time for processing what has happened.

If the ego has not accumulated any experience in behaviour towards certain objects, then these objects are not securely fixed in time. This explains past traumata which are always upon us, always immediate. We have never been able to outlive them because we have never been able to develop the behaviour necessary to control them, to outgrow them. (1964, p. 85)

We cannot dismiss the event with the help of the ego, saying, 'This happend ten years ago and I interpreted it in this way. . . .' When the event occurred we were unable to locate it in time and space with the help of the ego; it therefore pursued us, continually forcing itself on our minds. In other words, the ego must be allowed the requisite opportunity and time for controlling an anxiety-laden situation. The further back in time the unprocessed trauma lies, the more difficult it will be to control it now, since the present external situation has probably changed so much as to render almost inaccessible any possible solution (defence mechanism) based on present-day experience.

This is the theoretical explanation of the major role of severe events in childhood (such as the divorce or death of parents) in the development of depression in adult life. But the single stressful event in itself may not be alone in leading to depression in the adult; the very experience of being unable to control a situation is also an important factor. The trauma teaches us that *it is possible to lack control*; in other words, it disturbs the process by which we become aware of ourselves as agents of control.

Language

Language is the instrument employed by the ego. It is language that helps us to acquire control over behaviour repertoires; it is by means of language that we can create meanings and conjure up defence mechanisms. Without language we would have no 'real' ego; we would remain on the original level of behaviour (the level of the behaviour repertoire). I say 'real' because Becker appears to mean that before it has developed a language the child already possesses the beginnings of an ego ('the rudimentary ego is already there', 1971, p. 20). It is important to emphasize that language is not isolated from action, but that the ability to abstract depends upon our 'power to do' (1964, p. 87). The reverse also applies, i.e. that the development of a language facilitates further doing.

Language must have an inner consistency if it is to help its possessor to acquire self-esteem without anxiety. If his symbolic frame of reference is no longer tenable, the individual will find it more difficult to act. A typical example of the result of such a situation is the depressed person who turns to guilt-language in an attempt to hold on to the symbolic frame of reference. 'We have to understand this self-accusation not only as a reflection of guilt over unlived life but also as a *language* for making sense out of one's situation. . . . The depressed person uses guilt to hold on to his objects and to keep his situation unchanged' (1973, p. 213). Guilt feeling can be interpreted in part as a result of a failure in life, *and* as an attempt by the failed person to create order, at least linguistic order. Guilt language is directed mainly towards creating a consistent ego-perception and consistent meanings. In this way guilt feelings constitute the linguistic solution to a personal failure.

Thus Becker emphasizes throughout that language is crucial to the ability to control doing. The individual whose language is inadequate will also command a correspondingly narrow range of possible actions.

Defence mechanisms

Defence mechanisms are an important ego-function which help us in our attempts to master anxiety. One of the ego's 'general' functions is to promote the avoidance of anxiety, while defence mechanisms can be regarded as a special ego-function with which we try to deal with present or threatened anxiety. We could say that the two main objectives of defence mechanisms are to exclude certain possibilites and to master the possibilities that we do allow. To achieve the second of these objectives may mean convincing ourselves that a chosen action alternative will bring us self-esteem without causing us anxiety. As regards the first objective, Becker explains its importance as follows: 'There is no way to experience all of life; each person must close off large portions of it, must "partialize", as Rank puts it, in order to avoid being overwhelmed' (1973, p. 244).

The question, then, is whether we really succeed, in our own and other people's eyes, in excluding those portions of reality which yield the most anxiety and the least self-esteem. Does the form of 'rejection of reality' (1973, p. 209), that we have chosen, really work in the social context we are living in? The answers to these questions will depend not only on *how* we reject reality but also very much on *how great a part* of reality we reject.

The schizophrenic patient belongs to the category of people who reject relatively little, while the depressed person excludes large portions of reality. 'The creativity of people on the schizophrenic end of the human continuum is a creativity that springs from the inability to accept the standardized cultural denials of the real nature of experience' (1973, p. 63).

But there are probably some depressed people who have reached the point where they have accepted the 'true' nature of experience and have become depressed just on that account. According to Becker, the most important aspect of the 'true' nature of experience is the foreknowledge of our own death. Much of the work of the defence mechanisms consists of finding the best way of repressing this knowledge of our fundamental ontological position. A 'favourable' upbringing in these terms, so Becker suggests, would help the child to conceal his fear of death; it would help him to organize his repressions according to the standard patterns prevailing in the relevant culture. But it is when these repressions no longer function that self-esteem becomes more vulnerable with depression as a likely result. The defence mechanisms are probably more likely to become irrelevant and incapable of fulfilling their function if they were formed—and formed in a definite way—early in a person's life. And this development is, of course, even more probable in a very changeable culture such as our own.

10.4.3 Meanings

Becker postulates that we structure our experiences in meanings. Meaning can be defined as a vocabulary of choice, or a preparedness for action in relation to a specific object. A meaning is a behaviour pattern that the ego has processed with the help of language. We must exploit all four major ego-attributes in order to create meanings (i.e. the ability to abstract, the ability to divide reality into time sequences, the ability to wait and delay a response, and the ability to see oneself).

The decisive difference between behaviour repertoires (see p. 133) and meanings is that the latter are *conscious* behaviour patterns.

It is this framework of expectation and prediction that constitutes 'mind'. From a behavioural point of view, mind on any organismic level is *the total field of meanings.* . . . In man, they are elaborated into a field of conscious cause-and-effect; a network of symbolic ramifications which we are pleased to call conscious mind. (1964, p. 13).

This categorization into causes and effects is individual; an outsider may regard it as entirely irrelevant. The important point is that the individual conceives a certain factor as having a certain effect.

The depressed person is an example of someone trying to make sense of reality.

'One of the unconscious tactics that the depressed person resorts to, to try to make sense of his situation, is to see himself as immensely worthless and guilty' (1973, p. 79). 'Nobody could possibly like me, I'm so worthless.' The depressive person often explains his failure thus, as a result of his own incompetence; this seems to him to be the only answer he can find which makes sense of everything. Becker implies that the process is unconscious, which may appear to contradict his thesis that meanings are conscious, cause–effect sequences. But it is the process ('the tactical method') which is unconscious, and not the result of the process.

The most drastic solution to which the depressed person can turn in trying to make sense of his situation is suicide. To take one's own life is conceived as the only act likely to have any effect, the only act that seems meaningful. The depressed person has reached the stage where he feels that his own body is the only object left which he can consciously control. Rowe provides a further explanation that dovetails in with Becker's view, namely that suicide is an act that justifies and explains our previous actions. In this sense suicide can be regarded as a superordinate meaning that gives content and consistency to other meanings. Alvarez attributes to suicide the paradoxical significance of an act directed towards finding the calm and self-control which is not to be found in life. Perhaps we could say that suicide is a way of creating a meaning in the infinite term.

Drawing again on Alvarez, however, I should like to note the fundamental difference between suicide and depression: suicide is a question of to be or not to be, a decisive irrevocable choice. It therefore requires a certain strength and forcefulness, something which the severely depressed person usually lacks. We know that suicide is most common just as a person enters upon or leaves a state of depression. People can hardly be said to choose depression, at least not on the same conscious plane as the choosing of suicide or attempted suicide.

Let us return now to the concept of meaning: an important attribute of this is that it involves an abstraction, i.e. several elements are combined in accordance with a certain principle. This principle provides the cause–effect basis for prediction. To be able to ascribe meaning to an object or a phenomenon simply means that we have understood (or believed that we have understood) what the object can be used for or what the phenomenon can lead to.

Meaning is a crucial concept in understanding the development of depression. Loss of object and action means loss of meanings. Loss of meanings means a reduction in our opportunities for acquiring 'life significance and self-esteem'. A prerequisite condition for being able to give content and significance to our lives is thus that our need for meanings has been satisfied. '. . . "meaning" is the establishment of dependable cause-and-effect sequences which permit ego-mastery and action. Meaning is at the heart of life because it is inseparable from dependable, satisfying action' (1964, p. 113).

Control of meaning

It is important to keep many meanings in the conscious mind, so that we can continue to act when confronted by a difficult situation. However, it is even more important to be *reasonably* certain of these meanings. This certainty, or trust, gives us a strength or self-value which prepares us for coping with difficulties. Using Becker's terminology, I shall refer to 'access to many meanings' and 'different degrees of control of meanings'. Control consists of a 'specification' of the meaning: what idea or feeling do I have that a certain action will lead to a certain result? The ideal state, according to Becker, is to have control over the greatest possible number of meanings.

Becker introduces at this point a concept that greatly enhances the explanatory value of his theory. He postulates that if meanings are *too strictly* controlled, the individual reduces his store of meanings to a few fixed solutions or answers to possible actions. Thus I shall discuss below the three following aspects of meanings:

(1) Weak control of meanings
(2) Control of meanings
(3) Too much control of meanings.

If we also introduce the concept of meaning-games (see p. 133), then we have a continuum of thought constructs in our conscious mind (if . . . then) in which we believe in varying degrees. The thought construct in which we believe blindly is to be found furthest out to the right (if we envisage a simple left–right continuum).

Meaning-games	Weak control of meanings	Control of meanings	Too much control of meanings

Becker's ideal ⟶

Access to many meanings

Becker quotes the following from Kierkegaard (*Sickness*, pp.170–172): 'If one will compare the tendency to run wild in possibility with the efforts of a child to enunciate words, the lack of possibility is like being dumb . . . for without possibility a man cannot, as it were, draw breath' (1973, p. 79). If we possess a rich variety of meanings, we will also have more opportunities for choosing different action alternatives. But faced with an excess of possibilities, we may lose control over the situation, partly because the surrounding reality threatens to overwhelm us and partly because we do not have enough time to learn some of the action alternatives.

Why is it considered advantageous to have access to a reasonably large number of meanings? According to Becker's interpretation of Dewey, a high possibility of choice 'permits the forward-momentum of the organism in a blocked situation' (1964, p. 201). But in this case why do we not all strive to extend the range of our possibilities? (I am assuming here that all *should* strive for this goal, provided they could survey their whole life situation, since a wide range of possibilities helps to enhance self-esteem).

In order to avoid anxiety, people seek clear-cut and definite answers to questions regarding their own and other people's lives, and in this way they reduce the range of their possibilities, their meanings. This narrowing of the range to encompass only the certain and dependable often begins during the first years of life, as a result of the fear of object-loss. It is just this fear of the uncertain and unpredictable that so often compels the depressed to bind up their lives to a limited number of objects. Becker suggests that these objects (people) are intended to serve as a protective wall against an uncertain world.

Certain *and* predictable actions are necessary to our survival, or we could perhaps say that *predictable actions which are also certain* are necessary to life (and give the most statisfaction). With this last formulation we have perhaps approached a definition of *control*. We experience a sense of controlling a situation (our actions) when we feel able to make a sure prediction. But, and this is very important here, this is connected with the main human motive, namely to achieve self-esteem without anxiety: a *certain* prediction of possible actions is a major prerequisite for avoiding anxiety, and we will attain greater self-esteem if we can make certain predictions about *many* actions.

But what can a certain prediction be based on? '*Internal, free creation of matched means–end sequences.* Here the inidividual has full control over the means, and appraises them with reference to the goal' (1964, p. 205). Thus we experience the feeling of *personal* control over the means that lead to certain desired ends. Following Dewey, Becker refers to the opposite phenomenon as *external-coerced means–end relationships*. According to Becker, this is the perfect definition of alienation: mechanical action. Here the individual is not his own agent; the means which lead to a certain end are beyond his control. We could say that the external obstacles have become so overwhelming that he can no longer see that his own actions will lead to certain ends. We must have the power to control our actions, if we are to be able to make certain predictions.

Becker also implies in this context that meanings should be *consistent*, i.e. the means–prediction should make sense. And not only should each single meaning be consistent in itself if we are to achieve inner control; the totality of the meanings should be consistent as well. That all meanings should hang logically together—this is the goal towards which man strives. And the goal will obviously be easier to attain if the number of meanings is not too great.

Our ability to control meanings is also affected by their *continuity*. Meanings of which we have long experience are easier to control; at the same time, however, they are more difficult to change. 'When one gets down to the last twenty years of this life drama, it becomes more and more difficult to justify abrupt changes in continuity; there is too much preceding plot for it to be remanipulated with ease' (1964, p. 118). This should make it more difficult to master the loss of an object or an action in old age. On the other hand, older people have probably learnt to exert a firmer control over the object world, and by this time they probably also have more meanings to turn to. But consideration of the continuity of meanings may be relevant in discussing the great preponderance of depression among women in middle age and among men after retirement. Another explanation of this phenomenon, however, could be that the threat to self-esteem is great at just these times of life.

What are the most important features of our control over meanings? ' . . . the person's main task is to put his self-esteem as firmly as possible under his own control; he has to try to get individual and durable ways to earn self-esteem' (1971, p. 191). Man's primary motive, according to Becker, is to achieve self-esteem (see next section). From this it follows that the control he exerts over the ways in which he can achieve self-esteem is of great importance to the individual. In the passage quoted, Becker also mentions that the individual ways of controlling the path to self-esteem should be durable (i.e. should have continuity). And this in turn explains why people so often bind up their lives with a small number of dependable objects.

But control over meanings is not enough on its own. The individual also needs to be aware that he possesses this kind of control; only then can his sense of inner security benefit. In this context Becker cites the well-known case of the schizophrenic girl, Renée (Sechehaye, 1976). With the help of the psychologist (Sechehaye) the disorientated 18-year-old Renée returned to events and experiences in earliest childhood. She played with her old dolls and gradually became aware of the possibility of controlling something outside herself. Becker's point here is that even if we command few meanings and our self-esteem is fragile, we can begin to create an identity in adult life if we can only be made to realize the possibility of controlling our own actions. Thus Renée played with her dolls in order to 'secure object-oriented action, with no anxiety, and a felt manipulation through the exercise of one's powers' (Becker, 1964, p. 94).

Becker and Sechehaye interpret Renée's recovery slightly differently. To Sechehaye the important point was that Renée was able to recreate the first stages in the development of her personality in symbolic form, and to resurrect certain traumatic events. Sechehaye perhaps has more regard for the *content* of the experiences, while Becker mainly emphasizes the *process* that moulded the experiences.

It is not possible to separate the concept of internal control from that of external control. To be aware of being able to govern or predict meanings presupposes at least some control over external reality (control of external actions). Inner security (control of meanings) can perhaps be said to stem from outer security (i.e. the possibility of steering objects in a determined direction). But then the converse also obtains: we would probably be unable to attempt to steer reality, were we not convinced of our ability to make safe predictions.

Too much control of meanings

The depressed personality had access to a limited number of meanings, and generally controls these few meanings all too well. The depressed personality thinks he can make dependable predictions about the limited world around him. He has taught himself exactly what his world should look like, and this is just the danger: his disappointment is all the greater when his predictions fail to tally with reality, which is likely to happen fairly often in a changeable world. But to the depressed person dependable answers have become a necessity, and people's necessities are difficult to alter.

As Kierkegaard sums it up: 'The loss of possibility signifies: either that everything has become necessary to man or that everything has become trivial.' Actually, in the extreme of depressive psychosis we seem to see the merger of these two: everything becomes necessary *and* trivial at the same time—which leads to complete despair. (1973, p. 80)

It is not, perhaps, immediately obvious what Kierkegaard and Becker mean by saying that something can be both necessary and trivial. The life which the depressed person 'chooses' has become necessary, in the sense that he cannot imagine any other way of living. In its most extreme form, when he has allowed himself to be totally engulfed by other people's expectations, his life can become one of spiritual slavery. He has chosen security, but lost the ability to find life significance for himself. This is what constitutes the trivial element: nothing he does can enhance his self-esteem.

Bound as he is to dependable solutions or answers, the depressed person is incapable of critically interpreting his surroundings and of critically scrutinizing himself, both of which deficiencies are evidence of a strict control of meanings.

Why are many people so uncritical of new experiences, in the sense that they reject impressions without processing them? One reason is that they have learnt from their parents to look at reality, and to deal with it, in the way that seemed right to the parents. If the picture of the world that has thus been passed on reflects the culturally accepted norms and ideals of an earlier generation, the children will find it difficult as adults to examine new experiences critically. Since social realities change continually, the ways in which we can best achieve self-esteem without anxiety also change. The person whose world of experience is narrow will have a poor basis for understanding reality and, consequently, of discovering ways of achieving self-esteem without anxiety.

People who have learnt early in life to restrict their experiences to a safe and narrow world may well be compelled to step outside the walls they have set up. And in thus venturing out, they expose themselves to feelings of guilt. Guilt feelings differ from anxiety, which arises when we lack control over our actions, in reflecting the way we look upon the unacceptable aspects of our own behaviour in the light of our strongly controlled meanings. The depressed person finds it hard to recognize the existence of choice, since his alternatives are determined by other people. Furthermore, he is unable to examine the alternatives critically since, being unaware of any real choice, he has no grounds on which to base his criticism. When external circumstances force him to live in another way, he will feel guilty. He still cannot envisage any alternatives, and it is just this conflict which generates the sense of guilt. Guilt, it seems to me, leaves a person even less likely to rely upon himself than before, which makes him increasingly vulnerable to other people's demands. This in turn augments his guilt, and yet again we are faced with a vicious circle.

People whose meanings are few in number and strictly controlled will have little opportunity for looking at themselves from several viewpoints. Their self-image will be circumscribed: they cannot stand outside themselves and critically examine what they see. This inability to examine themselves critically is typical of the depressed. Their fear of revealing themselves makes them seem 'literally stupid' (Becker, 1973, p. 79). As we have seen, fear of this kind has often been established in childhood, which makes it difficult for the depressed person to find reasons for his depressive state within himself, since he has no clear insight into the underlying causes.

The depressed person's lack of self-insight is manifest in his language. 'Depressive self-accusation, in some, amounts to *a search for a vocabulary of meaning* in the face of an overwhelmingly frustrating situation. It is a form of language substitute, a type of stupidity by someone poor in words' (1964, p. 120). Our meanings are clothed in words, but the depressed person has so few meanings (i.e. word-combinations) among which to choose, that he cannot fail to regard himself as worthless. Becker seems to assume here (though this does not agree with his argument in *The Denial of Death*) that his worthlessness need have no real social equivalent. The reverse can equally well apply, namely that if a person is regarded by others as worthless, then he *feels* worthless, and thus becomes depressed. It is also possible to regard oneself as worthless in some broad existential sense.

But the important point in this context is that the depressed person has poor self-insight as well as limited access to meanings. 'The individual doesn't know the performance style in which he has been trained; he doesn't know why he feels anxious at certain eventualities; he doesn't know why he is trying to get the other person to do *just this* particular thing' (1964, p. 119). Becker refers in this passage to 'most people'. But in other contexts he appears to refer particularly to the depressed.

Becker does not distinguish between different states of depression. But in a footnote (1964, p. 135) he discusses the possible causes of manic-depression and touches upon the arguments we have been discussing here. The manic personality and the depressive personality resemble one another in several significant ways. They are uncritical in connection with social realities; they are uncritical in connection with themselves; they have a loose grip on self-esteem, they are caught up in a narrow range of social rules. The manic-depressive continually seeks self-esteem from sources outside the family, but never succeeds in arriving at a point where he feels safe. When the obstacles outside become too much for him, he is forced back on the family. There he acquires secure but weak self-esteem, due to the limited scope for action that the family allows. The manic state has turned into one of depression.

10.4.4 Human motives

According to Becker no human motives can be regarded as purely personal. This would mean that no drives steer behaviour in the adult, i.e. in those who have developed symbolic selves. It is not quite clear whether Becker means that the child who has not yet evolved a symbolical self is steered by drives.

> ... the individual has a private life, but since this life is only the 'inner pole' of the social motives, it is private only *by location*. . . . Shame arises in the *moment of acknowledgement* that the private is merely the 'inner pole' of the social. It is the confession that one *really has nothing private per se to oppose to someone's scrutiny*. (1964, pp. 189f)

In Becker's view, it is very difficult to make a clear distinction between the personal and the social. We can never develop any entirely personal motives; they all in some way come from outside. A sense of shame arises, as Becker says, when we discover that we possess no really private motives. It may be a little difficult to follow Becker's argument regarding shame, when it is taken out of context as in the above quotation. He cites the woman who undresses for a medical examination: she feels no shame at all, simply because the social situation demands that she should have no private motives. Becker suggests that women in our culture generally blush more easily than men because they are allowed to have fewer private motives.

However, there is one human motive that is universal—universal in that is applies to all people as people, and is unconnected with drives. According to Becker the fundamental human motive is *to strive for self-esteem without arousing anxiety*. I am not quite sure whether Becker is placing the main emphasis on the striving for self-esteem or the efforts to avoid anxiety, but he seems to suggest that the avoidance of anxiety is more important at the beginning of our lives and that as we develop our symbolic selves the striving for self-esteem becomes paramount.

Thus there are three main components in the fundamental human motive:

(1) Striving towards action
(2) Striving to minimize anxiety
(3) Striving to maximize self-esteem.

The first component was discussed in a previous section (see pp. 129–131). The two other main components will be discussed below.

Self-esteem

> ... the basic law of human life is the urge to self-esteem. (1971, p. 66)

The desire for self-esteem can perhaps be singled out as the overriding motive of the adult human being. In order to achieve self-esteem it is obviously necessary to *act* in some way. In the very attainment of self-esteem lies the avoidance of anxiety.

> [Self-esteem] is an inner self-righteousness that arms the individual against anxiety. We must understand it, then, as a *natural systematic continuation* of the early ego efforts to

handle anxiety; it is the durational extension of an effective anxiety-buffer.... The qualitative feeling of self-value is the basic predicate for human action, precisely because it epitomizes the whole development of the ego. (1971, p. 67)

Thus it is possible to avoid anxiety in two ways: (a) by directing actions towards the attainment of self-esteem, and (b) by utilizing defence mechanisms. It is also clear from this quotation that Becker regards the three components—action, anxiety, and self-esteem—as inextricably interconnected. Self-esteem is the fundamental predicate of action. He who lacks self-esteem is inevitably passive; in the extreme case he will sink into total apathy.

Becker thus sees depression as a *consequence of impaired self-esteem*. If self-value is lost, the individual has no basis on which to build a meaningful life. Lack of self-esteem lies behind the withdrawal of the depressive from the real world and the breakdown of the schizophrenic. Typical of the depressive (in particular of the psychotically depressed) is the difficulty in taking any action at all. The schizophrenic, on the other hand, throws himself into chaotic action. Weak self-esteem leaves him incapable of *processing* his actions.

The early self-esteem learnt in childhood is important in two respects. It provides the basic trust that we generally retain throughout our lives, and this trust plays an important role in the attainment of later self-esteem. How, then, do we acquire this first significant self-value? We evolve meanings as we discover blocked paths of action; in learning to maintain a forward momentum despite obstacles we have to learn to process and steer our conduct towards particular goals. But the goals for which we can strive are at first entirely controlled by our parents, and the child learns that self-esteem can be achieved by striving for certain goals in certain approved ways. In time the child discovers that reality embraces more than its parents and their definition of the real world; there are also other quite different motives for which one could or should strive.

We realize at an early age that we cannot always determine our own actions (which later means being able to choose ways of acquiring self-esteem); in the case of the depressive personality this realization is particularly strong. The restriction on our free choice comes from two sources. In early life when we are still helpless, we learn that our opportunities of attaining self-esteem in our own way are limited. Furthermore, the first motives we learn have not been actively and consciously processed by ourselves, and they will therefore always affect the direction of our future actions without our understanding why (and possibly without our realizing that they do). These motives are learned before we have developed an ego of our own. Becker seems to suggest that a developed ego cannot subsequently process motives that were learned at a stage when it (the ego) did not exist.

I should now say something about the nature of this early self-esteem whose acquisition, though vital and beneficial in many ways, also injects into us so many grounds for future conflict. What is it based on? Is it consistent and durable? 'Some people have more of what the psychoanalyst Leon J. Saul has aptly called "Inner Sustainment". It is a sense of bodily confidence in the face of experience that sees the person more easily through severe life crises and even sharp personality changes' (1973, p. 22). This 'inner sustainment', the possession of a self-esteem characterized by continuity and consistency, generally becomes part of us during childhood. It develops best when the child feels secure, when his attempts to investigate his surroundings are met with warmth and approval.

[Kierkegaard] knows that the child has to be protected against dangers and that watchfulness by the parent is of vital importance, but he doesn't want the parent to obtrude his own anxieties into the picture, to cut off the child's action before it is absolutely necessary. Today we know that such an upbringing alone gives the child a self-confidence in the face of experience that he could not have if he were overly blocked: it gives him an 'inner sustainment'. (1973, pp. 71–72)

If a parent transfers his own anxiety to his child, he will not promote that child's security. And if the child is not secure, he will be less able to venture out on his own into ways of achieving self-esteem.

The individual who enters adult life with a firm basic trust can remain comparatively independent of the approval of others; he will be well fitted to rely on himself, and therefore able to venture along his own varied paths towards self-esteem.

Becker points out that, paradoxical though it may seem, not everyone strives to acquire self-esteem. Many adults cling to a way of life that does nothing to enhance their sense of self-value, and this involves a fateful conflict with the fundamental human motives. Here we have the paradox of the depressed: they are bound up in situations which bring them no self-esteem.

This is how we understand depressive psychosis today: as a bogging down in the demands of other—family, job, the narrow horizon of daily duties. In such bogging down the individual does not feel or see that he has alternatives, cannot imagine any choices or alternate ways of life, cannot release himself from the network of obligations even though these obligations no longer give him a sense of self-esteem, of primary value, of being a heroic contributor to world life, even by doing his daily family and job duties. (1973, p. 78)

If the depressed person recognized the existence of other opportunities, he would (presumably) choose those that yielded most self-esteem. But if he had realized that other alternatives were available, he would not have become depressed. (And, as I have argued in previous chapters, the actual existence of real, external opportunities can affect the situation as well: the possibilities available for achieving self-esteem in a certain sphere (e.g. work) may be genuinely limited.) It is possible to interpret Becker's exposition of this point in several ways. The interpretation which seems to me most likely, and which agrees with what Becker has said elsewhere, is that because the individual is so exposed to the demands of others, she (because it is generally a woman) cannot see any alternatives; she thus becomes locked in an endless series of other-generated life duties which yield her very little self-esteem. The crucial feature of the depression is thus the lack of self-value. But, as we have seen, there has to be a negative shift in self-esteem to set off the development of a depression, and if the subject lacks the 'inner sustainment' that Becker has described here, and therefore has a meagre supply of self-esteem to fall back on, the risk of a depression actually occurring is probably much greater.

To understand the role of self-esteem in the development of depression we thus need to ask ourselves three questions: What constitutes the greatest threat to the self-esteem of the depressive personality? What characterizes the self-esteem of the depressive personality? What has moulded his experience of self-worth?

The questions—and the answers to them—are closely linked with one another, but should nevertheless be considered separately as far as possible since they are relevant to different stages in the development of the depressive disorder. To begin with the question which comes last chronologically: the greatest threat to the self-esteem of the depressive personality occurs in connection with a negative shift in the chains of meaning that provide for a securely based positive feeling of self-worth.

Who are the people whose self-esteem would be most vulnerable in face of such negative shifts? We have already accumulated ample evidence that people who lack basic trust are particularly prone to perceive threats to their self-value. Self-esteem flimsily supported on a poor foundation of basic trust is characteristic of the depressive personality. A self-value that is not firmly rooted in the individual's own inner life, but is constantly being confronted and affected by what other people think, is also likely to be affected by the too readily perceived threats. Thus the depressed personality lacks trust in his own ability. Another threat to his self-esteem, resulting in depression, can stem from his having bound his self-value up with a limited number of meanings and a limited range of action. It is then fairly obvious that if his limited world is shaken or upset, the result will be catastrophic.

Why is the self-esteem of the depressive personality such a tender plant? The answer to this question recalls what has been said above the development of the depressive personality itself, bringing us back again to the fundamental importance of basic trust. Without the gift of adequate warmth, physical as well as spiritual, during the first years of his life, the growing child will be hampered in accumulating significance and a richness of variety in his own life. If his spontaneous development is then circumscribed at school, at work, in his intimate relationships, and in society in general, so that he has little opportunity to govern his own actions, it is not very surprising if he ceases to believe that such personal control is possible. Furthermore, the depressive personality originally acquired his fragile self-esteem because he was referred to certain determined niches or fields of activity, often within the protective walls of the home. We can thus see yet again how all the elements in this complex picture overlap: it is seldom possible to isolate single factors and say that 'just *this* is the reason for the weak self-esteem, this is the cause of the depression'.

Heroism

Our striving for self-esteem is connected with a longing to be endowed with positive value. But Becker sees our superordinate goal as something higher than this. He speaks of our search for that he calls a *primary value* and he links this with his concept of the hero. The chief attribute of the hero is not, in Becker's eyes, that he is superior to other people. It is a question not so much of comparisons with other people as of the relationship between himself and the rest of the world, or the cosmos, as he perceives it to be.

Let us now examine the connection between the urge for self-esteem and the urge to be a hero. Heroism concerns my value in relation to the cosmos and self-esteem my value in relation to myself. Heroism can thus be regarded as an extension of self-esteem. To be a hero is to have *self-esteem in the infinite term, spatially and in the stream of time.*

He [the individual] must be able to answer the question *'How does the dignity, control, bearing, talent, and duty of my life contribute to the fuller development of mankind, to life in the cosmos?'* Now we can see that primitive and traditional hero systems provided a clear-cut answer to precisely this question; and we can also judge that modern society provides no easy answer, if it provides any at all. (1971, p. 125)

Ultimately heroism is a question of the meaning of life, at least of *my* life.

In what way can people achieve a sense of primary value? Becker's answer to this question is not altogether without ambiguity. At one point he says that we conceive of ourselves as heroes when we feel able to predict our actions and when we know which actions will generate most self-esteem. In other contexts Becker seems to require more of heroism: a kind of self-commitment, fearlessness in the face of what we most need and desire ('natural narcissism') together with satisfaction of the fundamental need for self-esteem. The child is probably more prone to see himself as a hero in this sense. To achieve the same result the adult needs a world view that helps him to handle the guilt he has accumulated in the course of his life, one that directs him towards the acquisition of a primary value. To provide such a world view and to show the way to the attainment of primary value—that, in Becker's view, is the task of psychology today.

[Rank and Kierkegaard] reached the same conclusion after the most exhaustive psychological quest: that at the very furthest reaches of scientific description, psychology has to give way to 'theology'—that is, to a world-view that absorbs the individual's conflicts and guilt and offers him the possibility for some kind of heroic apotheosis. (1973, p. 196).

A firm belief in God can supply a framework of the kind that Becker demands of psychology: if we are God's servants everything we do is heroic. I as an individual have no significance; I am created by God for God. By placing our lives in the hands of an external and infinite power, we also solve the problem of death. The religious hero system can promise us eternal life as individuals, added to which we also live on in the services we have performed for the great God.

It is difficult for the members of modern Western society to perceive themselves as heroes. The religious hero system has largely lost its power, and neither psychology nor any other hero system has succeeded in assuming its role. This partly explains modern man's heavy burden of anxiety: one of the ways in which we seek to avoid anxiety is by undertaking actions that generate self-esteem, and self-esteem in the infinite term has become increasingly difficult of access.

In this context Becker defines mental illness as a failure to be a hero, i.e. to become a person of primary value. He seems to imply that those whom we could call mentally ill fail to understand their own supreme desire, or, if they do understand it, they do not know how to realize their heroism. The depressed is a person who has become aware of his desire but sees no chance of realizing it; nor does he have any God in whom he can trust. He has failed in his heroic role. 'When the average person can no longer convincingly perform his safe heroics or cannot hide his failure to be his own hero, then he bogs down in the failure of depression and its terrible guilt' (1973, p. 212). We seem to catch a glimpse of an important point here, which to some extent explains the apparent contradictions in Becker's definition of heroism. A man can be a hero to himself. He then believes that the secure life he leads is of primary value. But it is only possible for him to be a 'real' hero in relation to some power which he perceives as embracing the whole cosmos, which satisfies his need for self-esteem in an infinite perspective of space and time.

Action without anxiety

If self-esteem is the fundamental positive motive, the urge to avoid anxiety is the fundamental negative motive. The two motives can also come into conflict with one another, as I shall try to show at the end of this section.

According to Becker, psychoanalytical theory is concerned exclusively with the way the child tries to master its anxiety. The child's anxiety is connected with its fear of losing the objects that surround it. At first this fear of object-loss is very physical in its focus; anxiety concerns the possible loss of objects that supply the child's primary needs: 'Without mother and father, no food.' In addition to the child's basic fear of object-loss, he has to suffer the uneasiness that accompanies the development of a symbolic ego: 'Who am I?' 'Will people like me enough?'

In the adult, anxiety is concerned not so much with the fear of object-loss as with the fear of failing in action. 'The child's early fear of object-loss has been skillfully transmuted by his training to the adult's fear of wrong action' (1964, p. 33). The child is mainly thrown upon the actions of adults, while the adult himself is thrown upon his own resources. With his now developed ego, the adult can remember earlier mistakes and become uneasy about future failures. The ego is in a way both the cause of anxiety and the means of controlling it. The ego can fulfil one of its functions, to wait and delay a response, only when it can master anxiety. The ego is based on language. Our ability to verbalize the real world is an important way of controlling it, and therefore of mastering our anxiety. Mastery of language is thus a major component in the control of anxiety.

The fewer situations the individual can verbalize, the more the anxiety. The schizophrenic who has the fewest objects-as-action-possibility has the most anxiety. The depressed person, on the other hand, has objects, but the rules are so inextricably entwined with the concrete object that there is no backing away from them, no grip on them for critical review, no symbolic dexterity possible. (1964, p. 179)

It is in order to avoid anxiety that the depressed person binds himself so firmly to objects, both linguistically and in action. When the depressed person comes up against a reality that calls for symbolic flexibility, he is often unable to cope. According to Becker, the ability to verbalize our realities means being able to place them in a means–ends sequence; we can predict what object will succeed what action. Inability to predict inhibits action, and action in turn is crucial to the attainment of self-esteem.

The depressed personality is abnormally prone to fear of anxiety; he therefore tries to force reality into a definite mould both in his perception of it and in the way he acts towards it. It is just this fear, this terror, that is so typical of the depressed personality: he is afraid of being angry, of making other people angry, of being rejected, of losing control. One explanation of his excessive wish to avoid anxiety lies in the lack of security that he suffered when he was growing up—his early years were spent in the fear of object-loss; another in his fear of losing sub-objects (see p. 128), of losing some parts of the care and approval he is used to. This is the kind of fear that comes to those who have found love to be conditional, dependent on the satisfaction of parental demands. The child does not feel loved for his own sake.

In conclusion, let us examine a little more closely the relation between self-esteem and anxiety. In Becker's texts the relationship emerges as a question of balance—perhaps a dialectic—between anxiety and self-esteem. If we are excessive in our efforts to avoid anxiety, we will reduce our opportunities for attaining self-esteem; but if we open ourselves to all possible opportunities in our search for maximum self-esteem, we will lose control over reality and will thus experience anxiety. The experience of anxiety interferes with our mastery of reality, and a certain degree of mastery is necessary to the attainment of self-esteem. Our best solution is therefore probably to learn to tolerate a moderate dose of anxiety.

10.5 SUMMARY, AND SOME CRITICAL COMMENTS

It is not easy to summarize Ernest Becker's theory of depression, since it is drawn from so many bases and involves the interplay of numerous factors on several levels. Having registered these problems, I shall introduce my tentative overview with a question: What does Becker mean by depression? It seems to me that depression to Becker has a three-fold source:

(1) Fear of losing self-esteem
(2) The process by which self-esteem is impaired
(3) The result of the process that has impaired self-esteem.

These three elements are more likely to occur, and thus to engender depression, if certain negative conditions obtain. It is not really possible to distinguish between these negative factors or levels (as I shall do artifically below) since they are intimately connected with one another. A change on one level has implications on others. Further, all the factors have to be set in a historical framework including the developmental history of the individual and the history of society. Nor, as I intended to illustrate in the model introduced at the beginning of this chapter (see p. 123), can we draw any clear boundaries between the inner life and life outside the self. Many of the problems that confront us in analysing Becker's theory stem from the fact that a phenomenon in the external world has to be qualified by an 'inner' interpretation. We find ourselves returning continually to the vain attempt to distinguish between life in society and life in the mind.

Phenomenology showed that man looked at his world from the inside; and existentialism showed how important to man was the symbolic constitution of that world. Science, which was *par excellence* the technique of getting at things from the *outside*, measuring, weighing and counting them, found itself face to face with a most curious object. . . . Man's phenomenal world is a mixture of the possibilities of both actions and dreams; a real world and an imagined world that cannot be unfused. (1964, p. 145)

Becker appears to me to envisage the likelihood of the development of a depression—the reaction with a depressive response to a negative shift in life conditions—in terms of the following factors. I also mention under the various headings the kind of contexts in which these factors may occur. The examples are mainly my own.

(1) *Low self-esteem* The depressed personality generally has low self-esteem, since he is extremely anxious to avoid anxiety. Because of his fear, or terror, of losing the immediate objects in his world (in particular his parents, partner, child) he has reduced the number of possible ways in which he could have acquired self-esteem.

(2) *A negative change that affects the meanings which provide him with a secure and/or strong sense of self-esteem* The depressed personality often has few vocabularies of choice at his command, and these few are therefore of relatively great importance to his self-esteem. Thus, if a negative event occurs in his life, the risk that this will affect the meanings on which his self-esteem depends is considerable.

(3) *Few meanings which are too strongly controlled* The individual who is strongly bound up in certain solutions to possible actions will naturally find it difficult to see any way out of a stressful situation. The depressed personality finds it difficult to stand outside himself and subject himself to a critical examination or to view reality from several vantage points.

(4) *Few controlled actions* The depressed commands few opportunities—or fails to exploit those that he has—for steering his own life. There is thus little in his life that is based on his own needs.

(5) *Rigid action patterns* Those who are prone to depression often lead very restricted lives; everything has to be (ought to be) done in an exactly specified way. The range of events that will probably lie outside this narrow envisaged area is therefore great and the risk of negative effects on self-esteem continually threatens.

(6) *Few significant relationships* The depressed personality has few confiding relationships with significant others. The loss of one of these few leaves him with drastically reduced opportunities for absorbing value and meanings into his life.

(7) *The societal setting provides a limited range of possible actions and/or of actions accessible to control* If society imposes narrow limits on the permitted and the possible, those who suffer most will be the society members commanding few resources of their own. The individual who is unable to affect the content of his work tasks, may come to believe that *all* action is beyond the range of his control.

(8) *Society is changing fast* The goals which were considered desirable by the previous generation may be in sharp contrast to present ideals; a child can have learnt from its parents a way of handling reality that is no longer valid. He thus has access to fewer actions by means of which he could acquire a secure sense of self-esteem.

In his work Becker demonstrates several pairs of extremes where the ideal lies in seeking a position of balance between the two. The predisposed depressive has failed to achieve this balance but has directed his life towards certain aspects at the cost of certain others. He has been too persistent in the avoidance of anxiety, and neglected the search for self-esteem; he has demanded rigid and definite answers to the problems and questions in his path, and neglected to promote his own flexibility and readiness for action; he has focused on durable, dependable actions and denied himself access to a rich variety of alternatives. These three opposing pulls can be found on the two levels we have discussed, on the inner psychological level and the external societal level—which two, as we have seen, overlap and interact in every individual. A fourth opposing pull may also exist *between* the psychological and the societal levels. In this case the depressed personality gears himself more to pleasing others than to enriching his own needs and experiences.

A theory intended to be all-embracing on the scale of Becker's will always risk exhibiting incompleteness or inadequacy in some of its parts. Paradoxically, it seems to me that Becker, the anthropologist, pays too little attention to the impact of social factors on our lives. His concept of society is diffuse and the connections he establishes between society and the individual are often very general. Some discussion of the social phenomena likely to promote rigid action patterns, to limit the range of action opportunities, and to increase the risk of threat to self-esteem would have been instructive. Are particular social groups especially vulnerable in these respects?

The other major weakness in Becker's theory is his comparative neglect of aspiration and ideals. These concepts, which are central to neo-Freudian theory, serve to illustrate the *relative* role of self-esteem and the influence of ideology on our mental set. What are the goals or ideals of the predisposed depressives? What has led them to harbour the *unrealistic* expectations that characterize their approach to themselves and the real world?

In the course of presenting Becker's theory I have mentioned a few specific criticisms: that he perhaps gives too much weight to the problem of death, that the presentation of his arguments is often unclear and his formulations tangled, and that some of his propositions are loosely anchored in empirical research. Perhaps, too, the theory is too bound up in the concept of action, in which respect it reflects much American thinking in this field. There is some attempt to introduce an emotional dimension into the theory (in the concept of sentiment, for instance) but this remains tentative. Self-esteem, anxiety, guilt, and depression are all obviously aspects of our emotional set but they appear in Becker's theory only as the consequence of particular action components. What Becker fails to discuss is the role of certain emotional blockages or deficiencies (inability to show aggression, love, etc.) in engendering depression in people who possess adequate and flexible repertoires of possible actions.

In conclusion, however, I must emphasize that I have found ample empirical confirmation that Becker's theory best explains *most* depressions, including different types of depressive diagnoses. At the same time I feel that many other 'purely' psychological theories, in particular the neo-Freudian theories, often have a greater explanatory value than Becker's in certain specific cases. A great advantage of Becker's theory, however, is that it opens the analysis of depression to fruitful contributions from other theories, and together with the results discussed earlier in the present book it provides us with an opportunity to proceed on a multidisciplinary basis to the description of the depressive process. This is the far from modest ambition that I shall hope to realize in the next chapter.

CHAPTER 11

Development of Becker's theory—a model for depression

Chapter 10 represents a first step towards a development of Becker's theory, in that I have attempted to structure Becker's often rather disconnected ideas and themes. I have identified and interpreted what I see as the essence of Becker's concept of depression, taking his works as my point of departure. In this chapter I start from the other end, namely from my own composite picture of depression. My theoretical base owes much to Becker's work, but I have also drawn on neo-Freudian theory for certain specific assumptions and on the broad spectrum of empirical research which I have described in earlier chapters. Together these sources provide the empirical and theoretical base for the following description of the depressive process.

How does a depressive development originate, what leads to the perpetuation of a depressive personality, and what ultimately precipitates a depression? I will first discuss and define the concepts on which my description of the depressive process is based. The emphasis of the analysis remains on social–psychological factors; the societal level and the purely intra-individual level are thus barely touched upon, and the biological level will not be discussed at all. It was, of course, necessary to limit the vast material in some way, and my decision to concentrate on social–psychological aspects reflects my view that these factors provide the most fruitful explanation of depression in the individual.

11.1 DEFINITION AND DISCUSSION OF CONCEPTS DERIVED FROM BECKER

It is not easy to distinguish and put names to the dimensions or concepts which I have identified as being central to Becker's theory. One important mechanism, for instance, is referred to by Becker as *to control, to be bound up in, to hold on to, to master*, and *to manipulate*. These expressions evoke a variety of associations, but a basic content is common to them all. By reducing the number of designations and trying to pin down the common content in relatively simple and clear definitions I hope to create a more immediately comprehensible terminology suitable to my present purpose. At the same time I acknowledge that in this way I also lose many of the openings—and much of the flavour—of Becker's rich and many-faceted theory.

Another problem that complicates any attempt to reach simple definitions of

Becker's concepts is the dual nature of his whole approach, embracing both the psychological and the societal levels. This is not simply because Becker sometimes appears 'unsystematic' in the way he presents his arguments; it is also because the phenomena he describes cannot easily be split between an external and an inner reality. Phenomena in external reality must be fused with the interpretation of reality in the conscious mind.

I decided to resolve this problem by bringing together factors on the societal and psychological levels into single, fused concepts: the concept of the rigid action patterns and the limited range of possible action. In both cases conditions in external reality are reflected in the inner life of the individual. On the other hand, when I particularize these general concepts, giving them a more concrete form, the distinction between the psychological and the societal levels once again becomes apparent.

11.1.1 Limited range of possible actions

By range of possible action I mean *a preparedness for action in relation to a particular object, in the first instance other people.* This preparedness for action is, or has been, anchored in external reality in the shape of symbolic (verbal and non-verbal) and non-symbolic actions. Preparedness for action thus refers to available actions and not to products of the imagination. Conversely, the available actions have to be consciously perceived by the individual as real possibilities to qualify as *action opportunities.* A definition as general as this naturally raises many questions. What limits our preparedness for action? How long must an action be conceivable and possible before it can be defined as preparedness for action? Is it enough for an action to be conceived as possible for a few seconds? Other problems are linked with the boundaries between internal and external reality. How can we decide whether preparedness for action is relevant (anchored in reality) or whether it is a product of the imagination? Or whether a preparedness for action that used to be relevant is still so? Can such preparedness be generalized, thus continuing to serve us? In this connection some of Becker's more intricate concepts can be of use, in particular those concerned with access to 'meanings', i.e. an understanding of the world and our place in it. Preparedness for action can be regarded as a continuum from relevance exclusively for the individual to relevance for all (general relevance). This kind of preparedness for action, based on the individual's access to meanings, can be regarded as a genuine action opportunity, since relevance in circumstances no longer prevailing can evolve into relevance to new circumstances. The individual remains flexible in a changing world.

11.1.2 Rigid action patterns

Rigid action patterns reflect a *firm, unbending action preparedness.* On the psychological level, this may mean that the individual regards one action opportunity as the only possibility in relation to a particular object in a particular situation. It is thus a question of the individual's perception or feeling of certainty, which corresponds to the perception of a single way of behaving in a particular situation in the real world. On the social level, we can speak of accustomed actions that are *very persistent*. Actions prone to become persistent are those which endure over a long period or which are frequently undertaken, which are regular or which occur in few situations, which occur in relation to few objects or can be steered in a particular direction. The sense of being in control of reality, of being able to steer it in a predictable direction, is an important element in the concept of the rigid action patterns. From this description it can also be seen that the rigid action patterns can also be defined in 'internal' and 'external' terms and that the two definitions overlap. It is necessary that the individual perceives himself as steering the action *and* that in some way he actually does so (or has been able to do so).

This definition raises the same sort of questions as the definition of the limited range of possible action, namely the question of duration and the link between interior and external certainty. A specific problem in this present case is that it may be possible to feel certain on an immediate level, without being able to predict with any assurance the consequences at a later date and in a broader perspective. The crucial question in defining the rigid action pattern is, of course, the *degree* of certainty and the *extent* to which action preparedness is controlled. Since we are dealing here with people's inner lives, it is impossible to set any boundaries. All we can do is to try to establish the degree of certainty that seems probable.

11.1.3 Self-esteem

Self-esteem is closely related to self-reliance, but it is also a much more complex concept. According to the American sociologist Brisett (1972), self-esteem consists of two social–psychological components: self-evaluation and self-worth. Self-evaluation involves the assessment of achievement in light of certain ideals, while self-worth is connected with the experience of control over one's own actions. In these terms, self-worth is more fundamental to the self, more concerned with the individual's 'innermost' feelings. 'One's sense of self-worth is obviously more intrinsic than extrinsic to the person and in this sense it differs from self-evaluation' (p. 261). Nevertheless, self-worth is also basically social, since it springs from interactions with others. Brisett points out that it is possible for a person to feel involved in an activity that is quite unconnected with himself (he plays a role rather than playing himself); in such a case self-evaluation may be affected but not self-worth. Generally, however, the two components coincide, since the situations in which we value ourselves highly are almost those situations over which we have control. The sense of being able to control our own actions is connected with the expectations of others in relation to ourselves, and our ability to influence others naturally depends on the weight they ascribe to us (whether they 'take us seriously'). Self-esteem in Becker's theory (which Brisett also discusses) coincides most closely with Brisett's self-worth, and this is the meaning I attach to the concept here.

We can now examine the various concepts we have been discussing in connection with the depressive state. According to Becker's theory, a limited range of possible actions, rigid action patterns, and low self-esteem are characteristic of the predisposed depressive. Furthermore, it is the threat to self-esteem, or the threat of reduction in self-esteem, which ultimately precipitates the depression. At this point the individual no longer feels himself to be master of his actions, he loses confidence in his own worth and sees his self-value at risk. Typical events which may elicit such a reaction are separation, loss of job, severe conflict in a personal relationship, or acute illness or handicap. I have already discussed the process whereby these and similar problems may result in a loss of self-esteem. Characteristic of them all is that they involve some real loss.

Maddi (1977), who has his roots in the existential tradition, discusses another possible threat to self-esteem. Even the most stereotyped and unbending character must sometimes sense that life is not all that it could be. Maddi refers to May et al. who have dubbed this accumulative feeling of missed opportunities 'ontological guilt'. Let us envisage an individual, very set in his ideas about the nature of life and convinced of his own inability to influence the real world outside this carefully restricted range. Even the slightest sense that life could mean more than this will—it seems to me—involve the questioning of his own worth (the same, perhaps, as questioning the meaning of life), and self-esteem will be threatened. This feeling is surely more likely to arise if on one single occasion the individual has caught a glimpse of some wider opportunity; he has known a moment of bolder self-realization. In such a case the sharp contrast between the briefly known richness of life and the circumscribed range of his usual world is what may lead to a depression, rather than a concrete loss such as those mentioned above.

11.1.4 Doing and undergoing

With the two concepts *doing* and *undergoing* we approach another dimension that is discussed in various contexts in Becker's work. I did not include these concepts in my presentation of Becker's theory, because he does not himself use them in his explanation of depression. It seems to me, however, that they can help us to understand the origins of the limited range of action opportunities, the rigid action patterns, and the low self-esteem which we have found to be determinants of depression.

The concepts of doing and undergoing are connected with the relation between external reality and the conscious mind. *Doing* refers to external reality and *undergoing* to the individual's mental life. Another way of putting this is that *undergoing* is an interior activity and *doing* an activity in the external world. 'The "great soul" seems to be one who has achieved both a richness of experience and a flexibility in actions: an apt proportion of the receptivity to undergo and the power to manipulate' (Becker, 1964, p. 142). Thus the ideal state occurs when the individual has a large supply of manipulated experiences (undergoing) and the ability to act flexibly (doing). But the point of Becker's distinction between *doing* and *undergoing* concerns the balance between external and inner activity. Too much doing means too little undergoing, and vice versa. We cannot organize our impressions if we are active or too inactive. In the latter case we simply do not have enough impressions to organize. Organized impressions are, in fact, what I (following Becker) have defined here as meanings. To be able to initiate action it is necessary to have access to meanings.

Why are doing and undergoing so often out of balance? 'The organism that continually finds gratification without delay, frustration, or set-back moves ahead without sufficient registering of experience. It doesn't relate its experience to an assessment of its powers' (1964, p. 23). This sounds like the description of a spoilt child: someone who gets everything he wants and who never has to investigate the world for himself, will never discover the limitations of his own powers. He will not be able to develop a strong ego. It is through the ego that we can organize our impressions into meanings. If, on the other hand, a person experiences too much frustration in the external world, he will turn inwards to achieve satisfaction (1964, p. 32), which will also inhibit the development of a strong ego. Thus there are two opposing states in the real world that can lead to the evolution of a weak ego. The development of a strong ego, the ability to abstract, is largely determined by access to extrinsic action or 'the power to do' (1964, p. 87). The ability to abstract is connected with the ability to classify objects according to their areas of use. A person who lacks experience of his own actions in relation to objects will naturally find such classification difficult. We can follow Piaget in concluding that over-fantasizing actually reflects in inability to see many correspondences, which thus characterizes people geared to undergoing. Behind this inability lies another more fundamental deficiency, namely the inability to place oneself in a social context (Berg, 1976, p. 133).

I suggest that the depressed personality evidences a deficiency in both doing and undergoing. In some contexts the depressed person is characterized by too much doing at the expense of undergoing: most of his life runs along familiar tracks, meeting no obstacles; there is no need to wait and consider what response to make (undergoing), and there is therefore no chance to discover the extent of his own potential. In other situations undergoing may come to dominate; all activity becomes inhibited since it arouses anxiety and causes frustration. The individual turns in on himself, conjuring up an often gloomy picture in his imagination of the consequences of the particular activity. What kind of people are likely to develop a pattern of excessive doing? A typical case among the depressed is the person who during his formative years lived almost exclusively for, and with, his parents. He had no opportunity—or at any rate was not encouraged—to test his own resources outside the family circle; on the other hand, he has become pretty adept at handling activities within its narrow range. This pattern is repeated when he builds a family of his own.

Imbalance between doing and undergoing can also often arise in our relations with ourselves, in particular with our own feelings. We talk about what we are doing, how we are feeling, but seldom with any true reflection. We move along in a flow of words that allows no time for stopping and relating our feelings to ourselves or to the real world.

It should now be apparent that *doing* and *undergoing* are closely related to *action opportunities* and *rigid action patterns*. To illustrate the connection between the two sets of concepts I suggest in the model shown in Figure 3 how rigid action patterns and a limited range of possible action may result from

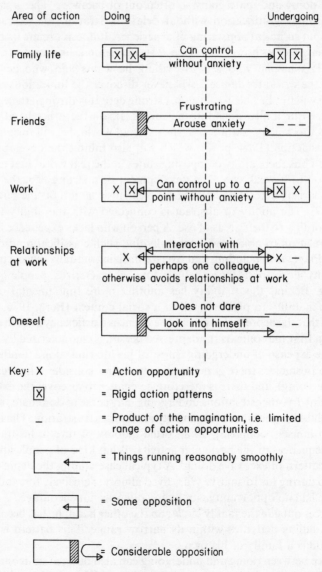

Figure 3 Example of the relation between doing and undergoing in the depressive personality

various negative relations (imbalance) between doing and undergoing. The example corresponds to what I have described as typical of the depressed personality: clear-cut organization of family life, a job that runs smoothly so long as it does not call for too much independent action, a limited number of relationships (probably only one), a general fear of seeking out people whose behaviour is not altogether predictable, and a fear of looking too closely into oneself. But what the model reveals most clearly is that in no area does the depressed person strike a satisfactory balance between doing and undergoing, and this is what lies behind the rigid action patterns and the limited range of action opportunities. The ideal picture should be:

$$\boxed{\text{X X X X X X} \longleftrightarrow \text{X X X X X X}}$$ within many areas,

what Becker calls 'the great soul'.

I have sometimes felt inclined to criticize Becker's theory for being too general, for being applicable to too broad a spectrum of psychological deviations: the narrow range of action opportunities, the rigid patterns of action and low self-esteem all occur in a wide variety of psychological disorders. What, we perhaps feel like asking, characterizes a neurotic compulsion as opposed to a depression? The concepts of doing and undergoing, in conjunction with the structuring of life into distinct areas of action, can help us to understand this and other differences. In the compulsive neurotic, for instance, we find fixations or compulsions of moderate strength in several areas $\boxed{\text{X X } \boxed{\text{X}} \longleftrightarrow \text{X X } \boxed{\text{X}}}$ A person suffering from phobia has a strong specific compulsion in a limited area ($\boxed{\text{X } \boxed{\text{X}} \longleftrightarrow \text{X } \boxed{\text{X}}}$). The schizophrenic, according to Becker, leans too much towards undergoing, and this probably applies in many areas of action ($\boxed{\text{ }}$). Still according to Becker, the opposite probably applies to the so-called psychopath ($\boxed{\text{X X} \longleftarrow}$ in many areas).

I have also found that Becker's theory can help us to understand the specific nature of depression if we apply it in conjunction with certain elements in neo-Freudian theory. In the following sections I shall argue that certain factors composing the concepts of the rigid action pattern and the limited range of action opportunities are particularly marked in the mental disorder we know as depression.

11.2 SOME ELEMENTS OF PSYCHODYNAMIC THEORY AND THEIR RELATION TO BECKER'S CONCEPTS

11.2.1 High unrealized ambitions

The predisposed depressive is distinguished by the unrealistic aspirations he cherishes: he expects from other people an inordinate amount of love, consideration, and attention. He also longs to be socially successful, popular, invincible at school and at work (see, for example Cohen *et al.*, 1954). What Bibring (1953) calls 'highly charged narcissistic aspirations' will thus include:

(1) the wish to be worthy, to be loved, to be appreciated, not to be inferior or unworthy;
(2) the wish to be strong, superior, great, secure, not to be weak and insecure; and
(3) the wish to be good, to be loving, not to be aggressive, hateful and destructive. (p. 24)

It is the failure to live up to these unrealistic ideals that can cause depression. High self-esteem ensues when aspirations and the opportunities for fulfilling them are not too far removed from one another; the danger comes when the gap is too great between what one wants to do and what one can do, with the consequent reduction in self-esteem.

Becker does not present his theory in exactly these terms, but another of his concepts comes close to that of the high narcissistic aspirations, namely the concept of heroism. Becker does not ascribe the desire to be a hero specifically to the depressive personality; but he does claim that the depressed person has failed in his heroic role. Recognizing the absence (or loss) of 'primary value', he becomes depressed. And naturally, if he has set the criterion of primary value far above the level of the possible, the discovery of failure—the absence of self-worth—will be all the more catastrophic.

We have already defined rigid action patterns as meaning that our preparedness for action is set in an unbending mould. We say 'Life *must* be like this to be meaningful', 'I shall be happy *if*...', 'A person in my position *cannot* be weak', etc. All this constitutes a special type of rigidity in our pattern of action: we have a settled notion about the shape of our lives; we have set our preparedness for action above all possibility of change and allowed it to determine—for us—the whole meaning of life.

High unrealistic ambitions can be equated with a limited range of action opportunities. If our preparedness for action has no feasible counterpart in the real world, the substance of our ambitions cannot represent a real action opportunity. Crying out for the impossible means failing to grasp the possible.

11.2.2 Past trauma

According to psychodynamic theory a childhood trauma can be reactivated by some similar event in adult life, to which the adult reacts with apparently exaggerated force. In his subconscious he has returned to the emotionally paralysing event that occurred in his childhood.

Börjeson (1979) cites past trauma as the main explanation of the depression in the following case:

The patient is a 25-year-old woman who a couple of years ago was denied custody of her child. In the acute phase the risk of suicide was considerable; an important element in this experience was that the separation of mother and child revived the woman's own experience of having been abandoned as a child by her own mother. However, the present crisis was overcome and she began to organize her life with social activities, studies and so on. She also managed to establish good contact with her son and his foster parents. But every time her son was due to visit her for any longish period, she became depressed and was unable to meet him. (p. 71; my translation)

Börjeson's explanation of this case was that the meetings with the boy revived his mother's 'betrayal' of him, and that this betrayal in turn reactivated her own original pain at being abandoned by her mother. Börjeson also suggests that the woman's depression was an intentional act, an attempt to protect herself from direct contact with the pain surviving from her own childhood.

Drawing on Becker I have expanded this explanation (Fredén, 1979), suggesting among other things that there was also a grave threat to self-esteem, and that the woman probably had a depressive personality (low self-esteem, limited range of action opportunities, etc.). Why was the child taken from her? This alone represents the negation of herself as both a person and a mother; she becomes—and feels herself to be—'worthless'. The experience of worthlessness, which is central to the depressive personality, is certainly revived when the mother is about to meet her child. Whether or not she already had a depressive personality, the crucial point in her case seems to me to be that the very act of looking after the boy forced her to acknowledge her rejection of him: at the end of their time together she would have to re-enact it and the life they had begun to build up together would inevitably have to be pulled down again. When this happened she would lose many action opportunities and consequently considerable self-esteem, since her life during the period with her child would be focused almost exclusively on him. Thus meeting her son represented a serious threat to her self-esteem.

Let us translate this process into theoretical terms: the past trauma leads in the first place to rigid patterns of action. At the time of the original trauma the individual protects himself from the intrusive pain, perhaps by convincing himself that this *cannot* be true, the reality *must* be something else. He finds it difficult to take in the whole sequence of events, difficult to orientate himself in it. He perhaps manages to cope with some small parts of the whole, and these he clings to with considerable force. In the grip of the rigid action pattern that thus develops he carries within himself the fear of a repetition of the trauma; he might, for example, lose someone he loves. The safest solution seems to be never to commit himself to anyone whom he might lose, and this curtailment naturally reduces the whole range of his action opportunities. To return to the case discussed above: recognition of the risk of losing action opportunities was possibly the precipitating factor in the woman's depression. But her reaction to this recognition would not have been so strong without her self-imposed conviction that she *could not have been* abandoned by her own mother and that her son was the *only* person who could give meaning to her life, and if she had not been so sure that depression *always* afflicted her just when she was about to see the boy (self-fulfilling prophecy).

11.3 EXTERNAL CIRCUMSTANCES

Man does not live in a social vacuum; our lives are dependent on the people with whom we come in contact and on our surroundings in the broadest sense. What external circumstances tend to push us towards rigid action patterns and a limited range of action opportunities?

11.3.1 The structure of society

What are the ideas and actions that command the most approval in our society? In the Western cultures success ranks as the overriding ideal. We must climb the social ladder, we must strive for greater happiness, we must develop our personalities, we must acquire material possessions. The yardsticks of success are 'increase' and 'growth'. Success on both the private and the public stage is achieved by beating others in competition. Linsky (1969) has shown that the incidence of depressive disorders is higher in communities where opportunities for occupational success cannot satisfy the aspirations engendered by the education provided. Linsky assumes that the depressed are people who have wholeheartedly adopted the success ideal but whose chances of fulfilling it have been blocked by the social realities.

Linsky's study reminds us of two ways in which the dominating ideas and actions in a society can affect the risk of depression in the individual: people can become excessively bound up in the dominating social pattern, or they can fail to learn it sufficiently well. Those who acquire influence and self-esteem and who benefit generally from the prevailing social pattern are probably also those who most readily adopt the dominating conception of the 'good life'. But they risk falling into a settled belief that everything will always be the same, and this limits their actions: they see no point in looking beyond the dominating social pattern. The others, who have not learnt or accepted the currently valid tenets of their society, will also find their actions circumscribed because for different reasons and in different degrees they may have been *compelled* to accept a way of living which limits their scope for action. These arguments thus suggest that people who can exert some influence over the societal process and who are not entirely satisfied with present conditions are in the best position as regards external circumstances to enjoy a rich variety of possible action alternatives.

Certain conditions and expectations may attach specifically to different strata in society, thus affecting the predisposition to depression in particular social groups. We have already discussed in various contexts the depressive picture at different social levels and I have suggested reasons for the apparently even spread of depression among these groups. I have assumed that people in the lower social strata have access to fewer actions over which they can exert control, i.e. they have less opportunity to influence their own situation. In the upper social strata, on the other hand, people are expected to exert more control over their actions, which means that they may come to expect life and the world around them to appear in a certain definite guise. Thus the members of the lower social strata generally enjoy fewer action opportunities than those above them on the social scale, while the upper strata tend to adopt action patterns that are over-rigid. I suggest that these two states cancel each other out, and that there is no preponderance of the depressed in any one social class. It would be interesting to try to distinguish the social contexts in which these tendencies (towards limited action repertoires or rigid action patterns) appear to be particularly marked. Which specific groups direct their lives strictly along lines that command prestige to the detriment of their 'true' wishes, and who are the people who are actually able to satisfy such aspirations? To answer this question we would have to examine the entire structure of society (power relationships, the economy, religion, various ideological sentiments, and so on), but a study on such a scale lies outside the scope of the present book.

11.3.2 The structure of the family

The functioning of the family naturally depends on the society of which the family is a part. In particular, the sex-role pattern in the family reflects the distribution of power and the female and male ideals that obtain in society as a whole. In our own Western society we find in the family the woman who exists mainly for others (husband and children), who sees that the family conforms to the social pattern expected of it. The risk is great that families who have adopted the traditional sex-role pattern will transfer the same pattern to the following generation, whose women will continue to lead dependent lives with the consequent restriction on their range of action. And we have seen (Chapter 5) that the main characteristic common to the childhood families of the depressed is *dependence*. People are made dependent on certain ideals and dependent on their parents for the fulfilment of the ideals; at the same time they are given little opportunity to build up their own strength or to formulate their own ideals (see also the case described below).

The structure of society also affects the role of the family by the very importance it ascribes—more perhaps today than before—to the family as a social unit. One of Becker's arguments is that Western society actually advocates the limitation of meaning to a limited number of objects. I interpret this as suggesting that in various ways our society promotes the restricted social unit, namely the nuclear family. The Christian religion emphasizes the role of the family as the pillar of society; economic life follows the same line, supporting the small consumption unit. Thus, as Becker points out, we have few objects in our immediate surroundings, few people to share in providing us with self-esteem. This also means that we have less protection in a crisis.

The risk of depression is aggravated by the speed of change in the modern world: the difference between the social patterns of yesterday and those of today is perhaps greater than ever before. Children learn approved actions from their parents, but the actions that will be able to provide the adult child with self-esteem will often be quite different, particularly if the parents were inflexible in clinging to the dominating social patterns of their own time. The children of such parents, who themselves live in a very changeable society, are particularly badly placed for acquiring new actions or meanings of their own.

The structure of the society and of the family into which we are born provides us with a set of external circumstances that is difficult for us to influence and which defines for us the limits of the possible. The following case is an example of the way in which just these external circumstances may have laid the foundations for the development of a depressive personality.

In her first interview F was a little hesitant at the outset, but once we had started talking she had a great deal to tell. Since she was 14 years old F had suffered long periods of persistent headaches. She had seen the doctor frequently about this, and just before the period we were discussing she had been referred by a private doctor to the neurological department at the hospital. From there she was referred to a small hospital, since her difficulties were believed to be connected with a weight problem. From this second hospital she was subsequently referred to the psychiatric clinic.

She had always believed that her depression stemmed from her headaches, but latterly she had begun to realize that her headaches might be a reaction to other problems. F mentioned repeatedly that other people's opinions of her were important to her, and that she perhaps listened too much to what other people said. She had not discussed her problems with anyone (neither husband, parents, nor anyone else). Both her parents have always dominated her; she has found them very demanding and has had little chance of asserting herself. In addition she has always felt somewhat overshadowed by her elder sister. She has never had a really close friend. It was her mother who decided what sort of work she should do (in an auxiliary branch of the medical profession). Her sister had worked at the same place earlier, before F arrived there, and everyone took it for granted that she would be as capable as her sister had been. Before the depressive period a couple of years ago she had been finding things very difficult at work. The atmosphere was often trying, because two of her colleagues didn't get on well.

F told me that she was often bullied at school; it used to give her stomach pains and made her very frightened. The bullying continued in her first jobs. F has always blamed her troubles on the headaches, particularly to the doctors. She has even blamed things on the headaches when she hasn't actually had one. As she has never been able to talk to anyone about the problems in her relationships with parents, sister, and colleagues, and her general unhappiness at work, the headaches have given her something to fall back on. It was easier to blame them than to try to tackle other, more sensitive issues. F has always felt very unsure of herself; it is important to her that other people should like her. She didn't like saying 'no' when she was asked to do things for other people, but often vented her feelings of frustration in aggressiveness towards those around her. She now realizes that the headaches have been a useful smokescreen to hide behind, when she has felt unable to cope with life.

I met F again a couple of years after the first interview. In the intermediate period she had been able to have continual discussions first with a psychologist and later with a psychiatrist. She was delighted to have been able to throw away her pills. She has found it extremely helpful to be able to talk about her problems to the same person every time. 'I can't pull the wool over their eyes; at the same time I can't be pushed, they have to be patient with me.'

F now produced a few more pieces of the puzzle, which make it easier to understand her problems. She was always overprotected by her parents after being very ill as a small child. At the same time, she felt that once she grew up her parents couldn't be bothered with her. They ran a farm, and F had to find things to do on her own. Ever since her schooldays she has always had difficulty in reading, writing, and arithmetic, and this has done a lot to impair her self-confidence. It hasn't helped that her job calls for skill in both reading and arithmetic. She has always believed that because she got bad marks for arithmetic at school, there was nothing whatsoever the could do to improve things.

F emphasized once again that she used to hide herself and her problems behind the headaches. Her aggressiveness to those around her had the same function: 'They won't turn on me if I show my claws first.' It took a long time before she could admit to her difficulties. She says that she must have been half asleep before; now she has woken up and discovered that what other people say is not everything: she must learn to look at life with her own eyes.

F's early years probably failed to provide her with a basic trust strong enough to help her to face her later problems. She does not appear to have been given the chance to test her own resources (she was overprotected), and when she later had to try out new actions, her parents failed to supply her with a secure base from which to make her forays. The attitude of her sister and schoolfriends added to her uncertainty. Other external circumstances that were difficult for her to master, and which probably led her into rigid action patterns and reduced her action opportunities, were her difficulties in reading and writing and the lack of supportive encouragement at school, the conflicts at work, and the attitude of the first doctors towards her 'illness'. She was also affected by prevailing social attitudes through her parents' emphasis on the success ideal, through the focus at school on performance rather than communal effort, and through the structure of her 'service' profession in which women are almost always occupationally subordinate to men.

11.4 THE DEPRESSIVE PROCESS

I have generally assumed in discussing depressive disorders above that an actual depression is seldom the result of a single isolated event. I have introduced the concept of the 'depressive personality' to describe people who have acquired certain experiences over a long period of time and who are at the greatest risk of reacting to a severe life event with a depressive response. A variety of factors in a composite process ultimately result in a depression. Some of the critical factors in this process have already been discussed in connection with our analysis of Becker's theory. I now suggest that different negative factors dominate at different times in the development of the depression. I have based the following model of the depressive process on the results of the discriminant analysis described in Chapter 2, combined with a synthesis of the investigations presented in the present book, with Becker's theory, with the statements of depressed people, and with some general social–psychological assumptions. One such fundamental social–psychological assumptions is that our conscious mental process and self-perception are the result of social interaction.

It is not, of course, possible to substantiate an abstract model of this type; it remains a construct. Nor can the human psyche be described fully in a model of any kind. Nevertheless, a theoretical model can provide a springboard towards a clearer understanding of the issues. Whether or not the present model does so must be left to the reader's judgement.

The idea for this model came to me originally when I was performing the discriminant analysis of the results of my earlier study (Fredén, 1978). It seemed to me that a very interesting grouping of the variables emerged. The most highly discriminant variables were those which I interpreted as doing *most* to impair action opportunities. Next come two variables which I interpreted as *mainly* affecting rigid action patterns. The third group of variables, which discriminate less clearly between the depressed and the non-depressed, seem to attach *mainly* to external circumstances which are not readily accessible to influence. The discriminating variables are ranked in order below with the main substance of my interpretation of each one. I will not describe here how I came to these conclusions about the specific variables, but the interested reader can refer to the analyses in the earlier chapters. As has been mentioned before, the questions put to the respondents concerned the period before the onset of a depressive or negative period.

In comparison with the non-depressed, the depressed showed higher ratings in the following dimentions:

	Interpretation
(1) Lack of depth in partner relationship	Limited range of possible action
(2) Occurrence of depression prior to the study period	Limited range of possible action
(3) Demand in partner relationship	Rigid action patterns
(4) Dominating parents	Rigid action patterns
(5) Initiates social activities	(Results contradictory)
(6) Experience of severe life events	External circumstances inaccessible to influence
(7) Non-significant partner bond	Limited range of possible action
(8) Mother working during respondent's childhood	External circumstances inaccessible to influence

(9) Lack of independent tasks at work   External circumstances inaccessible
to influence

Several conclusions can be drawn from this scheme. Perhaps the most obvious one is that access to a limited range of action opportunities has the greatest impact on the probability of a depression developing. Also important, though slightly less so, is the presence of rigid action patterns. And less important than either of these are external conditions that are difficult for the subject to influence. But a certain amount of caution is required before we can accept such an explanation.

The first reason for caution is that the period to which the questions (the variables) refer is the six-month period before the onset of an acute depression. But the depression may have been *in the making* for quite a long time, since a person entering upon a depressive process has often already been involved in a much longer-lasting process which I have called the development of the depressive personality. The questions in my study were concerned mainly with the period during which the individual feared a loss of self-esteem or when self-esteem had already suffered some impairment. But whatever it was that originally paved the way for the depression generally lies far back in time. Thus the explanation suggested above needs some adjustment. The following modified version appears reasonable (and is not contradicted by the discriminant analysis): namely that access to a limited variety of action opportunities has the greatest implications in an *acute crisis*, while the origins of the depressive personality are much more closely linked with restrictions imposed on the actions of an individual as a result of external circumstances over which he has little or no control.

The general depressive process as I envisage it can be divided into five stages (or perhaps we should call them elements, since there is no clear chronological order between the first four, but rather a continual series of interconnections);

(1) Restrictive circumstances extrinsic to the individual over which he can exert little or no influence
(2) Rigid action patterns
(3) Limited range of possible actions
(4) Self-esteem threatened or impaired
(5) Depression.

It should be noted that not all elements or stages, apart from the threat to self-esteem, are necessary conditions for the development of a depression. If the loss of self-esteem—or even the threat of loss—is more or less total, touching on the whole individual and affecting his whole life, most people would become depressed even without previous restrictions on their range of action opportunities or the presence of rigid action patterns. But the risk of depression is certainly greater if one or more of these stages has preceded the present threat to self-esteem. It is also important to remember that, as the argument in earlier chapters has many times confirmed, all these factors affect one another in a

170

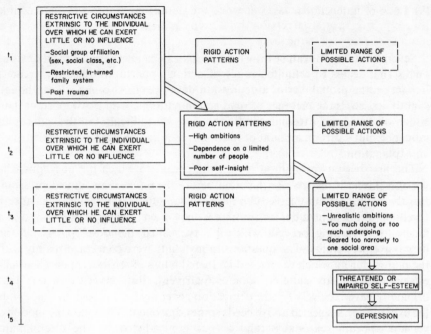

Figure 4 The depressive process

complicated pattern of interaction; there is no simple causal relationship. What we have identified here are important *general tendencies*.

Under some of the conceptual labels in Figure 4 I have entered certain factors that seem to me to affect the development of that particular state (rigid action patterns, limited range of action, etc.). The same point should be made here as in the case of the main determinants of depression: the risk of restriction on the range of actions, for instance, will be greater if more of these factors are present. These factors can perhaps also help us to identify the particular nature of the depressive process as compared with other psychological disorders.

Figure 4 thus illustrates the process that leads to the risk of depression in the individual. The most important factor in any period has been marked by double lines, the next most important by single lines, and the least important by broken lines. The first period or stage (t_1) towards the development of a depressive personality may have begun in the first years of life or in adulthood with the imposition of restrictive extrinsic limits on action opportunities. A woman brought up to adopt the traditional female role, for example, has inadequate opportunities for investigating the world for herself. A worker trapped by strictly systematized work routines is another example of the individual whose repertoire of possible actions and whose opportunities for directing his own actions towards desired goals are both severely limited by his social affiliation. The family into which he is born also represents, at least during the early years, a set of circumstances over which he has very little control. If his family is a closed system with very settled expectations regarding behaviour (norms) and little allowance for reciprocity in internal relationships (giving and taking), the growing child will naturally be formed in the same mould. The demanding attitude to children, the dominance and lack of openness, are passed on from generation to generation. Past trauma, another example of external circumstances over which it is difficult to exert control, may spring from conditions in society or in the family. The crucial factor here is probably some *single* event, sometimes just a chance event, which curtails the individual's repertoire of action and binds him to a particular type of behaviour.

Inflexible and restrictive external circumstances lead all too often to rigid patterns of behaviour (t_2). Since the scope for action has been narrowed down by the impositions of society and the family, it becomes important for the individual to succeed at least within these narrow confines, particularly as both society and the family have told him that happiness means finding the one great love or amassing great material wealth. Socially, the crucial element in the rigid pattern of action is that it leaves the individual dependent on a limited number of people for his self-esteem. This in turn means that on the psychological plane he often has poor self-insight. It is worth examining a little more closely the way in which these factors can interact.

Our culture, and our society as a whole, promotes and encourages the small social unit; as children we become dependent in the family on one or two people, and when we build a family of our own we are once again dependent on the other members for the experience of being loved and valued. In my earlier study I found that couples including one depressed partner often scored low on mutual confiding contact. Presumably the two people concerned were able to talk relatively openly with one another on certain topics. It is easier to discuss actions connected with external circumstances (the social level) than to talk about anything touching on the deep inner self (the personal level). Feelings, the experience of life's problems, the perception of the partner relationship—all these can be very hard to discuss together. And sadly it is just this sensitive area which is likely to be relevant to any subsequent depressive problems. The precipitating factor that finally reduces self-esteem to a critical level is generally a change in some aspect of life to which the individual particularly clings. One partner (perhaps the woman) may have convinced herself that her man will always be there, that he will always be the same as he was when she first met him, that he will go on providing a secure anchor in her life (perhaps the secure anchor that was missing in childhood). Here we have an example of high and unrealistic ambitions, and of the danger of building up our lives around a single other. In another case, a couple have perhaps never spoken to one another about their anxieties, about what might happen to either of them, or about any complicated feelings they may have developed about each other. Then something happens (gradually or suddenly) in one of their lives and now, when it has really become important, one partner has no idea how the other feels and thinks, reactions become mutually incomprehensible, and neither partner can predict the behaviour of the other. The secure self-esteem which they at least believed they possessed quickly collapses. The action opportunities on which their self-esteem was based are no longer available, life has lost its meaning. Here we have an example of rigid action patterns preceding the curtailment of action opportunities in the depressive process.

My argument is that it is necessary to be able to see alternatives (to have access to meanings) and to be able to exploit them (to have access to actions) when an untenable situation arises *regardless* of whether or not the individual clings rigidly to any of the alternatives. That restrictions on action opportunities and rigid action patterns develop in a process of mutual generation is another matter altogether (see Becker's hypotheses, p. 131).

Thus when self-esteem is threatened or reduced it is very important to have access to some alternative action which can replenish the stock (t_3). It may not be possible to redeem the threatened area of action, perhaps because it is too strongly controlled, but its relative importance (and therefore the effect of its loss) will not be as great if the individual has access to other actions which enhance his self-esteem. Moreover, access to a variety of action alternatives gives him an opportunity to understand the effect on his own feelings of the events that have occurred. This alone may help him to keep a sense of proportion and not to exaggerate the size of the threat.

What type of restriction on action opportunities is most critical in the depressive process? In the typical case there is likely to be much external activity in the conventional areas of life (e.g. the domestic structure, leisure-time activities) but feelings have not been brought out into the open. Thus in certain contexts there has been too much doing and in others too much undergoing. There is a lack of harmony between what the individual does and what he thinks, and the imbalance between the psychological and the social aspects is reflected on the psychological and social planes: if action opportunities are linked too firmly to external or interior activity (i.e. to doing or undergoing) the consequences of a threat to self-esteem can be more serious. Another facet of the limited range of action opportunities appears when the repertoire of action is restricted to a *single* social area. If, for example, a woman's action opportunities are limited exclusively to the home, she runs a greater risk of becoming depressed than she would if her repertoire of possible actions embraced several different areas (work, family, friends, etc.). A rather different restriction arises when an individual cherishes high ambitions which he has not learnt how to handle or which are beyond his abilities; this constitutes an absence of action opportunities that must weigh heavily upon him.

The first three stages or elements in the depressive process I have described are closely linked with the major human motives we have discussed earlier: external circumstances that are inaccessible to influence raise the avoidance of anxiety to the level of a primary goal, and self-esteem is reduced; rigid action patterns are enforced in order to keep anxiety and fear of the uncertain at bay; the limited range of action opportunities reduces self-esteem, which in turn renders the individual more vulnerable in any crisis involving a further threat to his already fragile sense of self-value.

Drawing on neo-Freudian theory I have assumed that threatened or impaired self-esteem (t_4) is a necessary condition of depression in the individual. But the threat to self-esteem is connected with the presence of rigid action patterns and a limited range of action opportunities. We can thus formulate the following hypothesis: *there is a greater probability of threat to self-esteem if the individual is rigid in his patterns of action, but the threat to self-esteem is much less likely to lead to depression if he has access to a variety of action opportunities.* If action patterns are rigid, only a limited number of fixed actions will contribute to the individual's self-esteem, only a few acts can provide him with a satisfactory feeling of mastery. But society and human relationships are changing all the time, and some action once mastered may cease to be valid. We can take the case of the elderly elementary-school teacher who has always lived for his school, who expects obedience and wants the pupils to listen quietly while he talks. In schools today the pupils are tougher, projects and joint activities are encouraged; the elderly teacher's established skills are becoming a burden to him since their value is constantly being called in question. All this must constitute a great threat to his self-esteem, but if he has a variety of other interest outside and perhaps even inside the school which continue to give him satisfaction and self-confidence, the risk of a depression developing need not be so very great.

We have already discussed various factors which can threaten or reduce self-esteem. The most menacing problems seem to be those that touch upon the inner life, e.g. separation, problems in the pair relationship, and family difficulties. In crises of this kind the individual is often cut off from objects or actions that previously brought him satisfaction; but what is probably more important is the change in his inner life that prevents him from finding happiness or security in the earlier actions. It is difficult for anyone else to find solutions for him since the reduction in self-esteem may not solely be linked directly to specific losses of possible actions. It is probably just when the threat to self-esteem is of a *complex* nature (internal and external) that it is particularly important to have access to a variety of action opportunities, particularly to action opportunities with strong inner roots (meanings).

It is thus when people neither *have* nor can *see* any alternatives with which to meet a threat to self-esteem that depression becomes a probability (t_5). The depression can be explained as an attempt to regain or compensate for lost self-worth (see, for example Curt Adler in Arieti and Bemporad, 1978). The depressed individual exploits his own weakness, craving satisfaction without the assumption of responsibility. Giving way to his depressive feelings thus provides one way of regaining control over his actions (and of achieving self-esteem). At the same time, however, his manipulations of others arouse feelings of guilt in those around him.

Irritated, yet inhibited and increasingly guilt-ridden, members of the social environment continue to give verbal assurance of support and acceptance. However, a growing discrepancy between the verbal content and the affective quality of these responses provides validation for the depressive's suspicions that he is not really being accepted and that further interaction cannot be assured. To maintain his increasingly uncertain security, the depressive displays more symptoms. (Coyne, 1976, p. 34)

The depression thus becomes a self-fulfilling prophecy. The depressed person is desperately seeking confirmation of his own importance in the interactions he maintains with other people, but his actions tend to have a negative effect on those around him, eliciting guilt-ridden reactions that make it difficult for them to show genuine consideration or to reassure the depressed person of his value to them.

The experience of depression can in turn affect the way in which the depressive continues to deal with the realities surrounding him. He has probably become afraid of future rejections; at the same time he has learnt—perhaps unconsciously—to exploit the manipulative techniques that depression involves. He may cling inflexibly to some objects or some people whom he can control, doing everything possible to avoid losing them. In this connection the reader should remember that the model described above allows for circular effects, i.e. the various stages in the depressive process can affect and reinvoke one another. To help someone out of the vicious circle of the depressive process it may be necessary to be able to step in on several levels and at several stages.

We can conclude this analysis of the depressive process by examining a case in which the different stages or elements seem to be distinguished fairly clearly.

P is a 25-year-old woman who has been depressed four or five times since 1971. She once spent six weeks in a psychiatric ward and was diagnosed as suffering from neurotic depression. The first depressive period occurred when P moved from the home she was sharing with her then boy-friend. At the time of the break she suffered from headaches and became irritable. P saw a neurologist about her headaches, and he referred her to the psychiatric clinic. P did not think she needed psychiatric help, but she followed the neurologist's advice. Her ex-boy-friend also advised her to see the psychiatrist.

P rang me up herself when she received an introductory letter about my investigation. She was eager for an interview and was worried in case we should be unable to reach her at her house. P is now living alone in one of the old parts of Uppsala, where she has been working for the last four years at a children's day centre. P had a difficult childhood. Her parents divorced when she was 2 years old and things were never easy with her step-father. He owned a small shop, where P's mother also worked. The shop ran into financial problems, and P's mother became depressed and had to seek medical help. It should perhaps be mentioned that P's only sister has also been depressed and was in touch with a psychiatrist after being divorced.

P seems to have been unable to liberate herself from her mother's influence; throughout her childhood she lacked a reliable father figure. The boy-friend with whom she lived at the beginning of the 1970s became her whole life. He was a policeman and had to move on account of his work. P went with him and organized her life completely to fit in with his. He was very dominating and jealous. Their leisure-time companions were almost all old friends of his. In fact, however, they spent most of their time on their own. P's problem is probably connected with her need to cope for herself. This is confirmed by the positive periods she mentions; two years ago she left another boy-friend and moved into the flat where she now lives. She thoroughly enjoyed being on her own and she began to meet her sister more often. She felt free to do what she wanted. She has now found lots of new friends and has plenty of new leisure-time activities that really interest her. She is also undergoing individual psychotherapy with a psychologist.

An interview with P's sister a few days later filled out the picture. As an outside observer the sister had considered P's relationship with her boy-friend to be a very good one. The two of them were all in all to one another; nothing else had any importance. After the separation P met several rather 'odd' people, including her own alcoholic father who introduced her into his circle of friends. When P met a new boy she would compare him with her former boy-friend; none of the new ones came up to scratch. During the depressive period P often visited her sister, but it was difficult for the sister to get through to her although P obviously found some sort of security in the other woman's company. P did not want to talk about her problems, and it was always the sister who brought up the subject. The sister also tried to get P not to drink strong liquor: whenever she drank P would suffer acute feelings of anxiety. She was afraid her mother would find out about her drinking. When P was depressed her mother didn't want to meet her. She was afraid of a confrontation with her daughter's problems. She had a bad conscience about P, suspecting that the step-father's attitudes were all part of the trouble. P's first boy-friend rang up P's mother and told her about the depressions and the drinking. Naturally P objected to this and disliked the feeling that people didn't trust her.

When I asked P's sister what in her view helped P to get over her depression she said it was the fact that P had embarked on a new way of life. She stopped going about with her old friends with their bad drinking habits. By that time P's sister was divorced and had more free time; the two sisters became closer. P's sister also mentioned work as a positive factor: P has always been appreciated by the children and their parents, and her job has forced her to keep on her toes.

The first stage in the depressive process, in which the individual is exposed to restrictive external circumstances that are inaccessible to influence, seems here to coincide with P's difficult and circumscribed family situation during childhood. These years were marked by the mother's depression, the conflicts between mother and step-father, the financial problems—all conditions which P must have felt powerless to alter. She may even have experienced her parents' divorce, when she was 2 years old, as a trauma; she was first abandoned by her father and later—as she may perhaps have felt—by her mother, who 'abandoned' her for the step-father. This first stage (or element) in the depressive process is also reflected in P's present social affiliation involving a typical female occupation and low-status job that requires her constant adaptation to terms dictated by other people.

The strong ties with the mother and the poor relationship with the step-father added to the lopsidedness of P's emotional world and made it more difficult for her to develop a life of her own. The second stage, which sees the development of rigid action patterns, is mainly reflected in P's clinging dependence on a single person: in childhood and adolescence this was her mother and in adult life her boy-friend. The expectations that these two nursed with regard to P simply compounded the rigid pattern of behaviour that her dependence upon them was engendering. The fear and anxiety that surrounded her drinking, the striving to do as she was bid, are signs that she had bound up her idea of self in others: 'If I want to be good, this is how I must behave.'

By binding up her life with that of her boy-friend, P set narrow limits on her own range of action opportunities (stage or element 3 in the depressive process). She never had the chance to develop actions of her own. P's progress since the depressive periods also suggests that what she previously lacked was any choice of actions based upon herself and her own needs. Following her entry upon a deeper and freer mode of contact with her sister, she was gradually able to build up the courage to start steering her own life. Another inhibiting factor, before this development, may have been the unrealistic nature of her ideas about the possibilities of love (stemming probably from the absence of a father figure) which seems to have become more marked as she compared all subsequent boy-friends with her own idealized conception of the first one.

The threat to self-esteem (stage 4) must have seemed overwhelming at the time of the separation, since P's whole life had been bound up in the relationship with the boy-friend. When the break came she was left almost without friends or interests of her own, i.e. she had no repertoire of alternative actions that could give positive value to her view of herself. She also found it difficult to explain and understand her own reactions, and the depression was a fact (stage 5). It seems to me that even the headaches and the visit to the neurologist were evidence of deficient self-insight. And once again her mother and her boy-friend had to tell her what the position was and what she should do about it.

CHAPTER 12

No way out?

What can be done for the depressed? Is there no way out of depression? How can we organize our lives and, ultimately, our society so that people do not become depressed? The reader must have had such questions in mind during our exmination of the mechanisms apparently underlying depression. Up to now we have concentrated on the causes of depression, although various ways of preventing depressive disorders and helping the depressed patient have naturally been glimpsed in the course of the argument. Now, however, it is time to consider these various measures in their own right, and to suggest which of them may in certain instances be more appropriate than others.

I must remind the reader that I am not a medical practitioner and that I therefore have no personal experience of the various forms of therapy. My aim is simply to indicate some of the therapies and preventive measures which are available and which accord with the theoretical conclusions we have reached in the course of this book. The reader who requires more specific advice could either turn to the books and papers listed in the References or contact an experienced psychotherapist.

Before discussing some general preventive measures I will briefly recapitulate the arguments propounded in the earlier chapters. The title of the Swedish version of this book, *Att sakna möjligheter*, means literally 'to lack opportunities'. This phrase goes to the heart of the problem of depression, on the perceptual as well as the social level. A depressed person often feels that no opportunities are open to him. He cannot see any meaningful way ahead; he cannot influence the people who constitute his world. He may feel that none of the objects or activities which previously gave him satisfaction are available to him any longer. And his sense of powerlessness, of helplessness, is not engendered in a social vacuum: the depressed individual does not only *experiences* a lack of opportunities—his opportunities for creating a meaningful life for himself *are* often genuinely restricted.

Naturally, there is no simple relationship here. What I have called a man's inner life (perceptions, experiences, and so on) and his external life (actions) affect one another continually in a complex process of interaction. Nor should we forget that man is *both* a social *and* a biological being. Biological factors alone cannot predispose a person to depression, but various biological conditions may affect his ability to cope with severe stress.

What kind of circumstances can result in the contraction of an individual's range of possible action and his loss of confidence in his own possibilities? If we limit ourselves to the depressed, we find that the partner relationship emerged as the most important factor in our empirical investigation—hardly a surprising result, since the partner is generally the most frequent companion, the person who has the greatest impact on the individual's self-esteem, who can provide him with secure ground for his sense of self-value. It is the loss of self-esteem that precipitates the depression. Self-esteem grows from the feeling of being master of one's own actions. If it is 'the other' who mainly decides what an individual does and how he should live, then what he does and what he believes he can do will surely be severely limited. This kind of narrowed range of opportunities is common among the depressed, although it need not necessarily have originated within the partner bond. On the contrary, the narrow range of possible actions has often become an established fact in childhood. People who had difficulty in testing their own resources in their early years, perhaps because of their parents' restrictive attitude, are often the same ones who later find it difficult to try their own wings in the partner relationship. A man (or woman) who enters into a relationship with a weak ego faces the risk that his limitations, real and perceived, will be reinforced. At the beginning of a new friendship many people are eager to *bind* themselves to the other person, adopting what they believe to be the other's meanings and opportunities, probably because their own repertoire of possible actions is inadequate. But this tendency to believe that one has understood and rendered certain and predictable other people's actions (and even one's own) can constitute a serious risk in a stressful situation. If a person has taught himself to regard 'the other' in a very definite light, he will see no alternative way of understanding unexpected developments in either or both of their lives.

I also found in my investigation that a large proportion of those who became depressed had difficulty in talking freely with their partners. People who cannot talk to one another are denied an important means of learning to understand their own situation, of recognizing the circumscribed nature of their opportunities. 'Why does he treat me like this? What makes him happy? What upsets him? Can I talk to him about my worries?' If two people can communicate with one another on these important issues, they will each find it easier to understand reactions in the other that differ from their own, since they have both learnt to know a *whole* other person. It will also be easier for them to extend their own opportunities, easier to see life from several vantage points.

In the previous chapters I have focused mainly on the partner relationship and, to some extent, on the relationship with parents. It is important to emphasize, however, that the arguments can be applied to any 'others' who occupy an important position in our lives: close friends, work colleagues, and so on. Work normally represents an important area of activities. People who have been compelled to accept a limited range of possible actions in their jobs probably run a greater risk of becoming depressed at work and even away from it. In my study I found among the depressed a preponderance of people whose jobs provided little in the way of responsible tasks. Another important sphere of action for a long period in our lives is school. Many people, it seems to me, lose confidence there in their own opportunities to 'make something of themselves'.

Thus conditions in the family, among friends, at school, and at work, can all contribute to the constriction of the range of possible actions in our inner lives and in our lives in the real world. Even if we lose a major component of our self-esteem we are less likely to become depressed if we have access to a wide range of possible actions and if we are confidently aware of their availability. Loss of self-esteem usually occurs because something which previously provided us with satisfaction is no longer available to us. But if we have other satisfying actions to which we can turn, the loss will not seem so severe. We have access to other ways of maintaining self-esteem. It is much harder to throw off the emotional and practical paralysis that accompanies depression if our access to action alternatives is severely limited. We may find ourselves caught in a vicious circle: because of our limited range of possible actions we lose confidence in our own possibilities; because we have no self-confidence we are afraid of trying out new actions; because we dare not test new actions, the range of those available to us shrinks even more until in the end the situation becomes untenable, life loses its meaning, and we sink into a severe depression.

The individual's social life forms part of the much wider context which we call society. Society defines the limits of the permissible; in other words it limits the range of actions available to its members. The underprivileged generally have less room within which to act; the privileged, on the other hand, often cling eagerly to a particular way of life, so that their behaviour is prone to set in rigid action patterns. Societies thus generate systems of rules and ideas (ideologies) and are subject to economic realities which affect groups and individuals *in different ways*, with the result that some of their members have greater access than others to a wide range of action alternatives while others are more likely to develop rigid patterns of action.

An important point to emerge from this summary is that measures for the prevention or amelioration of depression must be applied at several different levels. We can distinguish four main levels, all of which influence one another:

Level 1: Society and its institutions
Level 2: Primary groups (family, friends, school, work)
Level 3: External life—what people do
Level 4: The inner life—perceptions, motivations, and experiences.

Successful 'treatment' will require investigation of more than one of these levels. Let us consider, for example, a woman who feels she is no good at anything' and whose self-confidence is meagre. It may be possible to bring her to a revaluation of herself with the help of insight therapy or perhaps behaviour therapy. But what happens next? She presumably returns to her old activities at work or at home, activities which at least in the eyes of the primary group (and possibly matching what some of them actually want) often end in failure. Naturally, the risk of failure is less if the therapist has succeeded in reinforcing the patient's self-confidence, but the social situation which is undermining her self-confidence persists. Moreover, both she and her primary group are exposed to the influence of society: the economy determines her role as an object unable to influence her own work situation; the prevailing ideology determines her role as a subordinate dependent on her husband and tells her that happiness consist of commanding respect, of being able to consume, of making a husband happy. Conversely, if we want to help a person prone to depression it is not enough to recommend changes in society and in the subject's social situation; she carries within herself a self-image and an idea of reality which will not change simply because we change the world.

The rest of this chapter is divided into three sections. The first of these-—'Preventive measures'—refers mainly to level 1, society and its institutions. The two later sections—'How can we help the depressed?' and 'General therapeutic procedures'—are concerned chiefly with the relationships between levels 2, 3, and 4.

12.1 PREVENTIVE MEASURES

How can we change society and alter our way of life to reduce the risk of depression? A first aim must be to create opportunities (action alternatives) for people to influence their life situations in all contexts, great and small. Principles of child rearing and the societal context in which it occurs are both of great importance here. What legacy do our parents bequeath to us from the first years of our lives? Of crucial importance, particularly as regards the predisposition to depression in the adult, is that during the first years of life the child is able to try out new actions and investigate the world about him in an atmosphere of security and encouragement. Arieti (in Arieti and Bemporad, 1978) refers to a study reported by Parker (1962). Parker had compared the Ojibwa Indians with Eskimo tribes living under similar ecological and geographical conditions. It was found that the Ojibwa Indians had a high rate of depression, while the Eskimos had hardly any depressive disorders at all; on the other hand they demonstrated more frequent hysterical attacks. Child-rearing customs were quite different in the two tribes. The Eskimo children were treated kindly and protected from suffering. The children were not expected to earn the love of those around them; there were few restrictions on behaviour and great tolerance of sexual curiosity. The Ojibwa Indian children were reared according to quite other principles. The child was made to feel responsible for his misfortunes; he was expected to suffer in order to expiate his sins. In this way the Ojibwa Indian child learnt to be afraid of venturing upon new actions. His range of alternatives was cramped, which probably helps to explain his predisposition to depression in adult life.

From the socio-political point of view it is pertinent to ask which social groups are least well placed to provide their children with stimulation and basic trust. Immigrants, for instance, presumably start off at a disadvantage in this respect. Immigrant parents have abandoned their old social community in favour of an unknown and therefore uncertain future. The local language, which provides a means of comprehending and influencing the real world, is denied them. The immigrant generally has to accept low-status jobs which offer little chance of acquiring self-esteem. These and other factors obviously reduce the range of opportunities available to him, and it is hardly surprising if he feels trapped in a situation from which he can see no way out. Nor is this the end of the story: the parent who feels insecure, who can see no openings, will pass on the same pessimistic picture to his children (the social legacy). Immigrant children suffer from a double feeling of insecurity since the rules and *meanings* which they learn at school and from their friends often conflict with those of their parents. What, then, can give them a basic trust?

Others who probably find it difficult to provide themselves and their children with security and stimulation are 'immigrants' within their own country: people who have been compelled to leave their homes, perhaps to look for work elsewhere, and who therefore often find themselves living in a socially insecure setting. Life is also emotionally insecure for those without any jobs, and for families with two parents working outside the home and no adequate care available for the children. In all these examples the scope for action is limited for both children and adults.

The most obvious preventive measure is to organize society so that people do not have to move, so that they can keep their jobs, and so that adequate care is provided for their children. In other words, social policy should be orientated towards human needs (the need for security, continuity, community, self-esteem) rather than being subordinated exclusively to economic principles. It is also important that people should have more opportunity to control and assume responsibility for their own life situations. To be able to influence the work setting, to be able to choose where to live—such powers must surely extend the individual's range of possible actions.

Living arrangements should be organized so as to promote all possible areas of contact. Residential areas can be planned in such a way as to encourage people to meet one another, among other things by the provision of adequate premises for community activities. The tendency to withdraw into privacy needs counteracting. Similarly, tasks at work should be regarded as a common responsibility, and teamwork rather than individual activities encouraged.

Common to all these preventive measure is the implication that people should be able to control their own situations, that they need to be close to others with whom they can feel security and community of purpose. Society seems to me, however, to be moving in the opposite direction; powerlessness and the forces of individualism are on the march. Unless we can reverse this trend, the numbers of the depressed, the alcoholics, and the drug addicts are likely to increase.

What elements in a society tend to reinforce rigid action patterns in the individual? At first sight, development in our Western world may appear much more hopeful on this count. We live, so we are constantly being told, in a pluralistic society with many channels of communication and special organizations, and a wide spectrum of values is to be found in our culture. In contrast to this optimistic picture we have what Marcuse (1968) called the one-dimensional society, in which he includes both the capitalist and the communist worlds. Economic development—and even more markedly technological development —have become ends in themselves, swallowing up other possible cultural values such as creativity, community of purpose, intellectual freedom, and a just distribution of societal resources. Marcuse claims that the one-dimensional society has spawned the one-dimensional man who, caught up in mass production and mass consumption, identifies himself with society as a whole. Technology, mass production, and mass consumption swallow the *entire* man, while suffocating his 'true needs'. In both East and West the continual desire to consume makes men slaves to the ruling bureaucratic or economic interests. The individual is so manipulated and indoctrinated that satisfaction of his consumption needs comes to absorb all his thoughts, feelings and desires; he has no need to think, feel, or desire anything on his own. The message disseminated by the media is intended to elicit a specific response from the reader or listener; the scope for individual interpretation and association is reduced to a minimum. Thus Marcuse. The reader may well consider his view of society and modern man to be on the pessimistic side, but it accords very closely with the concept of the rigid action pattern as I have described it here.

Our society appears to project a very definite idea of what is meant by 'the good life'. It is a rather narrow and simple picture, promoting material welfare and consumption as the one and only road to happiness. Success is measured in money and in steps up the status hierarchy. Heroes are those who reap success in the market place, e.g. in the *entertainment* or *sports industries*. The symbols of heroic glory are clothes and other consumer goods; worship involves the exposure in the mass media of the hero's private life, which mainly means love with a capital L. The political parties all aim at roughly the same goals, differences between the parties being reduced to a minimum.

Power *per se* is the paramount value. Trade union organizations and political parties both fight to promote the material welfare of their own members. *One* way of life is assumed by all to be the best.

If we accept this description we can then ask ourselves which groups in society cling most firmly to the rigid action patterns. It seems to me that two essentially different groups should be mentioned. First, there are those who possess no resources, who have neither knowledge nor language at their disposal and who therefore lack the means to examine critically the ideals placed before them. Secondly, we have those who put the ideals on offer in the political and economic markets, who profit from promoting the political and economic goods.

Preventive action at the societal level would mean providing the first of these groups with the instruments and knowledge necessary for questioning the accepted conception of the 'good' or the 'right' life. One way of achieving this would be to inject into society, within the broadest cultural framework, the notion that no *single* way of life is necessarily the best. Mass-produced culture, whose primary aim is to sell, would have to accept restrictions, but culture in general (films, stage drama, literature, art) should all be given more scope. Other institutions such as the mass media and schools which disseminate ideas about the nature and potential of things, i.e. which spread the ideological message, should be free in the true sense of the word: free from market forces, free from political decision makers, and free from bureaucratic controls. By expanding the boundaries of those with little resources, by providing the underprivileged with the opportunity to question accepted ideas, we will also have made it more difficult for the other group to profit from the propagation of a single fixed ideal (consumption and 'success').

In one group in particular role expectations are especially prone to result in rigid action patterns, namely among women. And among the depressed we do in fact find a great preponderance of women. Women are often taught to adapt themselves to what other people (i.e. men) tell them to do or to be. As well as this expectation of general dependence on men, there is also the special and very definite expectation of finding the Great Love (in the extreme case the woman exists only for the man in her life). Naturally, men are also the subject of definite or rigid expectations, but in their case the expectations generally involve opportunities for action, opportunities to command. One potent way of preventing depression could thus 'simply' be to alter the traditional female (and therefore also the male) roles. There have been a great many developments in this area in recent years, particularly as a result of campaigning by the women's movement. But much still needs to be done: child care, wages in typically 'female' occupations, the relative number of women politicians, the mass-produced women's weekly magazines—in all these areas improvements or alternatives are badly needed.

Up to now we have been looking at preventive measures on the societal level. But measures can also be directed towards particular groups or individuals who are at great risk of becoming depressed. In the kind of society we have today, with its lack of community affiliations, we need 'professional' groups whose task is to reach people in common crisis situations, such as divorce, bereavement, or serious illness. The fundamental necessity is to help people to work through their problems, particularly in the absence of relatives or friends who could provide adequate support. Hinchcliffe *et al.* (1978) cite Gerald Caplan:

He has demonstrated that it is possible to organize in society, at a neighbourhood level, various agents who can be seen as resource people and who are available to others at risk in times of crisis. These resource people come from a variety of backgrounds, including professional workers, such as psychologists, social workers, medical personnel, and the clergy. (p. 130)

But the resource people to whom we can turn in times of crisis need not necessarily be professionals in the original meaning of the word. Hinchcliffe *et al.* mention the various lay groups which are appearing in increasing numbers in Western societies. They consist of people who because of their own experience of crises now want to pass on their knowledge to others in similar situations. There are groups for the divorced, for battered wives, for parents bereaved of a child, and so on; in all these groups the members work on a basis of their common experience of the various crises. The great advantage of these groups is probably that no member need feel at a disadvantage. An important element in the depressive syndrome is the feeling of failure and inferiority, so that if it is possible to feel on an equal footing in the therapeutic relationship, much has been gained.

And it is often more difficult to achieve this feeling of equality in relation to a professional therapist complete with status label and the symbolical white coat which marks the distance between patient and therapist, saying in effect, '*I* am here to help *you.*' Naturally, however, many psychologists, doctors, social workers, and others can also feel empathy for their patients and avoid exploiting their position of power. Added to which the professional therapist has the advantage of his knowledge of the depressive process and of the therapeutic procedures which can help to persuade the depressed person out of his blocked emotional state. Given this technical but real difference between therapist and patient, there is some risk attached to pretending to equality; the difference should rather be brought out into the open, after which the therapist should refrain as far as possible from exploiting his position.

Family therapy groups are a good example of crisis therapy as a preventive measure. Öberg and Öberg (1979) describes work with families in conflict over the custody of children. In most cases of divorce the court decides, after lengthy deliberations and investigations, which parent shall have custody of the children. The Öbergs point out that this means encouraging people to speak *ill* of one another instead of speaking *to* one another in order to reach the best solution for all parties. The weaknesses and faults of the parents are emphasized, with all the attendant risks of shattered self-esteem and subsequent depression. The aim of the Öbergs' crisis therapy was to get the husbands and wives to talk *to* each other, to collaborate and assume joint responsibility for the children. After undergoing this kind of therapy eleven of fifteen couples in their study reached agreement on the question of custody. I agree with the Öbergs practical suggestion that

parents in conflict over the custody of their children should be offered crisis therapy. It is important that the court and social welfare authority support such a procedure and require of the parents that they negotiate with one another, accept the necessity of compromise, learn to cooperate, and finally to make the decision on the custody of the children themselves. (p. 580)

Action of this kind may prevent the development of a depression in either one of the parents and will almost certainly help to prevent it in the children.

12.2 HOW CAN WE HELP THE DEPRESSED?

The most common methods of treatment for the depressed who seek professional help are psychodrug therapy and electroconvulsive treatment, neither of which methods need be described here. Psychodrug therapy can be very useful in reducing distress. The severely depressed person suffering from acute feelings of guilt, crushed by despair and unable to see joy anywhere, can be made to feel slightly better. Drugs can help him to take the first step out of the depths of depression, so that it becomes possible for him to start to discuss his situation. Bemporad (1978) points out that in cases of mild depression psychodrugs have a positive effect chiefly on somatic symptoms such as poor appetite, poor sleep, and psychomotor retardation. Psychotherapy, on the other hand, is most effective in getting patients to function socially and raising their self-esteem.

Arieti (in Arieti and Bemporad, 1978) acknowledges the value of psychodrugs in cases of severe depression, but stresses the importance of complementing them and following them up with psychotherapy to prevent the individual from retaining the psychological 'equipment potentialities and vulnerabilities' that provided the soil for the original depression.

The inherent risk attaching to drug therapy is that we may be satisfied with it: some symptoms have disappeared, the patient is beginning to function more efficiently, so why embark on long and time-consuming psychotherapy? Both patient and doctor may come to think along these lines. The patient is released from responsibility for his situation; he can simply take his tablets. The doctor need not start digging behind the depressive façade, a task which would call for hard work and considerable commitment on his part. But we can hardly be surprised if the patient suffers further depressions, and has to keep coming back to the psychiatrist for more help. The depressive behaviour and the depressive personality persist, everything is as it always was. The aim of the various therapeutic techniques discussed below is to discover the psychological mechanisms underlying a depressive development. I shall discuss three types of psychotherapy, namely individual therapy, group therapy, and family therapy in that order. Hitherto individual therapy has been the most common in practice, and family therapy the least, although the latter is now gaining ground. In common parlance 'psychotherapy' is generally associated with individual therapy, and perhaps in particular with therapeutic techniques based on Freud's psychoanalytical approach.

12.2.1 Individual therapy

Cohen et al. (1954) advocate a form of therapy based on the psychodynamic approach, but do not regard conventional psychoanalysis as appropriate to the treatment of manic-depressive patients. Words can easily put up barriers, they can be manipulated and used to cover up feelings. In trying to get at feelings, non-verbal approaches involving gestures, tone of voice, etc., may be more appropriate. The patients should be helped to understand that stereotyped conventional language and behaviour is a defence against anxiety. To this end the therapist talks openly of the transference from the patient to himself. In the course of the therapy the patient makes great demands on the therapist, who in the imagination of the patient becomes the sought-after parent figure. Arieti (1978) describes this situation by saying that the patient is looking for a 'dominant third', a person who in addition to the 'dominant other' is expected to satisfy the patient's needs. Arieti suggests that to begin with the therapist should meet the patient's demands, in order to soothe his initial distress, but that as soon as possible he should proceed to the role of the *significant third*, 'a third person with a firm, sincere, and unambiguous type of personality who wants to help the patient without making threatening demands or requesting a continuation of the patient's usual patterns of living . . . . He may indicate alternative possibilities but he does not demand their implemention' (p. 215–216).

Cohen *et al.* emphasize the danger that arises if the therapist promises too much. Sooner or later the patient will discover that his hopes are not being fulfilled, and he may experience a sense of failure even greater than before. Such disappointment will increase the risk of suicide. At the same time, the therapist must show that he believes in the patient, that he considers him important as a person.

We have concluded, on the basis of these considerations, that the manic-depressive can best be treated in a situation where certain rules are laid down for him in an active, vigorous and "involved" way by the therapist. We feel that his irrational demands should be recognized, labelled, and refused. We feel that the therapist should not make decisions for the patient nor attempt to give him advice on how to behave; in fact, the therapist's pressure should be in the opposite direction—that of the patient's working through his conflicts to the point of being able to make his own decisions. The rules should be laid down in terms of setting up a structure or frame of reference within which the patient would then be responsible for working out his own personal choices and decisions. (Cohen *et al.*, 1954, p. 135)

To both Arieti and Cohen *et al.* an important element in treating the severely depressed consists of freeing the patient of his dependence by bringing it out into the open. The patient should be made to understand that his previous satisfaction has always depended on his fulfilment of *other people's* needs and that at the same time he has been trying to make other people dependent on himself. The therapist must gradually help the patient to see that he has failed to learn to live according to his own needs. Everything he has done has been directed towards gaining the approval and love of the dominant other, or of achieving the dominant goal. In order to uncover the patient's *own* needs and to discover what he really wants out of his life the therapist can try to recreate the day-dreams, aspirations, and fantasies of his childhood and youth. The patient must be brought to understand the role of the dominant other as well as his own role in creating 'the climate and pattern of submissiveness'.

There appears, according to Arieti and Bemporad (1978), to be no essential difference between the therapy appropriate to the severely depressed and that appropriate to the mildly depressed, although drug therapy may perhaps be used more often to relieve the symptoms of severe depression. Bemporad (1978) shows that the mildly depressed patient should be helped to understand how dependent he is on others for self-esteem. The therapist can demonstrate to the patient his earlier dependence on others, and can even show him how he is now becoming the dependent party in their present therapeutic interaction. The aim of the therapy is to encourage the patient to achieve satisfaction as a result of his own independent activities. The therapist must be cautious about accepting the patient's picture of himself as helpless. Making himself appear small and helpless may be part of an attempt to manipulate others and to free himself of responsibility. This is why Bemporad advocates the avoidance of regression in therapy; instead the therapist should try to bring out the mature, strong sides of the patient's personality. His continual complaints must be actively checked by the therapist and attempts made instead to extend his range of possible actions.

Free association is not an appropriate technique here, since it all too easily leads the patient back into the old circle of complaints.

A tendency to see everything in the most negative light is typical of the depressive's way of thinking. Beck *et al.* (1979) describes it as a cognitive triad consisting of the patient's negative view of himself, his negative view of the world, and his negative view of the future. Both Arieti and Bemporad try to get the patient to reorganize his thinking, helping him to break his automatic train of thought:

'I am not getting what I should→I am deprived→I am in a miserable state.' The patient is guided to stop at the first stage of this sequence. ... Can the patient substitute this recurring idea and aim for another one, for instance, 'What ways other than aggressive expectation and dependency are at my disposal in order to get what I want?' (Arieti, 1978, p. 224)

Beck *et al.* (1979) has developed a cognitive therapy of depression based on the theory of negative thinking. Beck describes the way the person thinks as nondimensional, absolutistic and moralistic, invariant and irreversible—terms which he has borrowed from Piaget's description of children's thinking. This description of 'primitive' thought processes sounds like a characterization of what we have called here 'rigid action patterns'. Beck exemplifies typical negative thinking as follows:

1. In order to be happy, I have to be successful in whatever I undertake.
2. To be happy, I must be accepted by all people at all times.
3. If I make a mistake, it means that I am inept.
4. I can't live without you.
5. If somebody disagrees with me, it means that he doesn't like me.
6. My value as a person depends on what others think of me. (Beck *et al.*, 1979, p. 246)

These feelings increase in strength and significance as a person becomes more depressed. The therapist must provide the patient with evidence that his negative thought processes contribute to his depression, and show him that his conclusions may be inaccurate (rather than irrational). The therapist may do this by pointing out that when several interpretations of an event are possible, the patient always seems to select the most negative. Beck suggests that the therapist could well quote Bertrand Russell's observation 'that the degree of certainty with which one holds a belief is inversely related to the truth of that belief. Fanatics are true believers, scientists are sceptics' (p. 269). Further, the patient can be encouraged by the therapist to look for alternative solutions and interpretations. He can even be encouraged to act 'against his assumption', which is a very effective way of changing negative beliefs. If the patient is very scared of making mistakes, the therapist may persuade him to do something 'outlandish', upon which he will often discover that other people do not see his behaviour as outlandish at all.

Beck emphasizes the importance of including the patient's significant other in the therapy. The significant other should be asked about the patient's symptoms and about his behaviour in general. He should also have the therapeutic procedures explained to him. The therapy will include tasks for the patient to do at home, and the significant other can be asked to encourage him. The tasks may involve activating and organizing his time. It is very important that the patient should himself decide what to do, so that he does not sink back into passivity. He should be encouraged above all else to take up his old social skills, rather than be made to learn new ones. Arieti (in Arieti and Bemporad, 1978) also stresses the importance of activating the patient. The patient and the therapist should together plan a programme of successively more difficult activities.

Beck describes how negative thinking can also be tackled with the help of role games. The patient can be assigned the role of the significant other. What does he believe the other thinks of him? The role game gives the patient a chance to break out of his negative self-absorption and to see his situation from another point of view. The therapist can also assume the role of the patient, trying in this way to get him to change his critical attitude towards himself. This, too, can help the patient to see himself in a more favourable light.

In cognitive therapy a detailed empirical examination is first made of the patient's automatic thoughts, conclusions, and assumptions. The therapy is then directed specifically towards the target symptoms established by the investigation. The therapist is very much more active in interaction with the patient than is customary in traditional psychotherapy. Particularly at the beginning of the process, the therapist tries to guide the patient into those areas most affected by negative thinking. This kind of therapy has proved effective in cases of non-psychotic depression only, but in such cases it has frequently proved superior to drug therapy, as several of Beck's outcome studies have shown.

12.2.2 Group therapy

Certain group therapy techniques have features in common with individual cognitive therapy. Hollon and Shaw (in Beck *et al.* 1979) mention three types of difficulty which can be converted into advantages in group cognitive therapy. In group therapy there is a risk that participants may retreat into their own negative thoughts. They may feel unable to say the 'right thing', comparing themselves unfavourably with other members who seem to find it much easier to express themselves. But it is just in the group therapy sessions that such negative social cognitions can be brought out into the open and worked through. It might be expected, too, that the negative thinking of the depressed could affect other group members. Hollon and Shaw found it possible to keep the therapy so firmly task-relevant that no such effects were noted. A third type of possible difficulty could stem from the inability of the individual patient to see the similarities between his own and other people's negative thinking. Hollon and Shaw found, however, that as group members observed the negative cognitive sets of the others and saw also how these could be restructured, they became more able to register their own maladaptive reactions. Thus members learnt to reality-test their assumptions in the group situation.

A different type of group therapy, based on psychodynamic theory, has been described by Stein (in Flach and Draghi, 1975). Like cognitive group therapy his method is inappropriate in cases of acute and severe depression and, in particular, of psychotic depression. In group psychotherapy the discussion flows freely with little control from the group leader, whose main task is to interpret group interactions. The patient should come to identify himself with the group leader and, thus, because of their common identification with the leader, also with the other members of the group. In this way the patient establishes a number of new relationships, which sets up a counterweight to the object-loss which he has presumably suffered. Furthermore, the leader will come to represent an ideal which can replace the patient's own punitive conscience (superego). The gentle, tolerant, and protective leader accepts the patient, as his own bitter and condemnatory superego fails to do. This helps the patient to discover new alternatives; he is no longer so harshly controlled by his conscience and can therefore begin to recover from the painful loss of self-esteem. The leader intentionally limits his interaction with the group in order to facilitate transferences among the members themselves. The patient thus has a chance to act out the disappointment and anger previously buried in his subconscious; the members of the group become available to one another as 'multiple transference objects', perhaps a hated mother or the patient's demanding and unrealistic ambitions. The leader's task is to help to clarify the specific mechanisms and general pathological character traits that quickly become evident in the group. The discovery that others have shared the same reactions of rage and hatred towards disappointing figures in their lives helps the patient to accept his own failures and ambivalences more tolerantly (Stein in Flach and Draghi, 1975, p. 188).

12.2.3 Family therapy

Once the individual therapy is complete it would often be helpful to include a husband or wife in the sessions, as Arieti (1978) has recommended. This is particularly important if the partner is trying to obstruct the independence that the patient has achieved in the individual therapy. Arieti points out that the partner often transfers his own feelings of guilt and shame on to the patient, in order to inhibit the process of liberation. This is particularly often the case when the depressed subject is a woman whose husband is a dominating person, afraid of his own feelings. He wants to keep the wife he is used to: dependent, repressed, and easily controllable. In such cases it is very important that husband and patient meet the therapist together.

Hinchcliffe et al. (1978) recommend family therapy for all depressed people who live together with a spouse or other partner. People living together will be affected by one another's behaviour. The therapist can help the relatives of a depressed person to bring out into the open the feelings he arouses in them, without fear of their hurting the patient. Honesty of this kind can benefit both parties. Hogan and Hogan (in Flach and Draghi, 1975) summarize the advantages of family therapy as follows:

This approach allows direct examination of and therapeutic intervention into the disturbed relationship. In addition, it reduces the burden on the therapist of the negative approach of the depressed spouse, helps maintain motivation for therapy, and provides immediate access to the spouse who is not the designated patient when he or she reacts depressively to the designated patient's improvement. (p. 226)

According to these authors, family therapy is based on systems theory. This means that the patient's difficulties are not studied in isolation; the whole family system is regarded as part of the problem. A common characteristic of depressed families is a lack of open verbal communication. Direct demands or requests meet with disapproval. It is assumed that all members know the rules of the family system, and these rules are often expressed in body language. In such families it is thought that 'one makes requests of a stranger, not of a loved one' (p. 205). In this way open communication—making tangible demands on one another and showing independence—are seen as evidence of criticism and lack of love. Thus the task of the family therapy is to reveal the rules that hold the family together, and to get family members to talk openly about them. It is suggested that they speak *to* one another and not *about* one another. They are also encouraged to give open expression to their desires rather than simply expect the other family members to be able to interpret their wishes from indirect signs. Hogan and Hogan stress the importance of pointing out the positive aspect of the blocked intra-family communication, namely that it is often evidence of mutual caring.

Once the old rules governing the family system have been brought out into the open and explained, they must be redefined or replaced by new rules. The members of the family must acknowledge their mutual expectations. In the therapy setting the family can then work out new rules without feeling threatened. The therapist's task is to give the family a legitimate opportunity to change the rules and to see that feelings and mutual expectations are openly expressed (Hinchcliffe *et al.*, 1978).

12.2.4 Therapies and the depressive process

How do the various therapeutic techniques discussed above link up with the depressive process as described in the previous chapters? A common feature of all these therapies is their concern with the rigid pattern of action, particularly on the psychological plane. The result of releasing an individual from a situation of dependence or from a dominant other, from rigid cognitive patterns or an inward-looking family system, is that he becomes able to start developing independent actions, extending the range of his action alternatives. Family therapy seems to be alone in going beyond the individual level and in tackling the primary group that is so important to people's thoughts and actions. Family therapy perhaps also does most to create new action alternatives. Rules are reformulated and people are encouraged to communicate more openly with one another. Beck's cognitive therapy also emphasizes the importance of action geared to the individual's own needs and goals. To Bemporad an important element in the therapy is the highlighting of the subject's strengths, which reinforces his range of possible actions. Thus, psychotherapy according to Cohen *et al.*, Arieti, Bemporad, and the group psychotherapists in general is mainly concerned to help the depressed person to *realize his or her own possibilities*, while cognitive therapy is directed towards *creating these possibilities in the conscious mind and thought processes* of the subject, and family therapy towards creating them in the subject's *most significant social relationships*. The aim of the various preventive measures discussed above is to *keep open the possibility of a variety of action opportunities* and to *limit such factors as lead to rigid action patterns*. Once again I must emphasize that successful treatment will almost always require work on several levels. It may be necessary, for example, to combine psychotherapy, cognitive therapy, family therapy, and social change. At the same time it will be important to identify the level at which the therapeutic input is likely to prove most constructive and to concentrate the greatest effort there. Resources are always limited and must therefore be put to the best possible use. A crucial decision concerns the starting level: the main purpose at the diagnostic stage should be to try to pinpoint the level at which the fundamental problem is to be found. Is there a serious mismatch in the social situation? Is there a blockage following some earlier traumatic event? Or is there some other psychological disturbance?

12.3 GENERAL THERAPEUTIC PROCEDURES

How, then, both as 'professional' therapists and as fellow human beings, should we behave towards the depressed? When, for instance, does it become necessary to contact a professional therapist? The decisive factor here is the depressed person's own will to change, his acceptance of the necessity for therapy. Further, professional therapy should be considered first when other solutions have been tried, or when attempts to solve the problems together with relatives or close friends have proved ineffective. Therapy should not be regarded as the first obvious answer, as a way of shrugging off all responsibility in the home. The appropriate moment for calling in professional help will naturally also depend on the severity of the depression. In cases of psychotic depression, when the patient suffers from hallucinations and serious apathy, professional help should obviously not be delayed. If there is a risk of suicide, it is equally necessary to try to persuade the depressed person to undergo therapy, not only for his own sake but for the sake of his family or other close friends.

Professional help should always follow the lodestar of 'help to self-help'. Rowe (1978) points out that since people are generally afraid to speak openly to those who have power over them and who might therefore be able to restrict their freedom, the goal of the professional therapist must be to let the patient determine his own choice of paths, while helping him towards an understanding of his blocked positions. The therapist or the supportive relative or friend can help the depressed person to restructure reality in a way that appeals to him. The therapist can also follow up and discuss any practical changes which the patient himself touches upon. But the paramount goal remains, that the depressed person himself should assume responsibility for his own life and make the decisions that affect it. This creates action alternatives.

Once the decision has been made to seek therapeutic help, the next question concerns its location. Arieti (1978) says that in most cases hospitalization should be avoided. If there is a threat of suicide hospitalization can, of course, reduce the risk, and in hospital the severely depressed can be given adequate drug treatment. Hospitalization may also be justified if a severely depressed person lives alone, has no relatives or friends, and cannot look after himself. Bemporad (1978) points out that a long stay in hospital prevents the patient from undertaking independent action on his own account; it also delays his understanding and acceptance of his own responsibility for solving his problems by his own efforts.

Hinchcliffe et al. (1978) mention in their discussion of the family therapy approach that during a long hospital stay the other members of the family may establish a new equilibrium in the family system without the absent member. When the patient returns, changed or unchanged, there may then be some uncertainty in the new interrelationships. If, on the other hand, the therapy takes place within the family, or the hospitalized member returns home frequently and remains involved in the family, the whole system can be changed gradually and with the inclusion of all its members.

Home-based therapy also has advantages for the therapist. Large psychiatric institutions or mental hospitals provide an artificial and alien background; it is probably easier there for the patient to conceal certain interactions that would have been clearly in evidence at home. Treatment of the depressed should be located as far as possible in the environment where the problems are most marked. It is easier not only for the patient but also for the therapist to identify and understand the problems there, where the depression has its roots or where roots established earlier in life have been strengthened and confirmed. Furthermore, despite all the problems, it is probably here that the depressed person still retains a frail strand of security, and this can provide a platform from which he can start the struggle to work through his depression. And, ultimately, it is in this everyday setting that he will have to create *new actions*, new ways of living. Ideally the whole social network should be included and the depression consequently 'deprivatized'. Depression is something which concerns and touches on our common social situation; its implications go far beyond the life of the particular family, one of whose members has become depressed.

West (in Flach and Draghi, 1975) suggests ways in which a satisfactory rapport can be established with a depressed person. In establishing a therapeutic relationship a quiet approach is called for, 'warm and accepting, but also firm and objective'. A hearty, boisterous attitude intended to cheer the patient up is altogether inappropriate. We should be prepared to provide continual comfort and reassurance, showing at the same time that we understand the patient's difficulty in accepting our reassurance. In discussing openly the question of suicide, the therapist should never accept the patient's suggestion that death would be the best solution to his problem.

Beck (in Beck *et al.*, 1979) recommends that the therapist should regard the *depressed person's thoughts* as irrational, but not the *whole person*. For this reason psychiatric jargon that assigns the patient to a diagnostic category (masochistic, neurotic, hysterical, etc.) should be avoided. Such classifications carry a ring of permanence, whereas the whole therapy is based on the idea that change can be induced.

In seeking to relieve depression it is always harmful to categorize people, saying that they are manic-depressives, that they are frightened, weak, or lacking in initiative. Such categorization thrusts the patient back on to his own image of himself; it can become just another self-fulfilling prophesy. At the same time the man with a label round his neck will find it even more difficult to step outside himself and view himself from different vantage points. It is equally important not to categorize children, placing them in some negative or restrictive class (naughty, bad at arithmetic, slow).

Hinchcliffe *et al.* (1978) see a connection between the growing incidence of depression and attempted suicide in all the Western countries and three myths of modern man:

(1) that the emotional pain of stressful life events is unbearable and, (2) that medicine has the cure for such pain readily available in the freely prescribed psychotropic drugs. The combination of these two myths is becoming increasingly life-threatening. Perhaps one should add a third myth, which holds that all human relationships must be fruitful and satisfying—and certainly never boring and irritating. (p. 125)

If this is a true picture, as it probably is, it is clear that the possession of *realistic ambitions* is an important component in our defence against depression, and the attainment of such ambitions must be an equally important element in the resolution of existing depression. This, as we have seen, reflects the main propositions of the neo-Freudian theorists and others. What is crucial in life is not to emphasize happiness goals, success goals, reified goals—all of which in various way lie beyond and outside the individual—but instead to bring out the good that lies *within the individual*. This is particularly important in the case of the depressed, and if it can be combined with building up his belief in his own possibilities, showing him *that he has a self-worth*, that he can make something meaningful of his life, a way out of the depression can open before him.

References

Akiskal, H., and McKinney, W. (1973), Depressive disorders: Toward a unified hypothesis, *Science*, **182**, 20–29.

Akiskal, H., and McKinney, W. (1975), Overview of recent research in depression, *Archives of General Psychiatry*, **32**, 285–305.

Alvarez, A. (1971), *The Savage God*, Weidenfeld & Nicolson, London.

Angst, J. (1966), Zur Ätiologie and Nosologie Endogener Depressiver Psychosen, *Monographien aus dem Gesamtgebiete der Neurologie und Psychiatrie*, **112**, 1–118.

Arieti, S. (1979), Roots of depression: The power of the dominant other (interview), *Psychology Today*, **12**, 54–62.

Arieti, S., and Bemporad, J. (1978), *Severe and Mild Depression. The Psychotherapeutic Approach*, Basic Books, New York.

Ashcroft, G. W., and Glen, A. I. (1974), Mood and neuronal functions: A modified hypothesis for the etiology of affective illness, *Advances in Biochemical Psychopharmacology*, **11**, 335–339.

Bagley, C. (1973), Occupational class and symptoms of depression, *Social Science and Medicine*, **7**, 237–340.

Bart, P. (1974), The sociology of depression, in *Explorations in Psychiatric Sociology*, ed. P. Roman and H. Trice, F. A. Davis Company, Philadelphia, 139–157.

Beck, A. (1967), *Depression: Clinical, Experimental and Theoretical Aspects*, Harper & Row, New York.

Beck, A., Rush, J., Shaw, B., and Emery, G. (1979), *Cognitive Therapy of Depression*, Wiley, Chichester.

Becker, E. (1962), Toward a comprehensive theory of depression: A cross-disciplinary appraisal of objects, games and meaning, *Journal of Nervous and Mental Disease*, **135**, 26–35.

Becker, E. (1964), *The Revolution in Psychiatry. The New Understanding of Man*, Free Press, Glencoe.

Becker, E. (1971), *The Birth and Death of Meaning. An Interdisciplinary Perspective of the Problem of Man*, Free Press, New York.

Becker, E. (1973), *The Denial of Death*, Free Press, New York.

Becker, J. (1960), Achievement related characteristics of manic-depressives, *Journal of Abnormal and Social Psychology*, **60**, 334–339.

Bemporad, J. (1978), Severe and mild depression, in Arieti and Bemporad (1978).

Benton, R. (1972), The structure of the depressive response to stress, *American Journal of Psychiatry*, **128**, 1212–1217.

Berg, L.-E. (1976), *Människans födelse*, en socialpsykologisk diskussion kring G. H. Mead and J. Piaget, Korpen, Göteborg.

Bibring, E. (1953), The mechanism of depression, in *Affective Disorders*, ed. P. Greenacre, International University Press, New York, 13–48.

Birtchnell, J. (1971), Social class, parental social class and social mobility in psychiatric patients and general population controls, *Psychological Medicine*, **1**, 209–221.

Blaney, P. (1977), Contemporary theories of depression: Critique and comparison, *Journal of Abnormal Psychology*, **86**, 203–223.

194

Börjeson, B. (1979), Depression—när livet saknar mening, *Sociologisk Forskning*, nr 1, 66–72.

Brisett, D. (1972), Toward a classification of self-esteem, *Psychiatry*, **35**, 255–263.

Brown, G., and Harris, T. (1978), *Social Origins of Depression*, a study of psychiatric disorder in women, Tavistock, London.

Brown, G., Sklair, F., Harris, T., and Birley, J. (1973a), Life-events and psychiatric disorders. Part 1: Some methological issues, *Psychological Medicine*, **3**, 74–87.

Brown, G., Harris, T., and Peto, J. (1973b), Life-events and psychiatric disorders. Part 2: Nature of causal link, *Psychological Medicine*, **3**, 159–176.

Brown, G., NíBhrolcháin, M., and Harris, T. (1979), Psychotic and neurotic depression, *Journal of Affective Disorders*, **1**, 195–211.

Brown, G., Prudo, R., Harris, T., and Dowland, J. (in press), Psychiatric disorder in a rural and an urban population: (2) Sensitivity to loss, *Psychological Medicine*.

Burns, S. J., and Offord, D. R. (1972), Achievement correlates of depressive illness, *Journal of Nervous and Mental Disease*, **154**, 344–351.

Cadoret, R., Winokur, G., Dorzab, J., and Baker, M. (1972), Depressive disease: Life events and onset of illness, *Archives of General Psychiatry*, **26**, 133–136.

Caplan, G. (1964), *Principles of Preventive Psychiatry*, Basic Books, New York.

Carney, M., Roth, M., and Garside, R. F. (1965), The diagnosis of depressive syndromes and the prediction of E.C.T. response, *British Journal of Psychiatry*, **111**, 659–674.

Chwast, J. (1966), Depressive reactions as manifested among adolescent delinquents, *American Journal of Psychotherapy*, **21**, 575–585.

Cohen, M. B., Baker, G., Cohen, R., Fromm-Reichmann, F., and Weigert, E. (1954), An intensive study of twelve cases of manic-depressive psychosis, *Psychiatry*, **17**, 103–137.

Costello, C. G., Christensen S. J., and Rogers, T. B. (1974), The relationships between measures of general depression and the endogenous versus reactive classification, *Canadian Psychiatric Association Journal*, **19**, 259–265.

Coyne, J. C. (1976), Toward an interactional description of depression, *Psychiatry*, **39**, 28–40.

Cullberg, J. (1975), *Kris och utveckling*, Natur och kultur, Stockholm.

Drake, R., and Price, J. (1975), Depression: adaption to disruption and loss, *Psychiatric Care*, **13**, 163–169.

Erikson, E. H. (1963), *Childhood and Society*, Norton, New York.

Farbrega, H. (1974), Problems implicit in the cultural and social study of depression, *Psychosomatic Medicine*, **36**, 377–398.

Ferster, C. B. (1973), A functional analysis of depression, *American Psychologist*, **28**, 857–870.

Flach, F., and Draghi, S. (1975), *The Nature and Treatment of Depression*, Wiley, New York.

Forrest, A. D., Fraser, R. H., and Priest, R. G. (1965), Enviromental factors in depressive illness, *British Journal of Psychiatry*, **111**, 243–253.

Forrest, M. S., and Hokanson, J. E. (1975), Depression and automatic arousal reduction accompanying self-punitive behavior, *Journal of Abnormal Psychology*, **84**, 346–357.

Fredén, L. (1978), *Att sakna möjligheter*, with an English summary: To lack opportunities. A theoretical and empirical study of depressions starting from the social psychological theory of Ernest Becker, Almqvist & Wiksell International, Stockholm.

Fredén, L. (1979), Depression—att inte finna mening i praxis, *Sociologisk Forskning*, nr 3, 86–91.

Freud, S. (1957), *Mourning and Melancholia*, Hogarth Press, London.

Frumkin, R. (1955), Occupation and major mental disorders, in *Mental Health and Mental Disorder*, ed. A. M. Rose, New York.

Gardell, B. (1980), Alienation and mental health in the modern industrial environment, in *Society, Stress and Disease, Vol. IV, Working Life*, ed. L. Levi, Oxford University Press, London, 148–180.

196

Gecas, V. (1971), Parental behavior and dimensions of adolescent self-evaluation, *Sociometry*, **34**, 466–482.

Gibson, R. (1958), The family background and early life experience of the manic-depressive patient, *Psychiatry*, **21**, 71–90.

Gove, W. R., and Tudor, J. F. (1973), Adult sex roles and mental illness, *American Journal of Sociology*, **78**, 812–835.

Grünfeld, B., and Salvesen, C. (1968), Functional psychosis and social status, *British Journal of Psychiatry*, **114**, 733–737.

Gut, E. (1974), Grief in adult life, *Omega, Journal of Death and Dying*, **V** (4).

Hällström, T. (1973), *Mental Disorder and Sexuality in the Climacteric*, Scandinavian University Books, Göteborg.

Hammen, C., and Padesky, C. (1977), Sex differences in the expression of depressive responses on the Beck Depressive Inventory, *Journal of Abnormal Psychology*, **86**, 609–614.

Hare, E. H. (1955), Mental illness and social class in Bristol, *British Journal of Preventive Social Medicine*, **9**, 191–195.

Harrow, M., Fox, D., and Detre, T. (1969a), Self-concept of the married psychiatric patient and his mate's perception of him, *Journal of Consulting and Clinical Psychology*, **33**, 235–239.

Harrow, M., Fox, D., Markhus, K., Stillman, R., and Hallowell, C. (1969b), Changes in adolescents' self-concepts and their parents' perceptions during psychiatric hospitalization, *Journal of Nervous and Mental Disease*, **147**, 252–259.

Henderson, S., Duncan-Jones, P., McAuley, H., and Ritchie, K. (1978a), The patient's primary group, *British Journal of Psychiatry*, **132**, 74–86.

Henderson, S., Byrne, D. G., Duncan-Jones, P., Adcook, S., Scott, R., and Steele, G. P. (1978b), Social bonds in the epidemiology of neurosis: A preliminary communication, *British Journal of Psychiatry*, **132**, 463–466.

Henderson, S., Duncan-Jones, P., Byrne, D. G., Scott, R., and Adcook, S. (1980), Social relationships, adversity and neurosis: A study of association in a general population sample, *British Journal of Psychiatry*, **136**, 574–583.

Hinchcliffe, M., Hooper, D., Roberts, J., and Vaughan, P. (1975), A study of the interaction between depressed patients and their spouses, *British Journal of Psychiatry*, **126**, 164–172.

Hinchcliffe, M., Hooper, D., and Roberts, J. (1978), *The Melancholy Marriage*, Wiley, Chichester.

Hogan, P., and Hogan, B. (1975), The family treatment of depression, in Flach and Draghi (1975), 197–228.

Hollon, S., and Shaw, B. (1979), Group cognitive therapy for depressed patients, in Beck et al. (1979), 328–353.

Inghe, G., and Åmark, K. (1958), I Mentalsjukvården. Planering och organisation, Swedish Government Official Reports, *SOU 1958*: **38**, 183–197.

Jacobowsky, B. (1961), in Proceedings of the Scandinavian symposium on depression, *Acta Psychiatrica Scandinavica*, Suppl. 162, **37**, 253–260.

Jacobson, E. (1971), *Depression*, International Press, New York.

Jacobson, S., Fasman, J. and DiMascio, A. (1975), Deprivation in the childhood of depressed women, *The Journal of Nervous and Mental Disease*, **160**, 5–14.

Johansson, S. (1970), *Den vuxna befolkningens hälsotillstånd*, Låginkomstutredningen, Allmänna Förlaget, Stockholm.

Kaplan, H. (1977), Gender and depression: A sociological analysis of a conditional relationship, in *Phenomenology and Treatment of Depression*, ed. W. Fann, Spectrum, New York, 81–112.

Kendell, R. (1968), *The Classification of Depressive Illnesses*, Oxford University Press, London.

197

Kendell, R. (1969), The continuum model of depressive illness, *Proceedings of the Royal Social Medicine*, **62**, 335–339.

Kiloh, L. G., and Garside, R. F. (1963), The independence of neurotic depression and endogenous depression, *British Journal of Psychiatry*, **109**, 451–463.

Klerman, G., and Paykel, E. (1970), Depressive patterns, social background and hospitalization, *Journal of Nervous and Mental Disease*, **150**, 466–478.

Kringlen, E. (1972), *Psykiatri*, Universitetsforlaget, Bergen.

Kreitman, N. (1961), The reliability of psychiatric diagnosis, *Journal of Mental Science*, **107**, 876–886.

Kreitman, N., et al. (1961), The reliability of psychiatric assessment: An analysis, *Journal of Mental Science*, **107**, 887–908.

Leff, M. J., Roatch, J. F., and Bunney, W. E. (1970), Environmental factors preceding the onset of depression, *Psychiatry*, **33**, 293–311.

Lesse, S. (1968), The influence of socioeconomic and sociotechnologic systems on emotional illness, *American Journal of Psychotherapy*, **22**, 569–576.

Lewinsohn, P., and MacPhillamy, D. (1974), The relationship between age and pleasant activities, Journal of Gerontology, **29**, 290–294.

Linsky, A. (1969), Community structure and depressive disorders, *Social Problems*, **17**, 120–131.

Maddi, S. (1977), The existential neurosis,

Mangs, K., and Martell, B. (1977), *0 → 20 år enligt psykoanalytisk teori*, Studentlitteratur, Lund.

Marcuse, H. (1968), *One-dimensional man*, studies in the ideology of advanced industrial society, Beacon Press, Boston.

Mostow, E., and Newberry, P. (1975), Work role and depression in women: A comparison of workers and housewives in treatment, *American Journal of Orthopsychiatry*, **45**, 538–548.

Munro, A. (1966a), Some familial and social factors in depressive illness, *British Journal of Psychiatry*, **112**, 429–441.

Munro, A. (1966b), Parental deprivation in depressive patients, *British Journal of Psychiatry*, **112**, 443–457.

Murphy, H., Wittkower, E., and Chance, N. (1967), Crosscultural inquiry into the symtomatology of depression: A preliminary report, *International Journal of Psychiatry*, **3**, 6–15.

Nijhof, G. (1978), Social inequality and psychological disturbances, paper presented at 9th World Congress of Sociology, Uppsala.

Öberg, G., and Öberg, B. (1979), *Skilsmässa, sorg och förluster*, with an English summary: Loss, grief and separation. Crisis therapy as an alternative to custody investigations, Department of Education, University of Stockholm, BIG-report no. 35.

Parker, S. (1962), Eskimo psychopathology in the context of eskimo personality and culture, *American Anthropologist*, **64**, 76–96.

Parkes, C. M. (1972), *Bereavement Studies of Grief in Adult Life*, Tavistock, London.

Paykel, E. Myers, J., Dienelt, M., Klerman, G., Lindenthal, J., and Pepper, M. (1969), Life events and depression: A controlled study, *Archives of General Psychiatry*, **21**, 753–760.

Perris, C. (1966), A study of bipolar (manic-depressives) and unipolar recurrent depressive psychoses, *Acta Psychiatrica Scandinavica*, Suppl. 194.

Perris, C., and Espvall, M. (1973), Depressive-type psychic reactions caused by success, *Psychiatric Clinical*, **6**, 346–356.

Phillips, D. (1968), Social class and psychological disturbance: The influence of positive and negative experiences, *Social Psychiatry*, **3**, 41–46.

Ramsay, R. W. (1978), Bereavement—a behavioral treatment of pathological grief, *Psychologisch Laboratorium, Universitet van Amsterdam* (mimeo).

Rosenthal, S. H., and Klerman, G. L. (1966), Content and consistency in the endogenous depressive pattern, *British Journal of Psychiatry*, **112**, 471–484.

Rowe, D. (1978), *The Experience of Depression*, Wiley, Chichester.

Scher, J. M. (1971), The depressions and structure: An existential approach to their understanding and treatment, *American Journal of Psychotherapy*, **25**, 369–384.

Schless, A., Schwartz, L., Goetz, C., and Mendels, J. (1974), How depressives view the significance of life events, *British Journal of Psychiatry*, **125**, 406–410.

Schwab, J., Brown, J., Holzer, C., and Sokolof, M. (1967), Sociocultural aspects of depression in medical inpatients, *Archives of General Psychiatry*, **17**, 533–538.

Schwab, J., Brown, J., Holzer, C., and Solokof, M. (1968), Current Concepts of Depression: The Sociocultural, *International Journal of Social Psychiatry*, **14**, 226–234.

Sechehaye, M. (1950), *Journal d'une schizophrène*, Presses Universitaires de France, Paris.

Seligman, M. (1975), *Helplessness*, Freeman, San Francisco.

Shaw, D., MacSweeney, D., Johnson, A., and Merry, J. (1975), Personality characteristics of alcoholic and depressed patients, *British Journal of Psychiatry*, **126**, 56–59.

Siirala, M. (1974), Anthropological structure of depression, *Psychiatria Fennica*, 87–101.

Silverman, C. (1968), *The Epidemiology of Depression*, Johns Hopkins Press, Baltimore.

Slater, E., and Roth, M. (1969), *Clinical Psychiatry*, Balliere, Tindall, & Cassels, London.

Sörensen, A., and Strömgren, E. (1961), Prevalence (the Samsö Investigation), *Acta Psychiatrica Scandinavica*, Suppl. 162, **37**, 62–68.

Stein, A. (1975), Group psychotherapy in the treatment of depression, in Flach and Draghi (1975), 161–182.

Stenback, A. (1965), Object loss and depression, *Archives of General Psychiatry*, **12**, 144–151.

Surtees, P. G., and Ingham, J. G. (1980), Life stress and depressive outcome: Application of a dissipation model to life events, *Social Psychiatry*, **15**, 21–31.

Tyndel, M. (1974), Psychiatric study of one thousand alcoholic patients, *Canadian Psychiatric Association Journal*, **19**, 21–24.

Ullman, L., and Krasner, L. (1969), *A Psychological Appoach to Abnormal Behavior*, Prentice-Hall, New Jersey.

Viestad, A., Baumgartner, U., Engelstad, I., Knutsen, S., Lundstol, F. Nickelsen, G., Vogt, K., Brudal, L., Matthis, I., Naevestad, M., and Wrånes, H. (1977), *Oppror eller sykdom?*, Pax forlag A/S, Oslo.

Vinde, K. (1977), *Er I riktig kloge?*, Tiderna skrifter, Köpenhamn.

Warheit, G., Holzer, C., and Schwab, J. (1973), An analysis of social class and racial differences in depressive symtomatology: A community study, *Journal of Health and Social Behavior*, **4**, 292–299.

Watts, C. A. H. (1966), *Depressive Disorders in the Community*, J. Wright, Bristol.

Weissman, M., and Klerman, G. (1977), Sex differences and the epidemiology of depression, *Archives of General Psychiatry*, **34**, 98–111.

Weissman, M., and Paykel, E. (1974), *The Depressed Woman*, University of Chicago Press, Chicago.

Weissman, M., Prusoff, B., and Pincus, C. (1975), Symtom patterns in depressed patients and depressed normals, *Journal of Nervous and Mental Disease*, **160**, 15–23.

West, L. J. (1975), Integrative psychotherapy of depressive illness, in Flach and Draghi (1975), 161–182.

White, R. (1977), Current psychoanalytic concepts of depression, in *Phenomenology and Treatment of Depression*, ed. W. Fann, Spectrum, New York, 127–141.

Wing, J. K., Nixon, J. M., Mann, S. A., and Leff, J. P. (1977), Reliability of the PSE (ninth edition) used in a population study, *Psychological Medicine*, **7**, 505–516.

Woodruff, R. A., Robins, L. N., Winokur, G., and Reich, T. (1971), Manic depressive illness and social achievement, *Acta Psychiatrica Scandinavica*, **47**, 237–249.

Zung, W. (1973), From art to science, *Archives of General Psychiatry*, **29**, 328–337.

Index

202